Vocabulary
for Achievement
Introductory Course

Margaret Ann Ríchek

GREAT SOURCE
WILMINGTON, MA

Author

Margaret Ann Richek

Professor of Education Emerita, Northeastern Illinois University; consultant in reading and vocabulary study; author of The World of Words *(Houghton Mifflin)*

Classroom Consultants

Beth Gaby
English Chair, Carl Schurz High School, Chicago, Illinois

Chris Hausammann
Teacher of English, Central Mountain High School, Lock Haven, Pennsylvania

Malisa Cannon
Teacher of Language Arts, Desert Sky Middle School, Tucson, Arizona

Patricia Melvin
District Secondary Reading Specialist, Duval County Public Schools, Jacksonville, Florida

Sean Rochester
Teacher of English, Parkway Central High School, St. Louis, Missouri

Credits

Editorial: Ruth Rothstein, Victoria Fortune, Dan Carsen, Amy Gilbert, Ronda Angel Arking

Design and Production: Mazer Corporation

Text Design and Production: Mazer Creative Services

Illustrations: Chris Vallo/Mazer Creative Services; Susan Aiello, Irene Gotz, Gary Krejca, and Barbara Samanich of Wilkinson Studios, LLC

Cover Design: Mazer Creative Services

Cover Photo: Corel, Inc., and Mazer Creative Services

Definitions for the three hundred words taught in this textbook are based on Houghton Mifflin dictionaries—in particular, the *Houghton Mifflin Student Dictionary*—but have been abbreviated and adapted for instructional purposes.

All pronunciations are reproduced by permission from the *American Heritage Dictionary of the English Language, Fourth Edition,* copyright © 2000.

International Standard Book Number -13: 978-0-669-51754-5

International Standard Book Number -10: 0-669-51754-2

11 12 - 1689 - 14 13 12

4500345056

Contents

COMPLETE WORD LIST FOR INTRODUCTORY COURSE

Words About Vocabulary

WORD LIST

antonym	concept	context	derivative	effective
glossary	retain	specialized	synonym	terminology

To help you understand the lessons in this book, you need to know the words that we use to talk about vocabulary. The ten main words in this lesson, and the words that are related to them, give you the tools to learn new vocabulary in every sport, hobby, pastime, and school subject. Each word below is presented with its pronunciation, part of speech, and meaning, followed by a sentence showing it in use.

1. **antonym (ăn´tə-nĭm´)** *noun*
A word that means the opposite of another word
• The words *up* and *down* are **antonyms.**

2. **concept (kŏn´sĕpt´)** *noun*
A thought or an idea
• In 1945, Alan Turing developed the **concept** of a computer.

conceptual *adjective* Many writers do much of the **conceptual** work for a novel long before they sit down to write it.

conceptualize *verb* Leonardo da Vinci **conceptualized** the helicopter more than 400 years before the first one took flight.

3. **context (kŏn´tĕkst´)** *noun*
a. The words surrounding a word that make its meaning clear
• Depending upon the **context,** the word *mad* can mean "angry"
or it can mean "insane."
b. The situation surrounding something
• Noisy streets are common in the **context** of city life.

contextual *adjective* Using **contextual** analysis, scientists figure out unknown words in ancient languages.

4. **derivative (dĭ-rĭv´ə-tĭv)** *noun*
A word formed from another word
• The words *serving, servant,* and *service* are **derivatives** of the word *serve.*

derive *verb* Food, drink, wood, and rope are **derived** from the palm tree.

Ant- and *anti-* mean "opposite." The Arctic and Antarctic are on opposite ends of the earth.

antonyms

In this book, *derivatives* are often included with definitions of the main word. For example, the derivative *conceptual* is listed under the word *concept.*

5. **effective** (ĭ-fĕk´tĭv) *adjective*
   a. Able to accomplish a result; useful in bringing about a result
   • Draining swamps where mosquitoes breed has been **effective** in reducing malaria.
   b. Starting at a certain time
   • **Effective** May 1, there will be no parking on Main Street.

   effect *noun* The rain had the **effect** of lowering the temperature.

   effectively *adverb* If you want to study **effectively,** turn off the television.

   effectiveness *noun* Because of her **effectiveness** as mayor, Ms. Khan was elected again.

6. **glossary** (glô´sə-rē) *noun*
   A list of definitions for terms or important words used in a certain text
   • The **glossary** in the back of our science text defined the terms *force, dynamic,* and *vector.*

7. **retain** (rĭ-tān´) *verb*
   a. To hold or keep
   • Most of the villagers put containers on their roofs to **retain** rainwater.
   b. To hold in memory
   • Frequent review of new words will help you **retain** their meanings.

   retention *noun* Good working conditions help with the **retention** of employees.

8. **specialized** (spĕsh´ə-līzd) *adjective*
   Having one use among many possible uses; specific
   • Words like *foul* and *base* have **specialized** meanings in sports.

   specialize *verb* The stamp dealer **specializes** in British issues.

   specialist *noun* Pediatricians are **specialists** who treat children.

   specialty *noun* Vegetarian food is a **specialty** of this restaurant.

9. **synonym** (sĭn´ə-nĭm´) *noun*
   A word with the same, or nearly the same, meaning as another word
   • The verbs *finish* and *complete* are **synonyms.**

   synonymous *adjective* The adjectives *late* and *tardy* are **synonymous.**

10. **terminology** (tûr´mə-nŏl´ə-jē) *noun*
    Vocabulary particular to a certain subject
    • *Megabyte, software,* and *bug* are examples of computer **terminology.**

    term *noun* In tennis, the **term** used for a score of zero is "love."

Effect and *affect* are often confused. *Effect* is usually a noun: The moon has an *effect* on tides. *Affect* is usually a verb: The moon *affects* the tides.

Syn- means "the same." *Synonym* is the opposite of *antonym.*

WRITE THE CORRECT WORD

Write the correct word in the space next to each definition.

_____ 1. writing or speech surrounding a word

_____ 2. successful in bringing results

_____ 3. a word with an opposite meaning

_____ 4. a list of terms used in a text

_____ 5. an idea

_____ 6. special vocabulary of a subject

_____ 7. a word formed from another word

_____ 8. having one particular use

_____ 9. a word with a similar meaning

_____ 10. to hold or keep

COMPLETE THE SENTENCE

Write the letter for the word that best completes each sentence.

_____ 1. Her method for studying the vocabulary was clearly _____, because she aced the test.
   a. synonymous   b. contextual   c. conceptual   d. effective

_____ 2. Try making a list of all the technical _____ for one subject area.
   a. terminology   b. antonyms   c. derivatives   d. contexts

_____ 3. Grouping words around central _____ can help you form connections between words and their meanings.
   a. antonyms   b. derivatives   c. concepts   d. glossaries

_____ 4. Words that you already know may have _____ meanings in science or math.
   a. specialized   b. glossary   c. conceptual   d. derived

_____ 5. The _____ in the back of your textbook provides the meanings of key words.
   a. derivatives   b. synonym   c. context   d. glossary

_____ 6. You can use the _____ around an unknown word to figure out its meaning.
   a. context   b. derivatives   c. glossaries   d. terminologies

_____ 7. As you learn a word like *nation*, think about _____ such as *national*.
   a. contexts   b. antonyms   c. derivatives   d. specialties

_____ 8. It is sometimes helpful to think of a(n) _____, such as *child* for *youngster*.
   a. antonym   b. derivative   c. glossary   d. synonym

_____ 9. Thinking of _____, such as *begin* for *end*, may also help you remember words.
   a. derivatives   b. concepts   c. antonyms   d. specialties

_____ 10. Using the new words that you learn will help you to _____ their meanings.
   a. retain   b. specialize   c. derive   d. effect

Challenge: If you can't figure out the meaning of a word from its _____, then look it up in the _____ at the back of the book.

_____   a. concept…terminology   b. context…glossary   c. specialty…derivative

Dictionaries: Past and Present

Can you imagine sitting down to write a dictionary? How would you choose the words? How would you define them? Would you include slang?

(1) The *concept* of listing English words in alphabetical order and defining them dates back to 1604. However, Samuel Johnson's 1775 *Dictionary of the English Language* was the first modern dictionary. **(2)** It gave *contexts* for words by including quotations that used the words in sentences. **(3)** Johnson did not include scientific *terminology*, slang, or words from foreign languages. Johnson did have a sense of humor, though, and at times, he wrote definitions that were jokes! **(4)** But, for the most part, the definitions were excellent, making his dictionary an *effective* guide to English.

James Murray wrote the *Oxford English Dictionary*, which is still widely used today. Murray had an army of helpers, including his eleven children. Starting with the letter *a*, in 1879, he thought he would finish *z* by 1889. But ten years later, he was only at *ant!* Murray's dictionary took fifty years to complete.

Today, dictionaries are updated in computer databases. Words no longer used, like *pingle* (to eat with little appetite) and *jaunce* (to ride), have been taken out. New words, like *blog* (web log) and *text-messaging* have been added. **(5)** In fact, English has so many new words that a *specialized* dictionary is devoted just to them.

There are many different types of dictionaries. **(6)** You can use a simple *glossary* to find out the meanings of words in a text, or you can use a huge dictionary that lists over half a million words. Dictionaries are also designed for different age groups. The American Heritage series includes a *Children's Dictionary*, a *Student Dictionary*, and a *College Dictionary*, in addition to a full-length dictionary.

Most modern dictionaries are much more than just lists of definitions. **(7)** A word entry gives all the definitions of a word, along with its *derivatives* and pronunciation. Like Johnson's dictionary, many modern dictionaries have example sentences. **(8)** Some dictionaries provide a list of *synonyms* for many words. These can help you make your writing more effective. **(9)** Sometimes, dictionaries also include *antonyms* for entry words.

Modern dictionaries, like the *American Heritage Dictionary*, list words that were not in Johnson's dictionary, including scientific terminology, slang, and words from foreign languages. **(10)** Pictures are also used to help readers *retain* a word's meaning. Word histories show where words came from, giving readers an idea of how language changes over time. For example, the word *dinosaur*, comes from the Greek words *deinos* and *sauros*, which mean "monstrous lizard." Where did the words *peach* and *potato* originate? Take a moment to look them up, and as you go through the dictionary, look for more fascinating information about the English language.

Each sentence below refers to a numbered sentence in the passage. Write the letter of the choice that gives the sentence a meaning that is closest to the original sentence.

_____ **1.** The _____ of listing English words in alphabetical order dates back to 1604.
    a. idea   **b.** vocabulary   **c.** result   **d.** opposite

_____ **2.** It gave _____ for words by including quotations that used the words in sentences.
    a. special vocabulary   **b.** surrounding words   **c.** ideas   **d.** results

_____ **3.** Johnson did not include scientific _____.
    a. vocabulary   **b.** opposites   **c.** ideas   **d.** results

_____ **4.** The excellent definitions made his dictionary a _____ guide to English.
    a. similar   **b.** surrounding   **c.** useful   **d.** specific

_____ **5.** A(n) _____ dictionary is devoted just to new words in the English language.
    a. useful   **b.** opposite   **c.** idea   **d.** specific

_____ **6.** You can use a simple _____ to find out the meanings of words in a text.
    a. vocabulary   **b.** list of terms   **c.** similar word   **d.** word form

_____ **7.** A word entry gives each key word, along with its _____ and pronunciation.
    a. other forms   **b.** opposites   **c.** ideas   **d.** special vocabulary

_____ **8.** Some dictionaries provide a list of _____ to help you make your writing more effective.
    a. similar words   **b.** opposite words   **c.** ideas   **d.** results

_____ **9.** Sometimes, dictionaries also include _____.
    a. similar words   **b.** opposite words   **c.** ideas   **d.** results

_____ **10.** Pictures are also used to help readers _____ a word's meaning.
    a. change   **b.** surround   **c.** accomplish   **d.** remember

Indicate whether the statements below are TRUE or FALSE according to the passage.

_____ **1.** James Murray wrote the first English dictionary.

_____ **2.** Dictionaries have changed a lot since the first one was created.

_____ **3.** Modern dictionaries update their word lists by adding new words and taking out words that are no longer used.

WRITING EXTENDED RESPONSES

Some dictionaries are now on the Internet, and you can access them through computers. However, dictionaries are still being published in book form. Think of the advantages and disadvantages of both formats. Then write at least three paragraphs explaining which format you prefer, and why. Use at least three lesson words in your essay and underline them.

WRITE THE DERIVATIVE

Complete the sentence by writing the correct form of the word shown in parentheses. You may not need to change the form that is given.

_____ **1.** Choosing the right words helps us communicate _____. (*effective*)

_____ **2.** *Hot* is an _____ for *cold*. (*antonym*)

_____ **3.** The words *automobile* and *car* have _____ meanings. (*synonym*)

_____ **4.** Often you must understand a word's _____ use before you can determine its meaning. (*context*)

_____ 5. Many social studies and science textbooks have a _____ in the back. *(glossary)*

_____ 6. The words *slowness* and *slowly* are _____ from the word *slow*. *(derivative)*

_____ 7. Quick but frequent review helps with the _____ of difficult material. *(retain)*

_____ 8. A double play is a baseball _____ that means a team gets two men out on a single turn at bat. *(terminology)*

_____ 9. Your vocabulary has an _____ on your reading and writing. *(effective)*

_____ 10. A linguist _____ in the study of language. *(specialized)*

FIND THE EXAMPLE

Choose the answer that best describes the action or situation.

_____ 1. Something that *retains* water
    a. waterfall   **b.** rainfall   **c.** bucket   **d.** lamp

_____ 2. A *specialized* form of scissors
    a. hatchet   **b.** nail clippers   **c.** paper cutter   **d.** tweezers

_____ 3. A *synonym* for the word *correct*
    a. nice   **b.** wrong   **c.** right   **d.** mean

_____ 4. Something found in a *glossary*
    a. definitions   **b.** maps   **c.** study guides   **d.** charts

_____ 5. A *concept* that you might learn about in math class
    a. equal rights   **b.** multiplication   **c.** gravity   **d.** conductivity

_____ 6. A *derivative* of the word *good*
    a. bad   **b.** nice   **c.** goodness   **d.** excellent

_____ 7. *Terminology* used in cooking
    a. foul, offsides   **b.** boil, simmer   **c.** curl, straighten   **d.** chord, scale

_____ 8. Something that *context* most often sheds light on
    a. bicycles   **b.** meaning of words   **c.** solar cells   **d.** green plants

_____ 9. An *antonym* for *happy*
    a. content   **b.** happily   **c.** times   **d.** sad

_____ 10. An *effective* way to study
    a. sleep soundly   **b.** run laps   **c.** review notes   **d.** bake cookies

Words Taken from Animals

WORD LIST

beastly	hog	horseplay	hound	lionize
mammoth	parrot	pigheaded	scapegoat	sheepish

Words taken from the animal world make our writing and conversation more colorful and interesting. You have probably heard expressions like "eat like a *pig*" and "busy as a *bee*." A famous World War II general was called "The Desert Fox" by his enemies because he was so hard to catch. Like a fox, he slipped out of their grasp, appearing where they least expected him. As you read the words in this lesson, think about the animals the words come from. Try to imagine how they are connected to the vocabulary.

a beastly headache

1. **beastly** (bēst´lē) *adjective*
   a. Awful; very unpleasant
      • Tony's **beastly** headache made it hard for him to concentrate on the test.
   b. Looking like a beast
      • The monster in my dream was **beastly,** with huge, hairy arms and long, sharp teeth.

   beastliness *noun* The **beastliness** of the child's behavior at the party embarrassed her parents.

2. **hog** (hŏg)
   a. *noun* A greedy or selfish person
      • I love turkey and stuffing so much that I eat like a **hog** every Thanksgiving.
   b. *verb* To be greedy; to take more than one's fair share; to hoard
      • Don't **hog** all the space at the table!

3. **horseplay** (hôrs´plā´) *noun*
   Rough play
      • Stop that **horseplay** or somebody will get hurt!

In England, people often use the word *beastly* to mean "extremely," as in "a *beastly* hot day."

4. **hound** (hound) *verb*

To pursue or urge repeatedly or insistently

• She **hounded** her boyfriend until he agreed to cut his hair.

5. **lionize** (lī´ə-nīz´) *verb*

To greatly admire; to idolize

• Sports fans often **lionize** famous athletes.

6. **mammoth** (măm´əth) *adjective*

Enormous

• The ship glided toward a **mammoth** iceberg.

7. **parrot** (păr´ət) *verb*

To imitate without understanding

• When Max said, "Three times three is nine," his three-year-old brother **parroted** back, "Three times three is nine."

8. **pigheaded** (pĭg´hĕd´ĭd) *adjective*

Stupidly stubborn

• The **pigheaded** child refused to wear a coat, despite the freezing weather.

9. **scapegoat** (skāp´gōt´)

a. *noun* A person unfairly set up to take blame for others

• John and Cody broke the window but tried to make Tim the **scapegoat.**

b. *verb* To unfairly put blame on someone else

• Have you ever been **scapegoated** for something you haven't done?

10. **sheepish** (shē´pĭsh) *adjective*

Quietly embarrassed or guilty

• The six-year-old looked **sheepish** when his mom asked him who ate the cookies.

sheepishly *adverb* Moira looked at us **sheepishly** when we asked her who had forgotten the scissors.

WORD ENRICHMENT

Words from birds

Our feathered friends have given us numerous words and phrases. Some come from birds of prey. For example, a *vulture* is a person who profits from the problems of others. Similarly, *vultures* profit from the death of other animals by eating them. To *watch like a hawk* means "to watch intently," just as *hawks* watch the prey they are about to attack. To *soar like an eagle* is to achieve great heights or great success.

Bird-brained means "foolish," and to *eat like a bird* means "to eat practically nothing." These terms came about because of how birds appear—their heads are fairly small and their bodies are very light—but these descriptions are actually inaccurate. Birds are quite intelligent, and some eat their own weight in food each day!

WRITE THE CORRECT WORD

Write the correct word in the space next to each definition.

_____ 1. to pursue without stopping

_____ 2. enormous size

_____ 3. someone unfairly blamed

_____ 4. unreasonably stubborn

_____ 5. very disagreeable and nasty

_____ 6. embarrassed

_____ 7. to repeat without understanding

_____ 8. a greedy person

_____ 9. to greatly admire

_____ 10. wild play

COMPLETE THE SENTENCE

Write the letter for the word that best completes each sentence.

_____ 1. Don't _____ what other people have said; think for yourself.
a. hog b. hound c. parrot d. lionize

_____ 2. Carla stared in despair at the _____ pile of dirty dishes left after the party.
a. sheepish b. mammoth c. lionized d. pigheaded

_____ 3. The boys made Jerry the _____ for their tardiness, but it wasn't his fault.
a. hound b. horseplay c. scapegoat d. hog

_____ 4. The children didn't realize their _____ had gotten out of control until they heard the crash.
a. horseplay b. mammoth c. lionizing d. scapegoat

_____ 5. The child showed her _____ manners by demanding things without saying "please."
a. parroted b. sheepish c. mammoth d. beastly

_____ 6. Ted's sister _____ the computer all night, so he couldn't check his e-mail.
a. hogged b. parroted c. lionized d. hounded

_____ 7. The president of the movie star's fan club _____ her so much that she hung a picture of the star in every room in her house.
a. hogged b. lionized c. hounded d. parroted

_____ 8. Sue was determined to _____ her brother until he paid her back.
a. scapegoat b. parrot c. hound d. hog

_____ 9. Gary felt _____ for having dropped two easy passes in the game.
a. lionized b. sheepish c. pigheaded d. mammoth

_____ 10. "I don't care if you think I'm _____, I refuse to wear that silly costume!"
a. lionized b. mammoth c. beastly d. pigheaded

Challenge: Because Jhett had a habit of _____ the ball, his teammates made him the _____ when they lost the game, even though none of them had played very well.

_____ a. parroting…hog b. hounding…horseplay c. hogging…scapegoat

From Our Animal Friends

Animals play an important part in both our lives and our language. Many English words are taken from animal appearance and behavior.

The word *hound*, for example, takes its meaning from the behavior of dogs called hounds, which are used to help in hunting. They have an especially strong sense of smell and will chase the scent of an animal until they catch it. For this reason, to *hound* means "to chase, follow, or pursue until you've got what you want." **(1)** News reporters are known for *hounding* people for information.

The word *horseplay* comes from the rough way that horses, especially wild ones, often play with each other. Horseplay has come to mean "a good time that gets out of control, sometimes becoming dangerous." **(2)** *Horseplay* often ends with someone getting hurt. Sheep, on the other hand, are quiet and fairly easy to control. Perhaps this is why they give their name to a quiet state of embarrassment. **(3)** Children might act *sheepish* after getting carried away in horseplay.

Perhaps you have seen a parrot, or other talking bird, repeat the words it hears. The bird doesn't understand what it is saying. Therefore, to *parrot* means "to repeat something without understanding it." **(4)** A common example of *parroting* is when people sing songs written in another language, without knowing what the lyrics mean.

Pigs are another species whose behavior has lent meaning to words. Pigs are known to be so stubborn, or *pigheaded*, that they can put themselves in danger. **(5)** *Pigheaded* people can do harm to themselves and cause trouble for those around them. An adult pig, or *hog*, eats greedily, snatching food away from other hogs whenever possible. For this reason, *hog* has come to mean "someone who selfishly takes more than a fair share." **(6)** Young children often *hog* toys, refusing to let others play with them.

Thousands of years ago, the members of an ancient tribe used a goat as a symbol to "take away" their bad deeds. Over the goat they confessed things they had done wrong; then they released the goat into the desert. The goat was said to have carried away the bad things the people had done. In modern times, a person who is punished for something done by others is called a *scapegoat*. **(7)** At one time or another, each of us has probably been *scapegoated* for something someone else has done.

A *beast* is a dangerous wild animal. The adjective *beastly* can be used to describe a person or an animal that looks wild or dangerous. It can also be used to refer to unpleasant behavior. **(8)** Knocking other people out of the way to get to the front of a line is an example of *beastly* behavior. The "king" of beasts, of course, is the lion. It appears as a king or hero in many folktales. Therefore, to *lionize* means "to treat someone as if he or she were a hero." **(9)** Many young people today *lionize* athletes and strive to be like them.

Another animal that made a big impression was the mammoth, an enormous elephant-like mammal that is now extinct. This creature's huge size gave the word *mammoth* its meaning. Mammoths' skeletons were so large that some early humans used them as homes. **(10)** Think how shocked those people would be to see the *mammoth* mansions that some people live in today!

Each sentence below refers to a numbered sentence in the passage. Write the letter of the choice that gives the sentence a meaning that is closest to the original sentence.

_____ **1.** News reporters are known for _____ people for information.
     a. refusing   **b.** grabbing   **c.** pursuing   **d.** admiring

_____ **2.** _____ often ends with someone getting hurt.
     a. Enormous size   **b.** Rough play   **c.** Great admiration   **d.** A guilty look

_____ **3.** Children might act _____ after getting carried away in horseplay.
     a. greedy   **b.** stubborn   **c.** admired   **d.** guilty

_____ **4.** A common example of _____ is when people sing songs written in a language that they do not speak.

    a. playing   **b.** pursuing   **c.** imitating   **d.** admiring

_____ **5.** _____ people can do harm to themselves and cause trouble for others.

    a. Stubborn   **b.** Enormous   **c.** Unpleasant   **d.** Embarrassed

_____ **6.** Young children often _____ toys, refusing to let others play with them.

    a. blame   **b.** pursue   **c.** hoard   **d.** play

_____ **7.** Each of us has probably been _____ for something someone else has done.

    a. admired   **b.** blamed   **c.** urged   **d.** pursued

_____ **8.** Knocking others out of the way is an example of _____ behavior.

    a. guilty   **b.** greedy   **c.** enormous   **d.** awful

_____ **9.** Many young people today _____ athletes and work hard to be like them.

    a. pursue   **b.** idolize   **c.** hoard   **d.** blame

_____ **10.** Early humans would be shocked to see the _____ mansions that some people live in today.

    a. awful   **b.** embarrassed   **c.** enormous   **d.** stubborn

Indicate whether the statements below are TRUE or FALSE according to the passage.

_____ **1.** A hound is a type of dog used for hunting.

_____ **2.** Sheep are harder to control than horses.

_____ **3.** The word *scapegoat* comes from an ancient tribal practice.

FINISH THE THOUGHT

Complete each sentence so that it shows the meaning of the italicized word.

1. The police *hounded* the criminal until _____

_____

2. The *mammoth* building _____

_____

WRITE THE DERIVATIVE

Complete the sentence by writing the correct form of the word shown in parentheses. You may not need to change the form that is given.

_____ **1.** Stop _____ the whole couch and let me sit down! *(hog)*

_____ **2.** _____ can lead to serious injury. *(horseplay)*

_____ **3.** The _____ of the villain in the cartoon frightened the young children. *(beastly)*

_____ **4.** John _____ the French words without knowing what they meant. *(parrot)*

5. The civil rights leader was _____ for her bravery. (lionize)

_____

6. The two workers became the _____ for the crimes of the company president. (scapegoat)

_____

7. The four-year-old looked at his mother _____ after he spit out the medicine. (sheepish)

_____

8. The reporter _____ the senator until he got an interview. (hound)

_____

9. _____ stone statues stood at the entrance to the cave. (mammoth)

_____

10. It is _____ to refuse to wear braces when you really need them. (pigheaded)

FIND THE EXAMPLE

Choose the answer that best describes the action or situation.

_____ 1. Another way to describe what someone who is *parroting* is doing
   a. arguing back   **b.** whining loudly   **c.** laughing   **d.** imitating

_____ 2. Someone most likely to be *lionized* by teenagers
   a. lawyer   **b.** pop star   **c.** mail carrier   **d.** zookeeper

_____ 3. An example of a *mammoth* building
   a. skyscraper   **b.** hut   **c.** cabin   **d.** playhouse

_____ 4. An antonym for *pigheaded*
   a. stubborn   **b.** agreeable   **c.** angry   **d.** wrong

_____ 5. Someone who is likely to get *hounded* by reporters
   a. movie star   **b.** gardener   **c.** baby sitter   **d.** teacher

_____ 6. Something being done by someone who *hogs* cookies
   a. sharing with others   **b.** dividing them up   **c.** taking too many   **d.** baking them quickly

_____ 7. What might happen during *horseplay*
   a. reading   **b.** yelling   **c.** drawing   **d.** sleeping

_____ 8. Something a *scapegoat* might say
   a. "Thank you."   **b.** "Can I help you?"   **c.** "When is it due?"   **d.** "I didn't do it."

_____ 9. An example of *beastly* behavior
   a. washing your face   **b.** tripping someone   **c.** spilling juice   **d.** feeding a cat

_____ 10. An example of *sheepish* behavior
   a. jumping around   **b.** knitting quickly   **c.** looking away   **d.** yelling loudly

Liking and Disliking

WORD LIST

affable	awe	contempt	crave	detestable
enchanting	fascinate	loathe	rave	recoil

Robert Frost, the famous poet, described love as fire and hate as ice. No one can really measure feelings the way we can measure the temperature of fire or ice. Still, the emotional reactions described by the words in this lesson can be intense. If you were to measure them on an emotional thermometer, some would be very high, others low, and still others somewhere between those extremes. As you study these words, think about where they fall on your emotional thermometer.

1. **affable** (ăf´ə-bəl) *adjective*
   Pleasant; friendly
   • My **affable** neighbor often stops by for a friendly chat.

   affability *noun* Mario's **affability** made him a popular party guest.

   affably *adverb* Sylvia greeted me **affably**.

2. **awe** (ô) *noun*
   Wonder, fear, or respect for something impressive
   • The size and beauty of the Grand Canyon filled us with **awe**.

   awesome *adjective* When the king entered, an **awesome** silence settled over the room.

3. **contempt** (kən-tĕmpt´) *noun*
   Hateful scorn
   • The king was filled with **contempt** for his subjects who betrayed him.

   contemptible *adjective* People who mistreat pets are **contemptible**.

> To be in *contempt* of court is to disrupt a court of law or to openly disobey a court order.

4. **crave** (krāv) *verb*
   To need or desire strongly
   • After spending all day alone in the house, the puppy **craved** human affection.

   craving *noun* After dinner, I always have a **craving** for ice cream.

5. **detestable** (dĭ-tĕs´tə-bəl) *adjective*
   Inspiring or deserving hatred
   • The **detestable** ruler forced people to work as slaves in his mines.

   detest *verb* I **detest** the taste of spinach.

a craving

6. enchanting (ĕn-chăn´tĭng) *adjective*
Charming; having the power to attract
• The sunset over the pond created an **enchanting** scene.

enchant *verb* Fairy tales continue to **enchant** children.

enchantment *noun* Children's **enchantment** with the video game
made it a bestseller.

7. fascinate (făs´ə-nāt´) *verb*
To capture strong interest or attention
• Stories about my grandmother's childhood **fascinate** me because life
  was so different back then.

fascination *noun* We watched with **fascination** as the bees
gathered pollen.

8. loathe (lōth) *verb*
To hate intensely
• I **loathe** waiting in line at the supermarket.

loathing *noun* The baby showed his **loathing** for the bad-tasting
cough medicine by spitting it out.

loathsome *adjective* Many people think snakes are **loathsome**
creatures.

9. rave (rāv) *verb*
a. To praise enthusiastically
• She constantly **raves** about her daughter's great musical talent.
b. To speak wildly without making any sense
• His father **raved** angrily when Jason left the house without
  permission.

10. recoil (rĭ-koil´) *verb*
a. To shrink back in fear, dislike, or disgust
• I **recoiled** from the sight of the bloody cut.
b. To move or jerk backward
• The shotgun **recoiled** so hard that it knocked the hunter over.

WORD ENRICHMENT

Dropping *e* when adding a word ending

Many words in this lesson, including *affable, awe, crave, detestable,*
fascinate, loathe, and *rave* end in a silent *e*.

When adding an ending to a word with a silent *e*, drop the final *e* if
the ending you are adding begins with a vowel. *Affable* becomes *affability*
when *-ity* is added. (Notice that you must also add an *i* before the *l*.) *Loathe*
becomes *loathing* when *-ing* is added. *Fascinate* becomes *fascination* when
-ion is added.

However, if the ending begins with a consonant, keep the *e*. Following
this rule, *awe* becomes *awesome* when *-some* is added.

WRITE THE CORRECT WORD

Write the correct word in the space next to each definition.

_____ 1. hateful scorn

_____ 2. to draw back in disgust

_____ 3. to need or desire strongly

_____ 4. deserving hatred

_____ 5. to capture interest

_____ 6. to hate intensely

_____ 7. to praise with much enthusiasm

_____ 8. friendly

_____ 9. charming

_____ 10. wonder

COMPLETE THE SENTENCE

Write the letter for the word that best completes each sentence.

_____ 1. I _____ violent movies because they give me terrible nightmares.
  a. fascinate   b. rave   c. crave   d. loathe

_____ 2. The new student was very _____, so he made friends quickly.
  a. detestable   b. raving   c. affable   d. contemptible

_____ 3. Criminals who cheat the elderly out of their money are especially _____.
  a. affable   b. detestable   c. awesome   d. enchanting

_____ 4. Her voice was so _____ that people would come from all over to hear her sing.
  a. detestable   b. loathsome   c. contemptible   d. enchanting

_____ 5. The discovery of new planets _____ scientists.
  a. fascinates   b. loathes   c. raves   d. recoils

_____ 6. I stared in _____ at my brother's amazing painting; I had no idea he was
            so talented!
  a. contempt   b. loathing   c. awe   d. craving

_____ 7. My parents _____ about how great his painting was.
  a. recoiled   b. detested   c. craved   d. raved

_____ 8. After playing in the snow, I usually _____ hot chocolate.
  a. crave   b. recoil   c. fascinate   d. enchant

_____ 9. The horrible sight and smell of the moldy food made me _____.
  a. fascinate   b. detest   c. enchant   d. recoil

_____ 10. Jason's teammates glared at him with _____ after he accidentally scored
            a touchdown for the other team.
  a. contempt   b. enchantment   c. fascination   d. awe

Challenge: Some people actually _____ raw oysters, while others _____ at the sight
            of them.

_____   a. loathe…detest   b. rave…fascinate   c. crave…recoil

The Clever Leprechaun

According to legend, imaginary little people called leprechauns live among the hills of Ireland. **(1)** Tales of leprechauns have *enchanted* human beings for generations. Perhaps this is because these little creatures are said to hide pots of gold. **(2)** There are many stories about people who *crave* leprechaun's riches and have tried to steal their treasures.

In stories, leprechauns avoid human beings, so we think of them as unfriendly creatures. **(3)** In many tales, however, they are quite *affable* with each other. They are depicted singing and dancing at leprechaun parties. They are also supposedly very smart. **(4)** A famous story tells how a leprechaun used his *awesome* intelligence to keep a human being from getting his gold.

One day, a boy named Sean was walking down a country road when he noticed something small moving behind a rock. Sneaking up quietly, he saw a leprechaun busily working on a pair of shoes. **(5)** Sean was *fascinated* by this tiny creature, with his red top hat, his green waistcoat, and his tiny cobbling tools. Sean grabbed him. **(6)** The leprechaun *recoiled* as Sean held him up and looked at him carefully. **(7)** The leprechaun *loathed* being held captive.

"Let me go!" the leprechaun shouted, trying to wiggle free.

Sean remembered what people said about leprechauns. He was sure the leprechaun had some gold hidden away.

"Only if you give me your pot of gold!" demanded Sean.

Now the leprechaun knew he could not escape, so he thought hard. Then he pointed to a bush and said, "It's underneath there."

Sean looked at the bush and tried to memorize its appearance, but there was a whole field full of bushes that looked the same.

"I will need to go back for a shovel. How will I remember which bush you are pointing to?" asked Sean.

"If you let me go, I will take my red handkerchief and tie it to the bush," the leprechaun replied.

"Promise me you are not lying," said Sean.

"I promise," said the leprechaun.

So Sean released the leprechaun and watched as the creature tied his handkerchief to the bush. Then Sean rushed home and returned with a shovel. But when he got to the top of the hill, he saw a whole field of bushes, each with a red handkerchief tied to a branch.

(8) Sean ran from bush to bush, *raving* about "lies and tricks" as he searched for the gold. **(9)** Finally, he turned to the leprechaun and said, "You *detestable* creature! How could you do this to me?"

(10) The leprechaun laughed with *contempt* at Sean's foolishness. Once again, a human being had tried to steal a pot of gold, and a leprechaun had outsmarted him.

Each sentence below refers to a numbered sentence in the passage. Write the letter of the choice that gives the sentence a meaning that is closest to the original sentence.

_____ **1.** Tales of leprechauns have _____ human beings for years.
    a. disliked   **b.** delighted   **c.** angered   **d.** respected

_____ **2.** There are many stories about people who _____ leprechaun's riches.
    a. accidentally found   **b.** strongly dislike   **c.** desperately want   **d.** look down on

_____ **3.** In many tales, however, they are quite _____ with each other.
    a. hateful   **b.** disgusting   **c.** wild   **d.** friendly

_____ **4.** A famous story tells how a leprechaun used his _____ intelligence to keep a human being from getting his gold.
    a. impressive   **b.** interesting   **c.** disgusting   **d.** friendly

_____ **5.** Sean was _____ by this tiny creature, with his red top hat, his green waistcoat, and his tiny cobbling tools.
   a. respected   **b.** interested   **c.** disgusted   **d.** praised

_____ **6.** The leprechaun _____ as Sean held him up and looked at him carefully.
   a. spoke wildly   **b.** captured interest   **c.** screamed angrily   **d.** shrank back

_____ **7.** The leprechaun _____ being held captive.
   a. loved   **b.** enjoyed   **c.** hated   **d.** ignored

_____ **8.** Sean ran from bush to bush, _____ about "lies and tricks" as he searched for the gold.
   a. speaking wildly   **b.** giving praise   **c.** deserving hatred   **d.** avoiding others

_____ **9.** "You _____ creature! How could you do this to me?"
   a. delightful   **b.** wild   **c.** hateful   **d.** loveable

_____ **10.** The leprechaun laughed with _____ at Sean's foolishness.
   a. praise   **b.** scorn   **c.** wonder   **d.** desire

Indicate whether the statements below are TRUE or FALSE according to the passage.

_____ **1.** Leprechauns do not like to be around people.

_____ **2.** There are leprechauns living in Ireland.

_____ **3.** Leprechauns are very smart creatures.

WRITING EXTENDED RESPONSES

Leprechauns are imaginary characters. What other imaginary or legendary characters have you read about or heard about? Choose or invent an imaginary creature and write a descriptive essay about it. Your essay should be at least three paragraphs long. Make sure that you describe at least two aspects of the creature, such as its appearance, behavior, purpose (if it has one), or your attitude or feelings toward the creature. Use at least three lesson words in your essay and underline them.

WRITE THE DERIVATIVE

Complete the sentence by writing the correct form of the word shown in parentheses. You may not need to change the form that is given.

_____ **1.** This book is so _____ that I can't put it down. *(fascinate)*

_____ **2.** I _____ mowing the lawn. *(detestable)*

_____ **3.** My friend thought the play was boring, but I was _____ by it. *(enchanting)*

_____ **4.** Have you ever _____ something so badly that you felt you would do almost anything to get it? *(crave)*

_____ **5.** Ever since I got sick after eating a banana split, I have _____ bananas. *(loathe)*

_____ **6.** Her _____ made her an excellent hostess. *(affable)*

_____ **7.** Bullies who pick on those who are smaller and weaker are _____. *(contempt)*

_____ **8.** I act embarrassed when anyone _____ about my good grades, but I really like it. *(rave)*

_____ **9.** Aisha _____ at the sight of the Brussels sprouts on her plate. *(recoil)*

_____ **10.** The most _____ sight I have ever seen was the Northern Lights, dancing across the sky. *(awe)*

FIND THE EXAMPLE

Choose the answer that best describes the action or situation.

_____ **1.** An expression that conveys *awe*
    a. "Pass the salt."   **b.** "How much is it?"   **c.** "That's amazing!"   **d.** "Good night."

_____ **2.** Something a person who wants to satisfy a *craving* for dessert would do
    a. refuse pie   **b.** leave the table   **c.** wash dishes   **d.** eat ice cream

_____ **3.** Something likely to *enchant* small children
    a. traffic jam   **b.** puppet show   **c.** political debate   **d.** doctor's visit

_____ **4.** An example of *detestable* behavior
    a. kicking a dog   **b.** cheering loudly   **c.** losing homework   **d.** staying up late

_____ **5.** Something a person who *loathes* sports might play
    a. basketball   **b.** soccer   **c.** piano   **d.** baseball

_____ **6.** What a *raving* person is doing
    a. sleeping quietly   **b.** studying for a test   **c.** painting a mural   **d.** speaking wildly

_____ **7.** Something a brother might treat his sister with *contempt* for doing
    a. going to school   **b.** giving him a gift   **c.** tattling on him   **d.** cooking dinner

_____ **8.** Something that would cause most people to *recoil*
    a. a snake   **b.** a glass of water   **c.** a cookie   **d.** a book

_____ **9.** A word you might use to describe a *fascinating* movie
    a. boring   **b.** interesting   **c.** dull   **d.** irritating

_____ **10.** An example of *affable* behavior
    a. insulting someone   **b.** telling a joke   **c.** picking on someone   **d.** telling a lie

Using the Dictionary

Parts of Speech and Derivatives

A word's part of speech gives valuable clues to its use. Many words also have *derivatives,* which are closely related words formed from one base word. Base words and their derivatives are usually different parts of speech. Learning a word and its derivatives together helps you to multiply the words you master. Here is an example.

concept *noun*
- In 1945, Alan Turing developed the **concept** of the computer.

conceptual *adjective*
- Da Vinci did **conceptual** work on helicopters.

conceptualize *verb*
- It is hard to **conceptualize** four dimensions.

conceptually *adverb*
- This problem is **conceptually** difficult.

Learning the word *concept* helps you learn *conceptual, conceptualize,* and *conceptually.* In this book, derivatives are listed with their base words.

Common Parts of Speech

A **noun** is a person, place, thing, or idea.
- *Irene* is a *nurse.* (person)
- *Los Angeles* is an exciting *city.* (place)
- *Flowers* grow in *gardens.* (thing)
- Alan Turing developed the *concept* of the computer. (idea)

An **adjective** describes a noun. We can also say that an adjective **modifies** a noun.
- Da Vinci did *conceptual* work on helicopters. (*Conceptual* modifies the noun *work.*)
- The *happy* child played in the sunlight. (*Happy* modifies the noun *child.*)
- The dog was *wet.* (*Wet* modifies the noun *dog.*)

An **adverb** modifies a verb, adjective, or another adverb.
- The athlete ran *quickly.* (*Quickly* modifies the verb *ran.*)
- This problem is *conceptually* difficult. (*Conceptually* modifies the adjective *difficult.*)
- The flood spread *very* rapidly. (*Very* modifies the adverb *rapidly.*)

A **verb** expresses an action or a state of being.
- It is hard to *conceptualize* four dimensions. (*Conceptualize* is an action.)
- The class *is* interesting. (*Is* expresses a state of being.)

There are two types of verbs, *transitive* and *intransitive.*

A **transitive verb** requires a direct object and can't stand alone.
- Amy *bought* shoes. (The transitive verb *bought* is directed to the object *shoes.*)

An **intransitive verb** does not need a direct object.
- The dog *jumped.* (The intransitive verb *jumped* does not have an object.)

Using Suffixes to Form Derivatives

Derivatives are usually formed by adding **suffixes** to a base word. A suffix is a group of letters added to the end of a word. Fill in the sentences below following the model.

Most **adverbs** are formed by adding the suffix *-ly* to an adjective.
> Your work is *effective*. You are working *effectively*.

> Sean felt *sheepish*. He looked at his teacher _____*sheepishly*_____ .

Nouns can also be formed by adding suffixes to other parts of speech. Common suffixes used are *-ion* (or *-tion*), *-ness*, *-ity*, and *-ment*.

Adding *-ion* or *-tion*
> Please *define* this word. Make your *definition* a good one.

> The paper *fascinates* me. My _____ kept me reading it.
> (Did you remember to drop the *e?*)

Adding *-ness*
> She is a *frank* person. We know about her *frankness*.

> The diamond is *genuine*. We are sure of its _____ .

Adding *-ity*
> The car is *reliable*. We like its *reliability*.

> The judge is *impartial*. Her _____ is good.

Adding *-ment*
> Don't *appease* your enemies. *Appeasement* will only fail.

> You like to *manage* things. You should go into _____ .

In addition, the suffixes *-ance* (or *-ence*), *-er* (or *-or*), and *-ism* can also form nouns. Examples of words that contain these suffixes are *insurance*, *teacher*, and *patriotism*.

Adjectives are often formed by adding the suffixes *-ous*, *-able*, and *-ive*.

Adding *-able* or *-ible*
> We can *rely* on our car. Our car is *reliable*.

> We *detest* bad behavior. Bad behavior is _____ . (In this case, use *able*.)

Adding *-ive*
> Thank you for your prompt *response*. Your *responsive* reply saved us time.

> There was an *excess* of food. We gave away the _____ amount of food.

Adding *-ous*
> Students with *industry* are hard working. *Industrious* students get good grades.

> Her *vigor* comes from good health. Her _____ exercise helps her.

The suffixes *-al*, *-ful*, and *-ic* also form adjectives, as in *conceptual*, *resentful*, and *operatic*.

Verbs are often formed by adding the suffix *-ize*.

Adding *-ize*
> I have a *special* interest in rare coins. I *specialize* in rare coins.

> That information is *visual*. It is easy to _____ it.

Understanding derivatives gives you a powerful tool to increase your vocabulary.

Honesty, Fairness, and Openness

WORD LIST

bluff	fabricate	frank	genuine	impartial
integrity	obvious	plagiarize	reliable	suppress

The words in this lesson describe degrees of honesty, fairness, and openness, and other words that refer to a lack of those qualities. Learning this new vocabulary will help you to better understand and describe many situations that, for better or worse, can come up in everyday life.

1. bluff (blŭf) *verb*
   a. To fool or deceive; to mislead
   • Posing as a general, the man **bluffed** his way past the security guard.
   b. To try to frighten with false threats
   • Amy knew her dad was **bluffing** when he threatened to "lock her in the dungeon" for not doing the dishes.

> "To *call* a *bluff*" means "to expose someone's lie by asking that person to prove the claim."

2. fabricate (făb′rĭ-kāt′) *verb*
   a. To invent in order to deceive
   • I watched in horror as my friend **fabricated** a story about why we were late.
   b. To make or manufacture
   • Steel is **fabricated** from iron and carbon.

fabrication *noun* We were shocked to realize that her stories of heroism were complete **fabrications.**

3. frank (frăngk) *adjective*
Completely honest
• It can be hard for parents and children to have **frank** discussions.

frankness *noun* The child's **frankness** startled her grandmother.

frankly *adjective* A wise politician allows her aides to speak **frankly** to her.

4. genuine (jĕn′yōō-ĭn) *adjective*
   a. Real; not copied or fake
   • Hidden among the junk in the attic was a **genuine** Picasso painting.
   b. Sincere; honest
   • Her request that we stay for dinner seemed **genuine,** so we accepted.

genuineness *noun* Experts confirmed the **genuineness** of the ancient Chinese vase.

genuinely *adverb* We were **genuinely** shocked to learn he was the thief.

genuine Ming vase

5. impartial (ĭm-pär´shəl) *adjective*
Fair; not favoring one side over another
• The jury was instructed to weigh the facts in an **impartial** manner.

impartiality *noun* The coaches respected the **impartiality** of the referee.

> The word part *im-* means "not." When added to *part* in *impartial*, it means "not taking one part," or "being fair."

6. integrity (ĭn-tĕg´rĭ-tē) *noun*
a. Strong moral character; the state of sticking strictly to one's morals
• A person of **integrity** does not cheat on exams.
b. Wholeness; soundness
• Luckily, the hurricane had not damaged the **integrity** of the house.

> The word *integer* means "whole" or "complete." A person with *integrity* sticks to all (or the *whole* of) his or her morals.

7. obvious (ŏb´vē-əs) *adjective*
Easy to see; clear; apparent
• The frown on Melinda's face made it **obvious** that she was not happy.

obviousness *noun* Mom laughed at the **obviousness** of her son's lie.

obviously *adverb* Dad's messy shopping list was **obviously** written in a hurry.

8. plagiarize (plā´jə-rīz´) *verb*
To copy the words or ideas of another person and claim they are your own
• Don't **plagiarize** by copying whole paragraphs from a book or an article.

plagiarism *noun* After admitting to **plagiarism,** the author had to pay the person whose work he had copied.

9. reliable (rĭ-lī´ə-bəl) *adjective*
Dependable; able to be trusted
• My e-mail server is not always **reliable,** so I sometimes miss messages.

rely *verb* Many people **rely** on alarm clocks to wake them up.

reliability *noun* I valued the **reliability** of my old car, which started in any kind of weather.

10. suppress (sə-prĕs´) *verb*
a. To prevent something from being published or known
• The books of Boris Pasternak were **suppressed** in the Soviet Union, but published in the United States.
b. To end by force or effort
• Raisa wanted to look interested, so she **suppressed** her urge to yawn.

suppression *noun* We were shocked by the **suppression** of the news.

WORD ENRICHMENT

Kidnapping words

The word *plagiarizing* comes from the Latin verb *plagiarius,* meaning "kidnapper." A *plagiarist* "kidnaps" the words of others.

NAME _____   DATE _____

WRITE THE CORRECT WORD

Write the correct word in the space next to each definition.

_____ 1. to prevent publication

_____ 2. to tell a false story

_____ 3. strong moral character

_____ 4. completely honest

_____ 5. easy to see

_____ 6. to try to frighten with false threats

_____ 7. dependable

_____ 8. to copy the work of another

_____ 9. fair

_____ 10. real

COMPLETE THE SENTENCE

Write the letter for the word that best completes each sentence.

_____ 1. The young boy threatened to run away from home, but his mother knew he was _____.
a. plagiarizing   b. suppressing   c. frank   d. bluffing

_____ 2. Dictators often _____ the views of those who disagree with them.
a. suppress   b. plagiarize   c. rely   d. bluff

_____ 3. The jeweler frowned and said, "Unfortunately, that diamond is about as _____ as a three-dollar bill."
a. frank   b. genuine   c. obvious   d. impartial

_____ 4. Thinking quickly, the boy _____ a story about finding the toy he had stolen.
a. relied   b. plagiarized   c. suppressed   d. fabricated

_____ 5. People with _____ keep their promises.
a. plagiarism   b. impartiality   c. integrity   d. suppression

_____ 6. It was _____ to the audience that Marsha hadn't memorized her lines.
a. obvious   b. reliable   c. frank   d. impartial

_____ 7. The author was furious when he found out that another person had _____ his work.
a. bluffed   b. plagiarized   c. relied   d. fabricated

_____ 8. If you buy appliances that are _____, they won't need constant repair.
a. impartial   b. suppressed   c. frank   d. reliable

_____ 9. "To be _____, Mr. McNair, I think I deserve extra pay for babysitting so late."
a. obvious   b. suppressed   c. frank   d. fabricated

_____ 10. The _____ principal suggested a compromise that satisfied both of the students.
a. impartial   b. obvious   c. suppressed   d. plagiarized

Challenge: I thought Juanita was _____, but her story turned out to be _____.

_____ a. obvious…frank   b. bluffing…genuine   c. plagiarizing…impartial

Protecting Creativity

The laws of intellectual property deal with the protection of ideas. Music, books, art, paintings, and even advertisements are created using our minds, or intellects. Intellectual property laws help to assure that artists' work is not copied or used without the artist receiving money or credit.

Music can be easily copied and sold without the permission of those who made it. **(1)** *Frankly*, anyone who makes copies of music without the permission of the producers is stealing. But people who sell these copies are committing a more serious crime, for they are stealing a large amount of money. **(2)** At times, the low quality of the recording and the cover art make it *obvious* that a disc is a fake. **(3)** But sometimes the copy looks and sounds *genuine*. **(4)** Songs are copied from the original disc, and cleverly *fabricated* covers look identical to those created by the artists' record companies. Illegal copies are a particular problem across international boundaries. **(5)** Artists' organizations in the United States have called on the governments of other countries to *suppress* this type of theft.

Intellectual property laws now ensure that recording artists get paid if their songs are downloaded from the Internet. **(6)** *Reliable* Internet services sell songs for a fee, and part of this money goes to the artist.

(7) *Plagiarism* is another crime addressed by intellectual property law. One author, reading the preface of a book, was shocked to discover that he was looking at his own words! People have even copied entire books and published them as their own. **(8)** Perhaps the copiers want to *bluff* the public into thinking they are authorities in a field. Or they may be after money. Copyright agreements, which are part of intellectual

property law, protect authors by giving them legal ownership of their writing for a certain period of time.

Intellectual property cases are often difficult to decide. For example, should initials be protected? In one case, a new cable channel, "Stand-Up Comedy Television," announced that it planned to use the initials SCTV as its name. However, a television comedy show called "Second City TV" had already used those initials as a title. The television show's initials were originally protected by copyright, but this copyright may have expired. As you can see, this case is complicated. **(9)** It may end up in court, where a judge and jury will try to make an *impartial* decision.

Intellectual property includes music, books, art, and even initials. **(10)** The issues are so complex that even people of *integrity* can find themselves in difficult situations. Copyright and trademark laws have a long history of protecting creative work. In today's world, where copying and transporting ideas and products is so easy, new protections are needed. For this reason, the World Intellectual Property Organization has been founded to protect creative works in every country.

Each sentence below refers to a numbered sentence in the passage. Write the letter of the choice that gives the sentence a meaning that is closest to the original sentence.

_____ **1.** _____, anyone who makes copies of music without permission is stealing.
   a. Fairly   **b.** Honestly   **c.** Dependably   **d.** Sincerely

_____ **2.** The low quality of the recording and the cover art make it _____ that the disc is a fake.
   a. easy to see   **b.** completely honest   **c.** equal for all   **d.** fair and unbiased

_____ **3.** But sometimes the copy looks and sounds _____.
   a. fake   **b.** easy   **c.** whole   **d.** real

_____ **4.** Cleverly _____ covers look identical to those created by the record companies.
   a. dependable   **b.** manufactured   **c.** honest   **d.** apparent

_____ **5.** Artists' organizations have called on the governments of other countries to _____ this type of theft.
   a. copy   **b.** trust   **c.** end   **d.** favor

_____ **6.** _____ Internet services sell songs for a fee, and part of this money goes to the singer or band.
   a. Dependable   **b.** Favorable   **c.** Invented   **d.** Apparent

_____ **7.** _____ is a crime addressed by intellectual property law.
   a. Treating fairly   **b.** Ending by force   **c.** Inventing lies   **d.** Copying work

_____ **8.** Perhaps the copiers want to _____ the public into thinking they are authorities in a field.
   a. trust   **b.** fool   **c.** prevent   **d.** surprise

_____ **9.** It may end up in court, where a judge and jury will try to make a(n) _____ decision.
   a. fair   **b.** honest   **c.** real   **d.** clear

_____ **10.** The issues are so complex that even people of _____ can find themselves in difficult situations.
   a. dependability   **b.** hopefulness   **c.** strong character   **d.** fairness

Indicate whether the statements below are TRUE or FALSE according to the passage.

_____ **1.** Intellectual property is something created using one's mind.

_____ **2.** It is legal to copy music without paying for it.

_____ **3.** Copyright laws give writers legal ownership of their work.

FINISH THE THOUGHT

Complete each sentence so that it shows the meaning of the italicized word.

1. A person with *integrity* might _____

_____

2. It is difficult to be *impartial* when _____

_____

WRITE THE DERIVATIVE

Complete the sentence by writing the correct form of the word shown in parentheses. You may not need to change the form that is given.

_____ **1.** We _____ hoped he would come back to visit again. (*genuine*)

_____ **2.** The coach's _____ seemed harsh at first, but it helped make the team better. (*frank*)

_____ 3. The teacher was furious when he discovered the student's excuse was a complete _____. (*fabricate*)

_____ 4. After Kyle missed an important meeting, his boss began to question his _____. (*reliable*)

_____ 5. The judge's _____ was questioned because he was friendly with one of the defendant's lawyers. (*impartial*)

_____ 6. Terry received a failing grade on her paper because she _____ from a book. (*plagiarize*)

_____ 7. He was _____ too tired to run any farther. (*obvious*)

_____ 8. Because he was a man of _____, he refused to lie about what he saw. (*integrity*)

_____ 9. The five-year-old was _____ when he said he wasn't afraid of anything. (*bluff*)

_____ 10. The students _____ their laughter after the map fell off the wall. (*suppress*)

FIND THE EXAMPLE

Choose the answer that best describes the action or situation.

_____ 1. A person who is always expected to be *impartial*
   a. parent   **b.** friend   **c.** referee   **d.** lawyer

_____ 2. Something that a person of *integrity* would most likely do
   a. report a crime   **b.** plan a crime   **c.** commit a crime   **d.** ignore a crime

_____ 3. Something that a person who is *reliable* would most likely do
   a. get lost   **b.** arrive on time   **c.** arrive late   **d.** not show up

_____ 4. Something a dishonest politician might want to *suppress*
   a. his supporters   **b.** his accomplishments   **c.** his message   **d.** his past failures

_____ 5. Something a child might find it difficult to be *frank* about
   a. earning an A   **b.** doing her chores   **c.** breaking something   **d.** winning an award

_____ 6. An example of an *obvious* lie a student might tell about homework
   a. "I forgot it."   **b.** "I didn't do it."   **c.** "I left it at home."   **d.** "Robbers took it."

_____ 7. An example of *plagiarism*
   a. recording a song   **b.** copying a paragraph   **c.** inventing a lie   **d.** selling a disc

_____ 8. Something that is *fabricated*
   a. rock   **b.** bark   **c.** cloth   **d.** water

_____ 9. Something that might be very valuable, but only if it is *genuine*
   a. a new book   **b.** a garden hose   **c.** an ancient coin **d.** a pretty dress

_____ 10. A situation in which people are supposed to *bluff*
   a. masquerade ball **b.** dog show   **c.** wedding ceremony **d.** doctor's visit

26   **Honesty, Fairness, and Openness**

Amounts, Large and Small

WORD LIST

accumulate	ample	barren	comprehensive	extensive
meager	pervasive	sparse	surpass	trifle

Every day, we use words that describe amounts. Do we have enough time to complete our homework? Will the large amount of rain cause flooding? The words in this lesson describe size and quantity without using numbers. Some words refer to size (how large, how small), some refer to quantity (how many, how few), and others refer to degree (more than enough, not enough). Listen to the speech of people around you and notice the ways they use this vocabulary.

1. **accumulate** (ə-kyōōm´yə-lāt´) *verb*
   To pile up or collect
   • For years, my grandmother **accumulated** old newspapers in the attic.

   accumulation *noun* The squirrel had an **accumulation** of old string and scraps in its nest.

2. **ample** (ăm´pəl) *adjective*
   More than enough; plenty
   • "These shoes have **ample** room for growth," said the clerk.

3. **barren** (băr´ən) *adjective*
   a. Not capable of producing plants or crops; unproductive
   • The **barren** desert land had no trees or shrubs.
   b. Empty
   • The proposals were **barren** of any new ideas.

   barrenness *noun* The **barrenness** of the land kept the farmers poor.

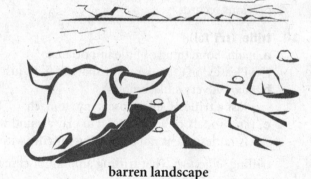

barren landscape

4. **comprehensive** (kŏm´prĭ-hĕn´sĭv) *adjective*
   a. Complete; including everything or the most important things
   • The principal made one **comprehensive** list of all the students in the school.
   b. Showing extensive or thorough understanding
   • After many years of study, his knowledge of the Civil War was **comprehensive.**

   comprehensiveness *noun* After reading the thousand-page biography, the critics were impressed by its **comprehensiveness.**

5. **extensive** (ĭk-stĕn´sĭv) *adjective*
Large; far-reaching
• The museum had an **extensive** collection of ancient pottery.

extend *verb* The Roman Empire once **extended** from England to Africa.

extent *noun* The full **extent** of the hurricane's damage was not yet known.

6. **meager** (mē´gər) *adjective*
Less than enough; a small amount
• The library's low budget resulted in a **meager** supply of books.

meagerness *noun* The **meagerness** of the meal left me hungry.

7. **pervasive** (pər-vā´sĭv) *adjective*
Found throughout; present all around
• A **pervasive** odor of bread told us that Mom was baking.

pervade *verb* Excitement about the nearby parade **pervaded** the classroom.

8. **sparse** (spärs) *adjective*
Occurring or growing far apart; not thick or dense; scattered
• In some deserts, plant life is very **sparse.**

sparseness *noun* The **sparseness** of Grandpa's hair allowed us to see the birthmark on his scalp.

9. **surpass** (sər-păs´) *verb*
To be better than expected
• This year's wheat crop **surpassed** last year's by two million bushels.

surpassing *adjective* Olympic runners keep **surpassing** previous records.

> *Surpassing* can also be used as an adjective, as in "It was a painting of *surpassing* beauty."

10. **trifle** (trī´fəl)
a. *noun* Something of little importance
• Please don't thank me for that gift—it's just a **trifle!**
b. *noun* A very small amount
• Just a **trifle** of spice upsets my stomach.
c. *verb* To talk or act jokingly; to play around with
• A rattlesnake is not something to **trifle** with.

trifling *adjective* That **trifling** amount of cinnamon won't affect the taste of the cake.

WORD ENRICHMENT

Thin words

The word *meager* comes from the Latin word *macer*, meaning "thin."
Macer is also the root of the English word *emaciated*, which means "extremely thin, often as a result of starvation."

WRITE THE CORRECT WORD

Write the correct word in the space next to each definition.

_____ 1. more than enough

_____ 2. something not important

_____ 3. to collect or gather

_____ 4. including everything

_____ 5. found throughout

_____ 6. far-reaching; large

_____ 7. few; scattered; growing far apart

_____ 8. to go beyond; to be better than expected

_____ 9. less than enough

_____ 10. unable to grow crops

COMPLETE THE SENTENCE

Write the letter for the word that best completes each sentence.

_____ 1. It wasn't worth arguing about; it was just a(n) _____.
   a. accumulation   b. meagerness   c. barrenness   d. trifle

_____ 2. The grass in the pasture was so _____ that the cows were practically starving.
   a. accumulated   b. comprehensive   c. sparse   d. surpassing

_____ 3. The audience of 1,000 people _____ our expectation of 500.
   a. trifled   b. surpassed   c. pervaded   d. accumulated

_____ 4. The applicants had to undergo a _____ medical exam to show that they had no health problems.
   a. comprehensive   b. sparse   c. barren   d. meager

_____ 5. The storm did such _____ damage to the barn that it collapsed.
   a. sparse   b. extensive   c. ample   d. barren

_____ 6. The dinner was _____ enough to feed the entire cast and crew.
   a. surpassing   b. sparse   c. ample   d. barren

_____ 7. The skunk's odor was so _____ that we had to have the whole house professionally cleaned.
   a. meager   b. ample   c. pervasive   d. barren

_____ 8. One small bag of nuts seemed like a(n) _____ supply for a party of fifty people.
   a. comprehensive   b. extensive   c. barren   d. meager

_____ 9. They wanted to _____ the biggest pile of pumpkins the town had ever seen.
   a. accumulate   b. pervade   c. extend   d. comprehend

_____ 10. Only penguins were able to survive on the rocky, _____ islands.
   a. trifle   b. surpass   c. comprehensive   d. barren

Challenge: It seems unfair that some people have such _____ resources, while others have a(n) _____ supply.

_____   a. ample...comprehensive   b. sparse...barren   c. meager...ample

The World's Largest Library

If you ever have a chance to visit the Library of Congress, you will see a library unlike any other. **(1)** Its collections are *extensive,* filling more than 530 miles of bookshelves in three buildings. The holdings include movies, photographs, computer programs, maps, diaries, letters, paintings, audio recordings, and special materials for handicapped researchers, as well as books. **(2)** To date, the library contains more than 128 million items—the most *comprehensive* collection of any library in the world.

Each year, more than one million people flock to see the library's exhibits. **(3)** A solemn air seems to *pervade* the rooms where some of the most important documents in American history rest—documents that were actually held by Washington, Adams, Jefferson, and other Founding Fathers.

(4) The Library of Congress was created in 1800, when Washington, D.C., was a new town, and its population was *sparse.* President John Adams approved $5,000 to start the library. **(5)** Compared with many private libraries of the time, its collection of three maps and 740 books must have seemed *trifling.* **(6)** But Thomas Jefferson had a vision of the Library of Congress becoming the most important *accumulation* of knowledge, wisdom, and art in the nation.

After part of the library was destroyed by fire, Jefferson offered his personal library of more than 6,000 books to the Library of Congress. **(7)** This purchase was *ample* enough to replace what was lost and greatly strengthened the collection. Many of Jefferson's books were destroyed in another fire, but those that survived are now a part of the library's Rare Books Collection.

Today, the Library of Congress has so many valuable resources that people can become confused about its purpose. Some think it is a law library used by members of Congress; some think it is a famous library for the blind; others think its sole purpose is to maintain The United States Office of Copyrights. In fact, it is all these things and much more.

(8) From its *meager* beginnings, the Library of Congress has grown tremendously. **(9)** It has gone from a tiny collection, set in a fairly *barren* cultural landscape, to a storehouse of one of the most richly developed cultures in the world. **(10)** Its size and scope have *surpassed* even the dreams of Thomas Jefferson.

And the U.S. Library of Congress is still growing, adding about 7,000 items per day. A giant among libraries, it is by far the largest and most important in the Western Hemisphere.

Each sentence below refers to a numbered sentence in the passage. Write the letter of the choice that gives the sentence a meaning that is closest to the original sentence.

_____ **1.** Its collections are _____, filling more than 530 miles of bookshelves.
  a. empty   **b.** large   **c.** small   **d.** scattered

_____ **2.** To date, the library contains more than 128 million items—the most _____ collection of any library in the world.
  a. unimportant   **b.** scattered   **c.** complete   **d.** empty

_____ **3.** A solemn air seems to _____ the rooms where important documents rest.
  a. spread throughout   **b.** gather together   **c.** go beyond   **d.** pile up in

_____ **4.** In 1800, Washington, D.C., was a new town, and its population was _____.
  a. growing   **b.** crowded   **c.** scattered   **d.** huge

_____ 5. Compared with many private libraries of the time, its collection of three maps and 740 books must have seemed _____.
    a. thorough   **b.** new   **c.** unimportant   **d.** large

_____ 6. Thomas Jefferson had a vision of the Library of Congress becoming the most important _____ of knowledge, wisdom, and art in the nation.
    a. reproduction   **b.** expectation   **c.** range   **d.** collection

_____ 7. This purchase was _____ to replace what was lost and greatly strengthened the collection.
    a. more than enough   **b.** not important   **c.** gathered together   **d.** less than enough

_____ 8. From its _____ beginnings, the Library of Congress has grown tremendously.
    a. empty   **b.** small   **c.** thorough   **d.** gigantic

_____ 9. It has gone from a tiny collection, set in a fairly _____ cultural landscape, to a storehouse of one of the most richly developed cultures in the world.
    a. growing   **b.** far-reaching   **c.** enormous   **d.** empty

_____ 10. Its size and scope have _____ even the dreams of Thomas Jefferson.
    a. spread throughout   **b.** lagged behind   **c.** gone beyond   **d.** gathered together

Indicate whether the statements below are TRUE or FALSE according to the passage.

_____ 1. The Library of Congress is located in Washington, D.C.

_____ 2. Thomas Jefferson created the Library of Congress in 1800.

_____ 3. Only members of Congress and lawyers can use the Library of Congress.

WRITING EXTENDED RESPONSES

Think of a library that you are familiar with, such as your school or your town library. How does it compare with the Library of Congress? In an essay of at least three paragraphs, compare and contrast the library you are familiar with and the Library of Congress. Some things you might compare are the sizes, ages, and purposes of the libraries. Use at least three lesson words in your essay and underline them.

WRITE THE DERIVATIVE

Complete the sentence by writing the correct form of the word shown in parentheses. You may not need to change the form that is given.

_____ 1. An _____ of string and rubber bands was piled in the drawer. *(accumulate)*

_____ 2. Maria _____ everyone's expectations when she won the spelling bee. *(surpass)*

_____ 3. The red food coloring began to _____ the bowl of white icing, turning it pink. *(pervasive)*

_____ 4. To the charity, the donation was huge, but to the billionaire, it was just a _____. *(trifle)*

_____ **5.** The doctor had to determine the _____ of the injury before she could decide how to treat it. *(extensive)*

_____ **6.** The _____ of the deliveryman's holiday tips disappointed him. *(meager)*

_____ **7.** _____ is usually not desirable in a lawn. *(sparse)*

_____ **8.** The _____ of the committee's report reassured lawmakers that all aspects of the issue had been considered. *(comprehensive)*

_____ **9.** Few settlers moved to the state because of the _____ of the land there. *(barren)*

_____ **10.** The pioneer family worked hard all summer to store _____ food for the winter. *(ample)*

FIND THE EXAMPLE

Choose the answer that best describes the action or situation.

_____ **1.** An area that would have *sparse* plant life
　　　a. rain forest　　　**b.** desert　　　**c.** jungle　　　**d.** woods

_____ **2.** What a *comprehensive* chapter test covers
　　　a. all of chapter　　　**b.** middle of chapter　　　**c.** end of chapter　　　**d.** beginning of chapter

_____ **3.** Someone who *accumulates* something
　　　a. forest ranger　　　**b.** life guard　　　**c.** stamp collector　　　**d.** pastry chef

_____ **4.** Something that would probably be considered a *trifle*
　　　a. love letter　　　**b.** joke　　　**c.** final exam　　　**d.** tax bill

_____ **5.** A situation that would probably cause a car to need *extensive* repair
　　　a. flat tire　　　**b.** out of gas　　　**c.** collision　　　**d.** stuck in snow

_____ **6.** Something that would most likely *pervade* the audience at a scary movie
　　　a. laughter　　　**b.** tears　　　**c.** happiness　　　**d.** fear

_____ **7.** Something that happens in a *barren* field
　　　a. crops won't grow　　　**b.** crops are moist　　　**c.** crops are gathered　　　**d.** crops grow well

_____ **8.** A *meager* crowd
　　　a. five people　　　**b.** fifty people　　　**c.** two hundred people　　　**d.** ten thousand people

_____ **9.** How an athlete could *surpass* her dream of making it to the Olympics
　　　a. making the team　　　**b.** winning a medal　　　**c.** getting injured　　　**d.** dropping out

_____ **10.** An *ample* amount of time to heat up a Five-Minute Meal
　　　a. 1 minute　　　**b.** 3 minutes　　　**c.** 6 minutes　　　**d.** 4 minutes

Agreement and Disagreement

WORD LIST

accord	consent	contrary	corroborate	friction
insolent	negotiate	pact	rapport	rift

More than one person often means more than one opinion. Sometimes we can't even make up our own minds about something! This means that disagreement is a fact of life. The words in this lesson relate to similarities and differences in opinion. As you study them, imagine how you could use them in your daily life.

1. **accord** (ə-kôrd´)
   a. *verb* To give or grant
   • Citizens are **accorded** certain rights by the Constitution.
   b. *noun* Agreement; harmony
   • His ideas are in **accord** with mine.
   c. *noun* A formal agreement or settlement
   • The strikers and their employers reached an **accord**.

   accordance *noun* In **accordance** with my parent's wishes, I declined the invitation.

2. **consent** (kən-sĕnt´)
   a. *noun* Agreement, acceptance, or permission given
   • Most schools require written **consent** from a parent or guardian before they allow students to go on a field trip.
   b. *verb* To agree to; to go along with
   • I **consented** to having my picture appear in the paper.

3. **contrary** (kŏn´trĕr´ē) *adjective*
   a. Opposite or opposed to; completely different
   • **Contrary** to their reputation, most bats are gentle creatures.
   b. Behaving stubbornly and in opposition to others
   • Three-year-olds often become **contrary** when it is time to take a nap.

   contrariness *noun* Your **contrariness** will cost you a place on the team.

4. **corroborate** (kə-rŏb´ə-rāt´) *verb*
   To support with new facts or evidence; to confirm
   • Five additional experiments **corroborated** the original finding.

   corroborative *adjective* **Corroborative** evidence strengthened the case against the defendant.

   corroboration *noun* We need **corroboration** for that claim.

My son/daughter has my permission to go on the field trip.

Mr. L

consent

5. friction (frĭk´shən) *noun*
Conflict or tension caused by a disagreement or clash
• Unkind remarks can cause **friction** between even the best of friends.

6. insolent (ĭn´sə-lənt) *adjective*
Rude; disrespectfully bold; insulting
• In an **insolent** gesture, the rebel refused to bow to the Emperor.

insolence *noun* I could not believe that her parents ignored her **insolence.**

7. negotiate (nĭ-gō´shē-āt´) *verb*
a. To discuss something in an attempt to reach agreement
• The United States helped **negotiate** a peace treaty in the Middle East.
b. To accomplish successfully
• The driver **negotiated** a difficult turn on the racetrack.

negotiation *noun* Treaty **negotiations** can be difficult.

negotiator *noun* That attorney is a good **negotiator,** especially in labor disputes.

negotiable *adjective* The price of this piece of jewelry is **negotiable.**

8. pact (păkt) *noun*
A formal agreement; treaty
• The **pact** between the two countries has been in effect for five years.

9. rapport (ră-pôr´) *noun*
A relationship of shared trust and understanding
• As the semester progressed, students developed a warm **rapport** with their teacher.

10. rift (rĭft) *noun*
A break in friendly relations; a disagreement
• In the 1800s, the issue of slavery caused a **rift** between the northern and southern states.

> *Friction* also refers to surfaces rubbing against each other. The *friction* between flint and steel can produce sparks.

> A *rift* can also mean "a narrow break or crack in rock."

WORD ENRICHMENT

Our Latin heritage

Nine of the ten words in this lesson—all except *rift*—have roots in Latin, the language spoken by the Romans of ancient times. Located in present-day Italy, the city of Rome was the center of a vast empire that stretched from Africa to Britain. In addition to spreading their language, the Romans brought orderly government to millions of people. They also introduced road-building techniques, mail delivery, and water supply systems. Ancient Roman walls, arches, and roads can still be seen in Europe.

WRITE THE CORRECT WORD

Write the correct word in the space next to each definition.

_____ **1.** to discuss in order to reach agreement

_____ **2.** a disagreement or break in relations

_____ **3.** opposite of

_____ **4.** a formal agreement

_____ **5.** conflict or clash

_____ **6.** shared trust and understanding

_____ **7.** to confirm or support with new facts

_____ **8.** rude; insulting

_____ **9.** to give or grant

_____ **10.** permission or acceptance

COMPLETE THE SENTENCE

Write the letter for the word that best completes each sentence.

_____ **1.** Copernicus's theory that the earth was not the center of the solar system was _____ to what most people believed at the time.
   a. insolent   **b.** contrary   **c.** negotiated   **d.** consented

_____ **2.** Randy was sent to his room for being _____.
   a. corroborative   **b.** negotiable   **c.** insolent   **d.** consenting

_____ **3.** The _____ between the sisters was so bad that they stopped talking to each other.
   a. rift   **b.** pact   **c.** accord   **d.** consent

_____ **4.** There was no evidence to _____ the suspect's alibi.
   a. accord   **b.** negotiate   **c.** consent   **d.** corroborate

_____ **5.** The members of the club made a _____ never to allow outsiders in their clubhouse.
   a. rift   **b.** rapport   **c.** pact   **d.** negotiation

_____ **6.** The _____ were difficult, but the two parties finally reached an agreement.
   a. corroborations   **b.** negotiations   **c.** pacts   **d.** accords

_____ **7.** The Constitution _____ the federal government fairly limited powers.
   a. negotiates   **b.** corroborates   **c.** accords   **d.** consents

_____ **8.** During the holidays, _____ among relatives can result in heated arguments.
   a. friction   **b.** negotiation   **c.** corroboration   **d.** accord

_____ **9.** The coach developed a great _____ with his players because he was fair.
   a. pact   **b.** rift   **c.** corroboration   **d.** rapport

_____ **10.** Students need parental _____ to join the Chess Club.
   a. friction   **b.** consent   **c.** insolence   **d.** pact

Challenge: When two sides disagree, they must _____ in order to reach a(n) _____.

_____   **a.** corroborate...insolence   **b.** consent...rift   **c.** negotiate...accord

Lesson 6   **35**

An Olympic Rift

In the world of sports, disagreements often arise. Players, fans and sports commentators frequently second-guess rulings by referees, umpires, and judges. Was the tennis ball on or outside the line? Was the pitch a strike or a ball? Was the catch good or was the football player's foot out of bounds? Differing opinions sometimes make for spirited debate. **(1)** When the stakes are high, people will openly challenge rulings, and serious *friction* can develop. At times, the public and the media pressure officials to launch an investigation and overturn rulings.

What happens when this drama is played out on an international stage? **(2)** Let's examine the *rift* that occurred during the 2002 Winter Olympics.

The Canadian figure skaters Jamie Sale and David Pelletier were competing for a gold medal. They skated a mistake-free program. The audience was on its feet, cheering this flawless and exciting performance. But their cheers quickly turned to boos and shouts of disbelief when the scoreboard showed that the talented Russian duo, Elena Berezhnaya and Anton Sikharulidze, had won the Olympic gold medal. **(3)** Even the broadcasters were not in *accord* with this decision. They agreed with the crowd that the Canadians should have won.

The Canadian pair appeared on talk shows in the days following the competition and talked about the results. **(4)** To their credit, they showed no anger or *insolence*. **(5)** On the *contrary*, they demonstrated good sportsmanship. **(6)** Interestingly, they had always enjoyed a good *rapport* with the Russian skaters and spoke well of them. After all, there was no indication that the Russian skaters were involved in any misconduct.

The public storm of protest led Olympic officials to review the judges' controversial decision. **(7)** When questioned, the French judge *corroborated* the suspicion that she had not scored the skaters fairly, and she was suspended for misconduct. **(8)** The International Olympic Committee and the International Skating Union then *negotiated* a satisfactory resolution. **(9)** *Consent* was given by the members of both organizations to award a second gold medal to the Canadian pair. Sale and Pelletier were delighted. **(10)** In addition, the officials made a *pact* to improve the way the sport of figure skating is judged.

Each sentence below refers to a numbered sentence in the passage. Write the letter of the choice that gives the sentence a meaning that is closest to the original sentence.

_____ **1.** When the stakes are high, serious _____ can develop.
   a. tension   **b.** conversation   **c.** feelings   **d.** love

_____ **2.** Let's examine the _____ that occurred during the 2002 Winter Olympics.
   a. competition   **b.** weather   **c.** disagreement   **d.** security

_____ **3.** Even the broadcasters were not in _____ with this decision.
   a. tension   **b.** agreement   **c.** amazement   **d.** time

_____ **4.** To their credit, they showed no anger or _____.
   a. harm   **b.** warmth   **c.** humor   **d.** rudeness

_____ **5.** _____, they demonstrated good sportsmanship.
   a. Quite the opposite   **b.** Predictably   **c.** With rudeness   **d.** Forever

_____ **6.** Interestingly, they had always enjoyed a good _____ with the Russian skaters.
     a. practice   **b.** disagreement   **c.** tension   **d.** relationship

_____ **7.** When questioned, the French judge _____ their suspicions.
     a. denied   **b.** announced   **c.** confirmed   **d.** outlined

_____ **8.** The IOC and the ISU then _____ a satifactory resolution.
     a. refused to consider   **b.** agreed upon   **c.** read about   **d.** disagreed about

_____ **9.** _____ was given by the members to award a second gold medal.
     a. Permission   **b.** Argument   **c.** Tension   **d.** Evidence

_____ **10.** In addition, the officials made a _____ to improve judging.
     a. score card   **b.** video   **c.** formal agreement   **d.** seating arrangement

Indicate whether the statements below are TRUE or FALSE according to the passage.

_____ **1.** No one was punished for the judging scandal of the 2002 Winter Olympics.

_____ **2.** Public opinion and the media can be powerful forces for change.

_____ **3.** The Russian figure skaters had to give up their gold medal.

FINISH THE THOUGHT

Complete each sentence so that it shows the meaning of the italicized word.

1. The *rift* began when _____

_____

2. I would never *consent* to _____

_____

WRITE THE DERIVATIVE

Complete the sentence by writing the correct form of the word shown in parentheses. You may not need to change the form that is given.

_____ **1.** His _____ made working with him very difficult. (*contrary*)

_____ **2.** To avoid _____, I do not discuss politics with my grandfather. (*friction*)

_____ **3.** "The rules in this house are not _____, young man." (*negotiate*)

_____ **4.** Counselors should have a good _____ with their campers. (*rapport*)

_____ **5.** Carlos _____ to the coach's request that he sit out the first half of the game. (*consent*)

_____ **6.** In _____ with the rules, no flash photography will be allowed. (*accord*)

_____ 7. Everyone hoped that the _____ would end the violence. *(pact)*

_____ 8. The student's _____ earned him a trip to the principal's office. *(insolent)*

_____ 9. The father and son did not speak for two years because of their _____. *(rift)*

_____ 10. I found _____ for the date in the encyclopedia. *(corroborate)*

FIND THE EXAMPLE

Choose the answer that best describes the action or situation.

_____ 1. Something that might be *negotiable*
   a. law   **b.** verdict   **c.** price   **d.** fact

_____ 2. What veterinarians should have good *rapport* with
   a. truckers   **b.** plants   **c.** police officers   **d.** animals

_____ 3. Something *contrary* to the truth
   a. evidence   **b.** lie   **c.** support   **d.** omission

_____ 4. An example of *insolent* behavior
   a. talking back   **b.** saying "please"   **c.** waiting patiently **d.** standing in line

_____ 5. Something most likely to cause *friction* between classmates
   a. homework   **b.** false rumors   **c.** desks   **d.** flint

_____ 6. Something a principal would NOT *consent* to at school
   a. throwing food   **b.** studying   **c.** playing sports   **d.** playing in the band

_____ 7. A synonym of *pact*
   a. truth   **b.** disagreement   **c.** box   **d.** treaty

_____ 8. A result of a *rift*
   a. bonding   **b.** hanging out   **c.** losing touch   **d.** shaking hands

_____ 9. Something that *corroborates* a crime suspect's alibi that he was at the movies
   while the crime was being committed elsewhere
   a. his own word   **b.** a popcorn box   **c.** a movie poster   **d.** an eyewitness

_____ 10. Something that two parties who've reached an *accord* would likely do
   a. continue to argue **b.** shake hands   **c.** buy a good car   **d.** start over again

Using the Dictionary

Parts of a Dictionary Entry

The dictionary is an important tool. It gives us a way to learn vocabulary meanings independently. It also gives us guides to pronunciation, spelling, and word usage.

A dictionary entry contains much information. Most dictionary entries contain seven parts. An example of these parts for the word *dizzy* is shown below.

diz•zy (dĭz´ē) *adj.* **diz•zi•er, diz•zi•est 1.** Having a sensation of whirling or feeling a tendency to fall; giddy: *A ride on the roller coaster made me feel dizzy.* **2.** Producing or tending to produce giddiness. **3.** Bewildered or confused: *dizzy with excitement.* *tr.v.* **diz•zied, diz•zy•ing, diz•zies.** To make dizzy: *So many facts and figures dizzied my brain.* [First written down before 830 in Old English and spelled *dysig,* foolish.] —**diz•zi•ly** *adv.* —**diz•zi•ness** *n.*

1. *The word.* The word *dizzy* appears in bold type. Dots (or sometimes extra spaces) show its division into syllables. *Dizzy* has two syllables, and they are divided between the two *z*'s.

2. *The pronunciation.* This appears between parentheses, or sometimes bars. Note the unusual symbols above the *i* and the *e*. The key to pronouncing these symbols is often found in the front of a dictionary and on every two-page dictionary spread. If you look at the key in the inside front cover of *Vocabulary for Achievement,* you will see that the *i* in the word *dizzy* should be pronounced like the *i* in the word *pit.* The *y* should sound like the *e* in the word *bee.* (The letter *y* is represented by a sound commonly given to *e.*)

   The pronunciation also tells you which syllable to stress. An accent mark (´) appears after the first syllable. This means you should stress the first syllable, *diz,* when you pronounce the word.

3. *Part of speech.* In the first skill feature of this book, you learned about parts of speech. To save space in dictionaries, parts of speech are abbreviated. Here are some common abbreviations.

n.—noun	*tr.v.*—transitive verb
adj.—adjective	*intr.v.*—intransitive verb
adv.—adverb	

   The word *dizzy* functions as two parts of speech. First, it is an adjective *(adj.).* But as you read the entry further, you will also see that it is a transitive verb *(tr.v.).*

4. *Listing of forms.* The dictionary usually lists *-ed, -ing,* and *-s* forms for verbs to help us spell them. It also lists *-er* and *-est* forms (or comparative forms) for adjectives. The plural spelling of a noun is given only if the plural form does not follow the general rule of pluralization.

   When *-er* and *-est* are added to *dizzy,* the *y* changes to an *i.* The dictionary lists these irregular forms in line 1: **diz•zi•er, diz•zi•est.** In line 3, when *dizzy* is used as a verb, the *-ed* and *-s* forms also change the *y* to an *i.* Again, these forms are listed: **diz•zied, diz•zy•ing, diz•zies.** These listings show how a dictionary can be used as a helpful spelling tool.

5. *Definitions.* Many words have several definitions. *Dizzy* has three different definitions when it is used as an adjective. It also has one definition as a transitive verb. Can you find them? (*Vocabulary for Achievement,* too, often gives more than one meaning for a word.) To help you use *dizzy* correctly, sample phrases and sentences are given in italics.

6. *The word history (etymology).* This is listed inside square brackets like this [ ]. Word history is sometimes called *etymology.* The word *dizzy* first appeared in print in the year 830, more than 1,000 years ago. It comes from Old English, which is a form of English no longer spoken. Many other words come from Latin, a language spoken in Rome about 2,000 years ago. Still others come from ancient Greek, spoken about 2,500 years ago. In an etymology, the most recent language before English is listed first, and the most ancient language is listed last. You will see some of these etymologies listed in later chapters of *Vocabulary for Achievement.*

7. *Related forms (derivatives).* Adding suffixes to the word *dizzy* forms derivatives that are other parts of speech. Adding *-ly* forms the adverb *dizzily.* Adding *-ness* forms the noun *dizziness.*

As you can see, a dictionary entry has a wealth of information.

Practice Using Dictionary Entries

Use the two dictionary entries below to answer the questions that follow.

pen•al•ty (pĕn´əl-tē) *n., pl.* **pen•al•ties.**
1. A punishment established by law or authority for a crime. **2.** Something, such as a sum of money, that must be given up for an offense. **3.** In sports, a punishment or disadvantage imposed on a team or competitor for breaking a rule. [First written down in 1462 in Middle English *penalte,* from Old French *penalite,* from Medieval Latin *poenalitas,* from Latin *poenalis,* penal; see **penal.**]

qua•ver (kwā´vər) *intr.v.* **qua•vered, qua•ver•ing, qua•vers** **1.** To shake, as from weakness; tremble; quiver. **2.** To speak in a quivering voice or utter a quivering sound. **3.** To produce a trill on a musical instrument or with the voice. *n.* **1.** A quavering sound. **2.** A trill that is sung or played on a musical instrument.
—**qua•ver•y** *adj.*

1. What part of speech is *penalty?* _____

2. Write the stressed syllable of *penalty.* _____

3. Give two languages in which the word *penalty* appeared before it was used in modern English. _____

4. Write the plural form of *penalty.* _____

5. The *y* in *penalty* is pronounced like the vowel in which common word? (See the pronunciation key.) _____

6. List the parts of speech that *quaver* may function as.
_____

7. The *a* in *quaver* is pronounced like the vowel in which common word? (See the pronunciation key.) _____

8. Write the past tense of *quaver.* _____

9. What part of speech is *quavery?* _____

10. In total, how many definitions does *quaver* have? _____

Movement

WORD LIST

brisk	linger	mingle	nimble	perpetual
saunter	scurry	sedentary	stride	totter

Words are like radio stations. Some stations send weak signals that do not come through clearly. The stronger the signal, the better the station can be heard. Well-chosen words send powerful signals that communicate clear messages to listeners and readers. A precise word leaves a strong impression. Which word seems stronger in the following sentences?

The horse goes. OR The horse gallops.
The man sat in the chair. OR The man slumped in the chair.

Like the verbs *gallop* and *slump,* the words presented in this lesson provide clear images of motion, or lack of it. Try to picture what the words describe.

1. **brisk** (brĭsk) *adjective*
   a. Moving quickly, as in walking
   • Amy walked at such a **brisk** pace that it was hard to keep up with her.
   b. Quick, businesslike
   • The doctor's **brisk** manner made it difficult for me to ask all my questions.

   briskness *noun* The **briskness** of the wind in Chicago reminded us of why it is called the windy city.

   briskly *adverb* The exercise coach moved **briskly** through the room, correcting everyone's pushups.

2. **linger** (lĭng´gər) *verb*
   To stay for a while before leaving
   • Fans **lingered** in the hotel lobby, waiting for the rap star to appear.

3. **mingle** (mĭng´gəl) *verb*
   To mix or join with others
   • The Senator **mingled** with the crowd, shaking hands and admiring babies.

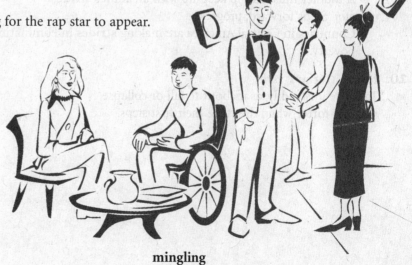

mingling

4. nimble (nĭm´bəl) *adjective*
   a. Having quick and skillful movements
   • The **nimble** gymnast jumped on top of the balance beam and did a handstand.
   b. Having a quick and skillful mind
   • He was **nimble** enough to add four-digit numbers without pencil or paper.

   nimbleness *noun* I love to watch the **nimbleness** of my grandmother's fingers as she knits.

   nimbly *adverb* The cat jumped **nimbly** from the tree to the top of the fence.

5. perpetual (pər-pĕch´o͞o -əl) *adjective*
   a. Lasting forever or for a very long time
   • The wealthy donor left a large sum to the college to ensure that the scholarship would be **perpetual.**
   b. Constant; continuing without interruption
   • The energetic toddler seemed to be in **perpetual** motion.

   perpetuate *verb* The monument **perpetuates** the memory of those who died in the war.

   perpetually *adverb* I seem to be **perpetually** overloaded with work!

6. saunter (sôn´tər) *verb*
   To walk in a slow, relaxed manner
   • Couples **sauntered** along the beach, enjoying the beautiful sunset.

7. scurry (skûr´ē) *verb*
   To run hurriedly with quick, short steps
   • The mice **scurried** away from the cat.

8. sedentary (sĕd´n-tĕr´ē) *adjective*
   Staying in one place; not moving around much
   • Computer programming is **sedentary** work.

9. stride (strīd)
   a. *verb* To walk quickly with long steps
   • The sheriff **strode** into the store, looking for the outlaw.
   b. *noun* A long step
   • A toddler must run to keep up with an adult's **strides.**
   c. *noun* Steps forward; progress
   • Countries in Central America are making **strides** in eliminating poverty.

10. totter (tŏt´ər) *verb*
   To move unsteadily, as if about to fall or collapse
   • Babies **totter** when they take their first steps.

> Notice that *scurry* sounds like *hurry.*

> To *take in stride* means "to cope with" or "to deal with calmly." The past tense of *stride* is *strode.*

WRITE THE CORRECT WORD

Write the correct word in the space next to each definition.

_____ 1. to walk with long steps

_____ 2. lasting forever

_____ 3. to run hurriedly

_____ 4. quick; businesslike

_____ 5. having quick, skillful movements

_____ 6. to walk in a slow, relaxed manner

_____ 7. to stay for a while

_____ 8. staying in one place

_____ 9. to move unsteadily

_____ 10. to socialize with others

COMPLETE THE SENTENCE

Write the letter for the word that best completes each sentence.

_____ 1. Because they grow so quickly, puppies are _____ hungry.
a. lingeringly   b. nimbly   c. perpetually   d. briskly

_____ 2. I like to _____ with lots of different people at parties.
a. saunter   b. totter   c. scurry   d. mingle

_____ 3. The injured bird _____ from side to side when it tried to walk.
a. sauntered   b. strode   c. mingled   d. tottered

_____ 4. Basketball players need to handle the ball in a _____ way.
a. nimble   b. perpetual   c. lingering   d. sedentary

_____ 5. I love to _____ alone in a quiet garden, enjoying nature.
a. scurry   b. linger   c. mingle   d. stride

_____ 6. We gathered from the _____ pace of her walk that she was in a hurry.
a. perpetual   b. sauntering   c. sedentary   d. brisk

_____ 7. When the company president _____ forcefully into the room, we all pay attention.
a. strides   b. scurries   c. totters   d. mingles

_____ 8. The kitten _____ after the rolling tennis ball.
a. sauntered   b. lingered   c. scurried   d. strode

_____ 9. While _____ through the park, we had a chance to watch the birds, squirrels, and people.
a. Sauntering   b. Mingling   c. Tottering   d. Scurrying

_____ 10. Mario remained _____, playing his video game for hours.
a. mingling   b. sedentary   c. perpetual   d. tottering

Challenge: Eliza _____ along, window shopping until she saw the bus arrive; then she _____ toward the bus to make sure she did not miss it.
_____ a. mingled...tottered   b. scurried...lingered   c. sauntered...strode

Tumbling to Achievement

(1) The crowd watches as the team *saunters* into place, wearing bright red uniforms. **(2)** One team member *scurries* up with a radio. As the coach introduces the team members, they start walking on their hands across the mats. **(3)** The *brisk* pace of the rap music seems to energize the athletes as they begin their routines. They twist through the air, do backward somersaults twenty feet above the ground, and hurl themselves through hoops.

Next, three team members form a pyramid. The top person puts his hands high in the air. **(4)** The audience gasps, thinking this formation is about to *totter,* but it holds steady. Then, a fourth member bounces off a trampoline and flies over the outstretched arms of the highest person. In the next routine, six team members form a pyramid three-levels high, but again, a seventh team member sails over everyone. The act finishes as a team member flies over the backs of all his other teammates—a flip of more than thirty feet!

The founder of this marvelous team, Jesse White, was born in Alton, Illinois, in 1934. At a community center near his childhood home, Jesse met retired teacher Fred Ross. Ross helped Jesse believe in himself. Jesse played high-school basketball, setting the school's record by scoring sixty-eight points in one game. **(5)** People remember his high leaps, spins, and *nimble* handling of the ball. **(6)** In fact, Jesse seemed to be *perpetually* moving.

He went on to play college basketball and professional baseball for the Chicago Cubs. He followed this with service in the army and a career in education. In 1998, he was the first African American to be elected Illinois Secretary of State. But Jesse White is probably best known for his work with children. **(7)** He has dedicated much of his life to helping them make *strides* toward success.

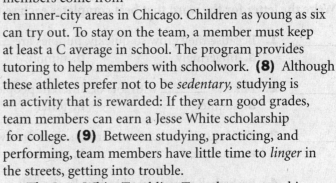

In 1959, he founded the Jesse White Tumbling Team, which is still going strong. Team members come from ten inner-city areas in Chicago. Children as young as six can try out. To stay on the team, a member must keep at least a C average in school. The program provides tutoring to help members with schoolwork. **(8)** Although these athletes prefer not to be *sedentary,* studying is an activity that is rewarded: If they earn good grades, team members can earn a Jesse White scholarship for college. **(9)** Between studying, practicing, and performing, team members have little time to *linger* in the streets, getting into trouble.

The Jesse White Tumbling Team has appeared in TV shows, commercials, and movies. They have traveled to Tokyo and performed in two presidential inaugural parades. **(10)** These experiences have enabled team members to *mingle* with many famous people. But perhaps most important, the Jesse White Tumbling Team has given thousands of children a chance for a better future.

Each sentence below refers to a numbered sentence in the passage. Write the letter of the choice that gives the sentence a meaning that is closest to the original sentence.

_____ **1.** The crowd watches as the team _____ into place, wearing bright red uniforms.
    a. rushes   **b.** socializes   **c.** walks slowly   **d.** walks quickly

_____ **2.** One team member _____ up with a radio.
    a. hurries   **b.** mixes   **c.** stays   **d.** jumps

_____ **3.** The _____ pace of the rap music seems to energize the athletes.
    a. skillful   **b.** relaxed   **c.** slow   **d.** quick

_____ **4.** The audience thinks this formation is about to _____, but it holds steady.
    a. shake   **b.** stay   **c.** hurry   **d.** walk

_____ **5.** People remember his high leaps, spins, and _____ handling of the ball.
    a. slow, steady   **b.** long, constant   **c.** quick, skillful   **d.** short, hurried

_____ **6.** Jesse seemed to be _____ moving.
    a. slowly   **b.** constantly   **c.** quickly   **d.** unsteadily

_____ **7.** He has dedicated much of his life to helping children make _____ toward success.
    a. commercials   **b.** attempts   **c.** quickness   **d.** progress

_____ **8.** Although these athletes prefer not to be _____, studying is an activity that is rewarded.
    a. sitting still   **b.** jumping around   **c.** walking quickly   **d.** moving unsteadily

_____ **9.** Team members have little time to _____ in the streets, getting into trouble.
    a. take long steps   **b.** mix with others   **c.** stay for a while   **d.** have skillful movements

_____ **10.** These experiences have enabled team members to _____ with many famous people.
    a. leave   **b.** socialize   **c.** run   **d.** fall

Indicate whether the statements below are TRUE or FALSE according to the passage.

_____ **1.** Jesse White started his tumbling team to help Olympic athletes practice.

_____ **2.** Jesse White has focused his entire career on coaching.

_____ **3.** Members of the team get to travel and meet famous people.

WRITING EXTENDED RESPONSES

The highly skilled movements of performers such as acrobats, athletes, and dancers are almost magical to watch. Think of a performance you have seen on TV, in a movie or video, or in person. Write a descriptive piece about this performance. Your essay should be at least three paragraphs long. Use at least three lesson words in your essay and underline them.

WRITE THE DERIVATIVE

Complete the sentence by writing the correct form of the word shown in parentheses. You may not need to change the form that is given.

_____ **1.** Even well-made buildings can be seen _____ during severe earthquakes. (*totter*)

_____ **2.** _____ through the museum, the family enjoyed the beautiful paintings. (*saunter*)

_____ **3.** The salesperson rang up our purchases _____, without a friendly word or a smile. (*brisk*)

_____ **4.** We would like to _____ this charming custom of reciting poems at dinner. (*perpetual*)

_____ **5.** We admired the _____ of the trial lawyer's mind. (*nimble*)

_____ **6.** The speed walkers _____ quickly down the lane. *(stride)*

_____ **7.** We _____ long after the sunset, watching the stars appear. *(linger)*

_____ **8.** People with _____ occupations should try to exercise regularly. *(sedentary)*

_____ **9.** I enjoy _____ with people at parties. *(mingle)*

_____ **10.** She was _____ around, trying to clean her house before company arrived. *(scurry)*

FIND THE EXAMPLE

Choose the answer that best describes the action or situation.

_____ **1.** An example of *lingering*
a. stopping to watch   **b.** beginning a run   **c.** driving too fast   **d.** chasing a ball

_____ **2.** Something that might make you walk *briskly*
a. being early   **b.** being relaxed   **c.** being sad   **d.** being late

_____ **3.** Something you might do right after you *totter*
a. run   **b.** skip   **c.** hurry   **d.** fall

_____ **4.** Something that seems to be in *perpetual* motion on a clock
a. the alarm   **b.** the second hand   **c.** the hour hand   **d.** the batteries

_____ **5.** Something you would NOT be doing when you are *sedentary*
a. skipping   **b.** sitting   **c.** studying   **d.** sleeping

_____ **6.** Something that requires *nimble* fingers
a. playing hopscotch   **b.** jumping rope   **c.** playing piano   **d.** singing songs

_____ **7.** Something you are doing when you are making *strides*
a. failing miserably   **b.** getting worse   **c.** giving up   **d.** getting better

_____ **8.** A reason you might *saunter*
a. lateness   **b.** bad weather   **c.** pretty view   **d.** urgent errand

_____ **9.** A situation in which you might *mingle* with people
a. taking a test   **b.** waiting in line   **c.** going to sleep   **d.** walking alone

_____ **10.** Something that children would probably *scurry* to do
a. catch candy   **b.** get cavities   **c.** mow lawns   **d.** take medicine

Anger and Forgiveness

WORD LIST

appease	condone	indignant	infuriate	malicious
penitent	reconcile	resent	retaliate	wrath

Anger and forgiveness are part of life. The words in this lesson relate to these common experiences. You will learn what it means when somebody is *infuriated* and what it means to ask whether that person can be *appeased*. You will understand why people *resent* actions that are *malicious*.

1. **appease** (ə-pēz´) *verb*
   To satisfy, calm, or soothe, usually by giving in to demands
   • The baby sitter **appeased** the toddler by giving him the cookie he wanted.

   appeasement *noun* Attempting to avoid World War II, European leaders allowed Nazi Germany to occupy some nearby nations, but this **appeasement** only made Hitler more bold.

2. **condone** (kən-dōn´) *verb*
   To allow, accept, or overlook something wrong
   • "I do not **condone** lying," the teacher told her students.

3. **indignant** (ĭn-dĭg´nənt) *adjective*
   Feeling anger about something unfair or mean
   • The **indignant** actor walked off the stage after the crowd began to boo.

   indignation *noun* Imagine my **indignation** when I saw how rude they were to my sister.

> *Appease* is usually used in a negative way to indicate that people "gave in" when they should not have done so.

infuriated

4. **infuriate** (ĭn-fyŏor´ē-āt´) *verb*
   To cause extreme anger; to enrage
   • His insults **infuriated** me.

5. **malicious** (mə-lĭsh´əs) *adjective*
   Deliberately harmful; done with a desire to harm or cause suffering
   • The **malicious** computer hacker disabled the hospital's record-keeping system.

   maliciously *adverb* The art student **maliciously** ripped the other contestant's pictures off the wall after losing the contest.

   malice *noun* In an act of **malice,** the man destroyed his neighbor's garden.

6. **penitent** (pĕn´ĭ-tənt) *adjective*
Regretful; sorry for bad deeds
• The **penitent** child apologized for breaking the lamp.

penitence *noun* He showed no sign of **penitence** for his crime.

7. **reconcile** (rĕk´ən-sīl´) *verb*
   a. To settle differences; to bring into harmony or agreement
      • Before making the final call, the referees gathered to **reconcile** their accounts of what had happened.
   b. To reestablish a close relationship; to make up
      • The two cousins **reconciled** after not speaking for two years.

reconciliation *noun* The father and son's **reconciliation** after their five-year rift was very emotional; everyone in the room was crying.

> When people must accept a bad situation, we often say they must *reconcile themselves to* it.

8. **resent** (rĭ-zĕnt´) *verb*
To feel angry or bitter at something
• The workers **resented** having to pay more for their health insurance.

resentful *adjective* Carla was **resentful** when her older brother got to go on the trip and she didn't.

resentment *noun* Because there had never been any **resentment** between them, everyone was surprised when they ended their partnership.

9. **retaliate** (rĭ-tăl´ē-āt´) *verb*
To respond to an injury or wrongdoing by inflicting another
• When Angela discovered that the dress she had loaned her sister was ruined, she **retaliated** by keeping her closet door locked.

retaliation *noun* In **retaliation** for her insult, I refused to talk to her.

> *Retaliate against* and *retaliation for* are common phrases.

retaliatory *adjective* The general considered whether his troops should launch a **retaliatory** attack.

10. **wrath** (răth) *noun*
Violent, resentful anger; rage
• In myths, humans often suffer the **wrath** of gods they have offended.

wrathful *adjective* Cinderella is saved from her **wrathful** stepmother.

WORD ENRICHMENT

Our ancient Greek heritage

Many English words come from ancient times. In Greek mythology, the *Furies* were spirits who retaliated for injustice. The English words *fury* and *infuriate* come from this root. Many other words and stories we know today can be traced back to ancient Greece, including the subject of this lesson's reading selection. The *Iliad*, which was about the Trojan War, was written by the Greek poet Homer.

WRITE THE CORRECT WORD

Write the correct word in the space next to each definition.

_____ 1. with intent to harm

_____ 2. rage

_____ 3. to allow a wrong

_____ 4. angry about an injustice

_____ 5. to feel bitter about something

_____ 6. to fight back

_____ 7. to settle differences

_____ 8. to calm by giving in

_____ 9. regretful

_____ 10. to enrage

COMPLETE THE SENTENCE

Write the letter for the word that best completes each sentence.

_____ 1. Lewis was _____ when his teacher unfairly accused him of cheating.
  a. appeased   b. penitent   c. indignant   d. condoned

_____ 2. Because of the _____ nature of his crime, the judge gave him a harsh sentence.
  a. penitent   b. indignant   c. resentful   d. malicious

_____ 3. The young boy _____ his older sister by reading her diary.
  a. condoned   b. infuriated   c. reconciled   d. appeased

_____ 4. If you accept a gift you know is stolen, you are _____ stealing.
  a. condoning   b. resenting   c. reconciling   d. infuriating

_____ 5. Maria convinced her friends to _____ so they could all go to the movies together.
  a. retaliate   b. reconcile   c. infuriate   d. condone

_____ 6. The _____ daughter apologized for having forgotten her mother's birthday.
  a. resentful   b. infuriated   c. wrathful   d. penitent

_____ 7. The teacher _____ the overworked students by moving the test from Friday to Monday.
  a. resented   b. condoned   c. appeased   d. retaliated

_____ 8. If you get angry and _____ when you've been wronged, you will cause problems for yourself.
  a. appease   b. retaliate   c. reconcile   d. condone

_____ 9. Do not play with that bear cub, or you will certainly suffer its mother's _____.
  a. reconciliation   b. penitence   c. wrath   d. appeasement

_____ 10. Juan _____ having to clean up the mess that his brother made.
  a. reconciled   b. retaliated   c. appeased   d. resented

Challenge: Marta was _____ when her brother showed no _____ after destroying her drawing.

_____
  a. appeased...resentment   b. penitent...wrath   c. infuriated...penitence

Eris's Revenge

According to Greek myth, the goddess Eris ruled over disagreements and fights. She was called the Goddess of Discord because arguments and unhappiness followed her wherever she went. She carried around a beautiful, shiny apple, called the Apple of Discord. When she threw it among friends, she caused disagreements; when she threw it among enemies, she started battles. **(1)** If people wanted to make peace, she ruined their attempts at *reconciliation*. **(2)** If a person who had done something wrong felt *penitent*, she would prevent him from apologizing.

Eris was very unpopular, so she did not receive many invitations. **(3)** When she was the only goddess not invited to the wedding of Peleus, her *wrath* knew no bounds. **(4)** *Indignant* at being snubbed, Eris plotted

her revenge. **(5)** After some thought, she decided how to *retaliate*. **(6)** Suddenly appearing at the wedding, she *maliciously* threw her apple into the center of the room, with a note attached that said "For the fairest."

Of course, this caused a tremendous argument. Aphrodite, goddess of love; Hera, queen of the gods; and Athena, goddess of wisdom, each believed that she deserved the apple. After arguing for a while, the goddesses turned to Zeus, the king of the gods. They asked him to decide who most deserved the apple. But Zeus was wise. **(7)** He knew if he picked one goddess, the other two would *resent* him forever. **(8)** It was impossible to *appease* all three.

So Zeus sent for a young prince, Paris, who was said to have an eye for beauty. Not content to be judged by their beauty alone, each of the three goddesses offered Paris a gift. Hera promised to make him a wealthy king of many lands. Athena assured him that if he picked her, he would be a great warrior. Aphrodite offered him the most beautiful woman in the world. After considering the prizes, Paris awarded the apple to Aphrodite.

Unfortunately, Helen, the most beautiful woman in the world, was already married to King Menelaus of Sparta. **(9)** When Paris ran off with Helen, Menelaus and the rulers of the neighboring cities were *infuriated*. **(10)** Feeling that they could not *condone* this behavior, they declared war on Troy, the city where Paris lived. By starting the bloody Trojan War, Eris got her revenge.

Each sentence below refers to a numbered sentence in the passage. Write the letter of the choice that gives the sentence a meaning that is closest to the original sentence.

_____ **1.** If people wanted to make peace, she ruined their attempts at _____ .
     a. arguing   **b.** agreement   **c.** bitterness   **d.** fighting

_____ **2.** If a person who had done something wrong felt _____ , she would prevent him from apologizing.
     a. sorry   **b.** angry   **c.** violent   **d.** injured

_____ **3.** When Eris was the only goddess not invited to the wedding of Peleus, her _____ knew no bounds.
     a. calmness   **b.** forgiveness   **c.** injury   **d.** rage

_____ **4.** _____ at being snubbed, Eris plotted her revenge.
     a. Feeling sorry   **b.** Feeling angry   **c.** Giving in   **d.** Settling differences

_____ **5.** After some thought, she decided how to _____ .
     a. bring about harmony   **b.** forgive the injury   **c.** return the wrong   **d.** debate the issue

6. Eris _____ threw her apple into the center of the room, with a note attached that said "For the fairest."
   a. kindly **b.** with evil intent **c.** violently **d.** with forgiveness

7. He knew if he picked one goddess, the other two would _____ him forever.
   a. be angry with **b.** give in to **c.** feel sorry for **d.** disagree with

8. It was simply impossible to _____ all three.
   a. feel sorry for **b.** harm **c.** anger **d.** satisfy

9. Menelaus and the rulers of the neighboring cities were _____.
   a. very calm **b.** extremely angry **c.** very sorry **d.** badly hurt

10. Feeling that they could not _____ this behavior, they declared war on Troy.
   a. settle **b.** calm **c.** allow **d.** return

Indicate whether the statements below are TRUE or FALSE according to the passage.

1. Eris's resentment at not being invited to a wedding led to the Trojan War.

2. Eris was used to being invited to many weddings.

3. The apple was awarded only on the basis of the goddesses' beauty.

FINISH THE THOUGHT

Complete each sentence so that it shows the meaning of the italicized word.

1. One way to *reconcile* a difference of opinion would be to _____

_____

2. Nothing *infuriates* me more than when _____

_____

WRITE THE DERIVATIVE

Complete the sentence by writing the correct form of the word shown in parentheses. You may not need to change the form that is given.

1. I know she was mad about the joke I played on her, but her _____ went too far. (*retaliate*)

2. The child showed no _____ for the damage he caused. (*penitent*)

3. The parents _____ their child so often that she became spoiled. (*appease*)

_____ **4.** He _____ attacked his opponent's character in an effort to turn voters against her. *(malicious)*

_____ **5.** If the coach does not punish his players for unsportsmanlike conduct, then he obviously _____ that type of behavior. *(condone)*

_____ **6.** The drummer _____ his neighbors by playing in the middle of the night. *(infuriate)*

_____ **7.** "This is not the correct change!" she said _____ to the cashier. *(indignant)*

_____ **8.** Jack fled down the beanstalk after awaking the _____ giant. *(wrath)*

_____ **9.** Lin had _____ Carra ever since Carra got the lead part in the play. *(resent)*

_____ **10.** After their _____, the two enemies became friends. *(reconcile)*

FIND THE EXAMPLE

Choose the answer that best describes the action or situation.

_____ **1.** Something that police officers do NOT *condone*
  a. running   **b.** cheering   **c.** stealing   **d.** playing

_____ **2.** Something a *malicious* person would most likely try to cause
  a. harm   **b.** joy   **c.** laughter   **d.** wonder

_____ **3.** Behavior that would make other people in a library *indignant*
  a. writing   **b.** reading   **c.** studying   **d.** yelling

_____ **4.** A state or situation in which a wild animal might become *infuriated*
  a. being healthy   **b.** being well fed   **c.** being cornered   **d.** being seen

_____ **5.** An emotion felt by a criminal who is *penitent*
  a. joy   **b.** guilt   **c.** fear   **d.** anger

_____ **6.** How a malicious person might provoke the *wrath* of a cat
  a. pet its back   **b.** pull its tail   **c.** let it out   **d.** feed it tuna

_____ **7.** Something two friends who have *reconciled* might do
  a. fight   **b.** glare   **c.** yell   **d.** shake hands

_____ **8.** A word that might describe someone right before he or she *retaliated*
  a. humiliated   **b.** congratulated   **c.** praised   **d.** supported

_____ **9.** A way to cause *resentment*
  a. give compliments   **b.** help someone   **c.** trick someone   **d.** warn someone

_____ **10.** A likely result of constantly *appeasing* a child who wants candy
  a. healthful habits   **b.** many cavities   **c.** constant whining   **d.** weight loss

Words from Spanish

WORD LIST

barrio	escapade	fiesta	guerrilla	lariat
mesa	mustang	poncho	siesta	stampede

At one time, Spain ruled a vast empire in South, Central, and North America. The empire was established when Spanish rulers sponsored voyages to find trade routes and treasures in the "New World." Spain financed the explorations of Christopher Columbus, Juan Ponce de Leon, Hernando Cortez, and Francisco Pizarro, as well as many others. As speakers of Spanish conquered native civilizations and settled in new lands, the language spread. The empire is gone, but Spanish is still the official language of most countries in the Americas. Millions of people in the United States also speak it, so it is not surprising that English is filled with words borrowed from Spanish.

1. **barrio** (bä´rē-ō´) *noun*
   A Spanish-speaking neighborhood of an American city or town
   • The streets of the **barrio** were filled with ice-cream vendors on bicycle carts.

2. **escapade** (ĕs´kə-pād´) *noun*
   An adventure filled with mischief and often danger
   • In one **escapade,** Robin Hood stole gold from King John's castle and bought food for the poor.

3. **fiesta** (fē-ĕs´tə) *noun*
   A celebration; a festival
   • People sang, ate, and danced at the **fiesta** for Mexican Independence Day.

4. **guerrilla** (gə-rĭl´ə)
   a. *noun* A soldier in a small, unofficial army that fights by surprise attack
   • The **guerrilla** hid in the forest, waiting for enemy forces to approach before launching an offensive.
   b. *adjective* In the style of surprise attacks by small bands of soldiers
   • During the American Revolution, the Minutemen used **guerrilla** warfare against the British army.

> Do not confuse *guerrilla* with *gorilla*. A gorilla is an ape.

siesta

5. **lariat** (lăr´ē-ət) *noun*

A lasso; a long rope with an adjustable loop at one end, used for catching horses, mules, and cattle

• Many cowboys carry a **lariat** on their belts to help them catch stray cows.

6. **mesa** (mā´sə) *noun*

A high hill with a flat top and steep sides

• **Mesas** are common in the Colorado Plateau of Utah.

7. **mustang** (mŭs´tāng´) *noun*

A small, hardy wild horse of the North American plains

• Currently, about 50,000 **mustangs** live in ten western U.S. states.

8. **poncho** (pŏn´chō) *noun*

a. A short, blanket-like cloak with a hole in the center for a head, but no sleeves

• The versatile **poncho** can serve as a jacket, blanket, or saddle cloth.

b. A sleeveless rain cloak with a hood

• As it started to drizzle, we slipped on our **ponchos.**

9. **siesta** (sē-ĕs´tə) *noun*

A nap taken after lunch

• In many Spanish-speaking countries, most people take **siestas** in the afternoon when it is too hot to work outdoors.

10. **stampede** (stăm-pēd´)

a. *noun* The sudden running of a herd of frightened animals

• The raging thunder turned the herd of horses into a deadly **stampede.**

b. *noun* The sudden rush of a crowd

• A **stampede** of fans raced on the field when their team won the game.

c. *verb* To rush suddenly in a crowd.

• The cattle **stampeded** across the field.

The Spanish brought Arabian horses to the Americas. Some escaped and bred, eventually producing *mustangs*.

WORD ENRICHMENT

Where do Spanish words come from?

Most Spanish words come from Latin, the language spoken by the ancient Romans. Much later in history, some Native American words also became part of the Spanish language. As the Spanish encountered new things in the Americas, they often adopted the Native American words. These words eventually became part of the Spanish language. Some have even been borrowed again from Spanish into English. For example, the words *tomato* and *chocolate* come from Nahuatl, the language of the Aztecs. *Potato* comes from the Taino language once spoken in the Bahamas.

WRITE THE CORRECT WORD

Write the correct word in the space next to each definition.

_____ **1.** a celebration

_____ **2.** a reckless adventure

_____ **3.** a soldier in an unofficial army

_____ **4.** the sudden rush of a herd of animals

_____ **5.** an afternoon nap

_____ **6.** a lasso

_____ **7.** a Spanish-speaking neighborhood

_____ **8.** a high, flat-topped hill

_____ **9.** a sleeveless, blanket-like cloak

_____ **10.** a wild horse

COMPLETE THE SENTENCE

Write the letter for the word that best completes each sentence.

_____ **1.** From the top of the _____, we could see for miles in every direction.
a. lariat **b.** stampede **c.** poncho **d.** mesa

_____ **2.** Herds of _____ roamed freely in the hills.
a. mustangs **b.** ponchos **c.** siestas **d.** mesas

_____ **3.** As soon as it started to rain, I put on my waterproof _____.
a. lariat **b.** mustang **c.** poncho **d.** escapade

_____ **4.** After a big lunch, Juan yawned and said, "It's time for a(n) _____."
a. stampede **b.** lariat **c.** escapade **d.** siesta

_____ **5.** "Here comes the _____," joked the saleswoman as she opened the doors for the big sale.
a. guerrilla **b.** stampede **c.** barrio **d.** mustang

_____ **6.** At the _____, Mariachi bands played as people danced and mingled.
a. mesa **b.** guerrilla **c.** fiesta **d.** siesta

_____ **7.** _____ warfare is often very effective against a large army.
a. Guerrilla **b.** Escapade **c.** Barrio **d.** Mustang

_____ **8.** In the 1950s, children across the country waited eagerly by their radios each week to hear about the Lone Ranger's next _____.
a. mesa **b.** guerrilla **c.** escapade **d.** barrio

_____ **9.** Life in the _____ was difficult, but the immigrants worked hard to get ahead.
a. fiesta **b.** escapade **c.** mustang **d.** barrio

_____ **10.** With an expert motion, the cowboy threw his _____ around the cow's neck.
a. mustang **b.** lariat **c.** fiesta **d.** guerrilla

Challenge: The day after the late-night _____, everyone took a long _____.
a. fiesta...siesta **b.** escapade...barrio **c.** siesta...stampede

Traditions from Mexico

Charros are Mexican cowboys known for their elegant costumes and great horsemanship. Charros are important figures in Mexico because they link the country with its Spanish heritage.

In the 1500s, Spanish conquerors brought horses and cows to the Americas. The Spanish built huge ranches in Mexico and hired Spanish and Native American workers as *rancheros,* or ranch-hands, to handle their cattle. **(1)** The rancheros' job involved roping and branding cattle, guiding them across prairies, and avoiding dangerous *stampedes*. **(2)** Many people think that the rancheros invented the *lariat*. **(3)** In addition to using these ropes to catch cattle, rancheros probably used lariats to capture *mustangs* that roamed the plains. The skills required of rancheros were highly prized in Mexico, and contests called *charreadas* gave charros an opportunity to show off their expertise.

The Mexican revolution of 1910 changed this tradition. **(4)** In a farmers' rebellion involving much *guerrilla* warfare, huge ranches were broken up into small farms. There was less need for rancheros. Still, many people wanted to continue the charreada. In 1921, an association was formed to promote charreadas. Today, these contests are considered the national sport of Mexico.

(5) In many ways, a charreada is a *fiesta*. It starts with a grand parade featuring charros dressed in elegant, silver-trimmed costumes. Vendors sell food and crafts. Riders guide their horses in a dance to Mariachi music. Nothing dampens the crowd's enthusiasm. **(6)** If it gets chilly, people just put on their *serapes,* which are similar to *ponchos*.

A traditional charreada has nine events. In the first, charros compete to see which riders can bring their horses from a full gallop to an instant stop. This is followed by roping and riding contests. **(7)** After sitting in the hot sun all morning, people may long for a *siesta,* but they rarely leave before the thrilling ending. **(8)** The last contest is a daring *escapade* featuring a charro who jumps from his own horse onto a wild horse and rides it—if he can hang on—until it stops bucking.

Rodeos are an Americanized version of charreadas. The word *rodeo* is taken from the Spanish word meaning "to surround," as cowboys do when they round up cattle. Rodeos and charreadas are somewhat different. Rodeos are usually competitions between individuals, and they test practical skills such as roping. But charreadas involve team competition and focus on showmanship and style. Both charreadas and rodeos have strict professional organizations that regulate the events. **(9)** If you live near the *mesas* of the Southwest, you are much more likely to attend a rodeo. **(10)** However, charreadas are becoming popular in *barrios* throughout the western United States.

Mexico is very proud of its charros. As one charro said, "We are the warriors of Mexico. Our ancestors fought for our independence and freedom, and we celebrate our patriotism by being brave and strong charros!"

Each sentence below refers to a numbered sentence in the passage. Write the letter of the choice that gives the sentence a meaning that is closest to the original sentence.

_____ 1. The rancheros' job involved avoiding dangerous _____.
     a. swinging ropes   **b.** running herds   **c.** adventures   **d.** celebrations

_____ 2. Many people think that the rancheros invented the _____.
     a. sleeveless cloak   **b.** afternoon nap   **c.** horse   **d.** lasso

_____ 3. Rancheros probably used their lariats to capture _____ that roamed the plains.
     a. wild horses   **b.** enemy forces   **c.** running herds   **d.** dangerous bandits

4. The farmers' rebellion involved much ——— warfare.
   a. celebratory   **b.** dangerous   **c.** surprise-attack   **d.** high hill

5. In many ways, a charreada is a ———.
   a. celebration   **b.** nap   **c.** neighborhood   **d.** soldier

6. If it gets chilly, people just put on their *serapes*, which are similar to ———.
   a. celebrations   **b.** long ropes   **c.** high hills   **d.** sleeveless cloaks

7. After sitting in the hot sun all morning, people may long for a(n) ———.
   a. sleeveless cloak   **b.** wild horse   **c.** afternoon nap   **d.** dangerous adventure

8. The last contest is a daring ———.
   a. horse   **b.** adventure   **c.** soldier   **d.** herd

9. If you live near the ——— of the Southwest, you are more likely to attend a rodeo.
   a. high, flat hills   **b.** long ropes   **c.** neighborhoods   **d.** loud parties

10. Charreadas are becoming popular in ——— throughout the western United States.
   a. fancy costumes   **b.** daring adventures   **c.** afternoon naps   **d.** Spanish neighborhoods

Indicate whether the statements below are TRUE or FALSE according to the passage.

1. Charros are Mexican cowboys known for their style and showmanship.

2. Charreadas began after the Mexican Revolution of 1910.

3. Charreadas and rodeos are similar but not exactly the same.

WRITING EXTENDED RESPONSES

Although you may not have been to Mexico or the Southwest or seen real cowboys, you have probably read stories about them or seen them in movies. Can you imagine life as a cowboy? Write a short story in which the main character is a cowboy who wants to compete or is competing in a rodeo or charreada. Use at least three lesson words in your story and underline them.

WRITE THE DERIVATIVE

Complete the sentence by writing the correct form of the word shown in parentheses. You may not need to change the form that is given.

1. In Mexico, ——— are common in September, when Mexicans celebrate their Independence Day. *(fiesta)*

2. "Make sure you bring your ——— in case it rains," Mama called to the boys. *(poncho)*

3. When the wolf emerged from the woods, the herd of sheep ——— across the field. *(stampede)*

_____ 4. The hot, dusty streets were deserted because everyone was taking a ———. *(siesta)*

_____ 5. Most cowboys hang their ——— from their saddles. *(lariat)*

_____ 6. Salsa music is especially popular in certain ——— across the country. *(barrio)*

_____ 7. ——— interrupted the desert landscape like tables scattered across a dance floor. *(mesa)*

_____ 8. "One of these days your ——— are going to get you in real trouble," Jorge's father warned. *(escapade)*

_____ 9. The ——— took their enemies by surprise by attacking in the middle of the night. *(guerrilla)*

_____ 10. The herd of ——— running free across the plain took my breath away. *(mustang)*

FIND THE EXAMPLE

Choose the answer that best describes the action or situation.

_____ 1. The time of day when people take *siestas*
    a. early morning   **b.** afternoon   **c.** late at night   **d.** early evening

_____ 2. Weather in which people would most likely wear *ponchos*
    a. cold and rainy   **b.** hot and steamy   **c.** sunny and dry   **d.** hot and snowing

_____ 3. Something a *guerrilla* would be most likely to do
    a. march in formation   **b.** dance a jig   **c.** hide in the woods   **d.** blow a horn

_____ 4. Something that might be caught with a *lariat*
    a. fly   **b.** mouse   **c.** snake   **d.** calf

_____ 5. A reason people might *stampede*
    a. to see a celebrity   **b.** to pay taxes   **c.** to take a walk   **d.** to go to sleep

_____ 6. A place where you would most likely see a *mustang*
    a. restaurant   **b.** city   **c.** pet store   **d.** prairie

_____ 7. Something that most resembles a *mesa*
    a. cup   **b.** tree   **c.** table   **d.** pencil

_____ 8. A reason for a *fiesta*
    a. a birthday   **b.** a protest   **c.** a funeral   **d.** danger

_____ 9. The language you would most likely hear in a *barrio*
    a. French   **b.** German   **c.** Spanish   **d.** Russian

_____ 10. Something an *escapade* would most likely involve
    a. mischief   **b.** relaxation   **c.** sleep   **d.** standing in line

Using the Dictionary

Looking for the Right Definition

Finding the right definition in a dictionary is not always as easy as it might appear. Here are some guidelines to help you.

Looking for the Correct Entry

Finding the right entry word in a dictionary can be tricky. At times, derivatives are listed under their base words. For example, if you wanted to find *slowly*, you would look under *slow*. If you wanted to find *penalization*, you would look under *penalize*. So if you don't find a word when you first look, try a shorter base form.

Write the entry word you would look under to find *omnivorously*. _____

In addition, some **homophones** that are spelled and pronounced the same can have different meanings. The word *chow* can mean a type of dog. Its homophone, also spelled *chow,* is a slang word for food. The dictionary lists both definitions of *chow*. *Chow¹* is listed as a dog and *chow²* as food.

Write the definition number that lists *chow* as a reddish-brown pet. _____

Looking for the Correct Definition

Once you have located the correct entry, you may find that the word has many definitions. Some definitions for the word *dominant* are listed below. You will see that the *American Heritage Dictionary* provides sentences that illustrate word meanings.

dom•i•nant (dŏm´ə-nənt) *adj.* **1.** Having the most influence or control: *the dominant dog in the pack.* **2.** Most prominent, as in position: *The tallest buildings are dominant in a city's skyline.* **3.** Of or based on the fifth tone of a musical scale: *the dominant chord in the scale of C major.*

Suppose you came across this sentence: The *dominant* mountain in the range stood several thousand feet tall. If you are uncertain of the meaning of *dominant* in this sentence, the following strategies will help you find the correct definition.

1. *Read all of the definitions in the entry.* You need to know all the possibilities. Be careful that you don't make the common error of just choosing the first definition.

2. *Read the sentence, substituting each definition for the word "dominant."* The wrong definitions just won't make sense in the sentence. This includes definitions that apply to the wrong part of speech.

If you do this, you will see that the correct definition is number 2, "Most prominent, as in position." The sentence would read "The most *prominent* mountain in the range stood several thousand feet tall." This definition makes the most sense in this context.

Which definition above best fits the following sentence?

The *dominant* tone of a scale in A major is E. _____

Practice

Using the dictionary entries below, write the correct definition, including the number and the part of speech, that best fits the word as used in each sentence.

ex•qui•site (ĕk-skwĭ′zĭt) *adj.* **1.** Characterized by intricate and beautiful design: *an exquisite vase.* **2.** Acutely perceptive or discriminating: *exquisite taste in art.* **3.** Intense, keen: *took exquisite pleasure in the success of their children.* —**ex•qui•site•ly** *adv.*

cou•ple (kŭp′əl) *n.* **1.** Two things of the same kind; a pair: *a couple of shoes.* **2.** Two people united, as in a marriage or interests: *a young couple just starting a family; a dance couple.* **3.** Informal. A few; several: *vacation for a couple of days; have only a couple of dollars.* —*tr.v.* To link together; attach; join: *Hard work coupled with good luck can make a business successful.*

ma•jor•i•ty (mə-jôr′ĭ-tē) *n., pl.* **ma•jor•i•ties.** **1.** The greater number of part of something; a number more than half of the total: *The majority of the class did well on the test.* **2.** The amount by which a greater number of votes exceeds the remaining number of votes: *The candidate won by a majority of 5,000 votes.* **3.** A political party or group that has the greater number of members or supporters: *The party is a majority in the city.* **4.** The status of having reached the age of legal responsibility.

1. The pain from the injury was *exquisite.*

_____

2. My grandfather gave an *exquisite* carving to my parents.

_____

3. His *exquisite* ear for music allowed him to hear one off-key singer in the choir.

_____

4. If you *couple* dedication with talent, you may become a professional musician.

_____

5. I had a *couple* of gloves, but I lost one.

_____

6. The elderly *couple* was popular with their neighbors.

_____

7. I have only a *couple* of minutes to relax before I leave.

_____

8. He reaches his *majority* when he is 21.

_____

9. At our school, girls are in the *majority.*

_____

10. Ted won the race for the student council by a *majority* of fifty votes.

_____

Friends and Foes

WORD LIST

acquaint	aloof	amiable	betray	enmity
idealize	protégé	recluse	solitary	treacherous

One common saying is, "A thousand friends are not enough, but one enemy is too many." The words in this lesson will help you better understand and express the complexities of human relationships.

1. acquaint (ə-kwānt´) *verb*
To make familiar with; to inform
• To present a good case at trial, a lawyer must be **acquainted** with the facts.

acquaintance *noun* She was an **acquaintance** from my old school.

2. aloof (ə-lōōf´)
a. *adjective* Unfriendly; emotionally or physically distant
• **Aloof** people tend not to smile or say hello to others.
b. *adverb* Standing apart, but within view
• The new student stood **aloof** from the rest of the class.

aloofness *noun* The celebrity's **aloofness** with fans cost him his popularity.

3. amiable (ā´mē-ə-bəl) *adjective*
Good-natured and friendly
• The candidate's **amiable** nature won him many votes.

amiability *noun* Jason's **amiability** at parties made him a popular guest.

4. betray (bĭ-trā´) *verb*
a. To be disloyal or unfaithful
• He **betrayed** his country by fighting for the enemy.
b. To reveal
• Your careless work **betrays** your lack of concern.

betrayal *noun* Telling my secret to others was a **betrayal** of our friendship.

5. enmity (ĕn´mĭ-tē) *noun*
Deep hatred
• In ancient Scotland, there was much **enmity** between warring clans.

aloof

Amiability and *enmity* are antonyms.

Remember that *enmity* exists between *enemies*.

6. idealize (ī-dē´ə-līz´) *verb*

To think of as perfect

• At times the public **idealizes** sports heroes, forgetting that they have faults like other human beings.

ideal *adjective* My **ideal** neighborhood has front yards filled with leafy trees.

7. protégé (prō´tə-zhā´) *noun*

A person who is helped by a more experienced or powerful person

• The professional violinist was thrilled when her **protégé** won first prize in the young artists' competition.

> *Protégé* is a French word, so it is pronounced differently than an English word. The feminine form of the word is *protégée*.

8. recluse (rĕk´lōōs´) *noun*

A person who withdraws from society to live alone; a hermit

• After the accident, Mr. Smythe became a **recluse,** avoiding all contact with his neighbors.

reclusive *adjective* The **reclusive** woman refused to answer the telephone or the doorbell.

9. solitary (sŏl´ĭ-tĕr´ē) *adjective*

a. Living or being alone
   • The prisoner was forced into **solitary** confinement.
b. The only one
   • She was the **solitary** sixth grader in the choir.

solitude *noun* I like to have at least half an hour of **solitude** every day.

> *Solitary* expresses being alone or the only one. Do not use this word to express "loneliness."

10. treacherous (trĕch´ər-əs) *adjective*

a. Dangerous; having unknown dangers
   • We couldn't go sailing because the seas were too **treacherous.**
b. Unfaithful; disloyal
   • She was a **treacherous** friend because she often spread false gossip.

treachery *noun* The wolf used **treachery** to trick Little Red Riding Hood.

WORD ENRICHMENT

Do you speak French? (The answer is yes.)

The English language has borrowed many words from French. One example is *protégé*. Another is *cliché* (pronounced klee-SHAY), which means "an overused, worn-out expression or idea."

The French have a long tradition of fine cooking, and many English words having to do with food come from French. A certain type of cooking is known as a *cuisine* (kwee-ZEEN). A gathering often starts with *hors d'oeuvres* (or-DURVS), or appetizers. Later, an *entrée* (ON-tray), or main course, might be served.

WRITE THE CORRECT WORD

Write the correct word in the space next to each definition.

_____ 1. unfriendly; distant

_____ 2. to be unfaithful to

_____ 3. hermit

_____ 4. to believe to be perfect

_____ 5. a student of a more experienced person

_____ 6. alone

_____ 7. dangerous or disloyal

_____ 8. friendly

_____ 9. hatred

_____ 10. to make familiar with

COMPLETE THE SENTENCE

Write the letter for the word that best completes each sentence.

_____ 1. When you _____ a person, you don't see his or her faults.
    a. acquaint   **b.** idealize   **c.** betray   **d.** recluse

_____ 2. The public expressed deep _____ toward the general who betrayed them.
    a. enmity   **b.** amiability   **c.** reclusiveness   **d.** acquaintance

_____ 3. Be careful when you swim; the currents are _____.
    a. solitary   **b.** treacherous   **c.** aloof   **d.** ideal

_____ 4. Although Shira had dozens of _____, only three of those people were close friends.
    a. recluses   **b.** ideals   **c.** acquaintances   **d.** enmities

_____ 5. The woman had a(n) _____ lifestyle and spent much of her time alone.
    a. amiable   **b.** treacherous   **c.** ideal   **d.** solitary

_____ 6. Jordan's skills improved when he became the _____ of a famous tennis player.
    a. protégé   **b.** recluse   **c.** enmity   **d.** betrayal

_____ 7. _____ people tend to avoid parties, parades, and other social gatherings.
    a. Idealistic   **b.** Reclusive   **c.** Treacherous   **d.** Amiable

_____ 8. Jerome is such a(n) _____ host that he can make anyone feel welcome.
    a. reclusive   **b.** aloof   **c.** solitary   **d.** amiable

_____ 9. Vanessa felt _____ when her best friend insulted her behind her back.
    a. betrayed   **b.** amiable   **c.** acquainted   **d.** reclusive

_____ 10. When Jason stayed _____ from the crowd, people shouted, "Come join us!"
    a. aloof   **b.** amiable   **c.** ideal   **d.** acquainted

Challenge: The recording of what Vanessa had said about Kate _____ Vanessa's _____.

_____   **a.** idealized...amiability   **b.** betrayed...treachery   **c.** withdrew...seclusion

Snakes: Friends or Foes?

There is no question about it. Snakes have a bad reputation. **(1)** Why do so many people feel *enmity* toward snakes? **(2)** There are several reasons why snakes are often seen as *treacherous*. In some cultures, the snake has had a villainous image since storytelling began! **(3)** In many traditional tales, snakes *betray* anyone who trusts them. Of course, humans have practical reasons to fear snakes, too. Some, like rattlers, cottonmouths, and vipers, can be dangerous and even deadly.

(4) Unfortunately, most people never bother to *acquaint* themselves with the positive aspects of these creatures. For example, snakes can serve as guards. A Virginian once used a boa constrictor to protect his business. In Sweden, three deadly snakes in a display case guarded a sapphire worth $500,000. Both employers accurately judged fear of snakebite to be an effective weapon against crime.

The very poison (or venom) that we fear can actually help save human lives. Ancrod, a compound found in the venom of the Malayan pit viper, can be used to prevent blood from clotting. The substance is given to people who have suffered strokes or heart attacks. It thins the blood and reverses the clotting response.

People often fear meeting snakes in the wild. Yet snakes pose almost no threat under natural conditions. **(5)** They are *reclusive* creatures who leave their burrows, caves, or trees only for warmth and food. **(6)** For the most part, snakes lead *solitary* lives.

While some people avoid snakes, others keep these slithery creatures as pets. Pet snakes are usually gentle, but feeding them can be a challenge. Most eat animals such as mice and insects. **(7)** Experienced pet owners often help their *protégés* learn about the snakes' diet. **(8)** Some believe that snakes' lack of affection makes them less than *ideal* pets. **(9)** Many snake owners, however, don't mind their pets' *aloofness*. **(10)** Some even say that their snakes show signs of *amiability*!

On occasion, snakes have been respected symbols. A flag featuring a serpent and the motto "Don't tread on me" waved from colonial American ships. Since ancient times, a staff with two snakes wound around it has been a symbol of the medical profession. Still, fairly or unfairly, the snake remains one of the animal kingdom's most hated species.

Each sentence below refers to a numbered sentence in the passage. Write the letter of the choice that gives the sentence a meaning that is closest to the original sentence.

_____ **1.** Why do so many people feel _____ toward snakes?
  a. anger   **b.** friendly   **c.** hatred   **d.** unfaithful

_____ **2.** There are several reasons why snakes are often seen as _____.
  a. clever   **b.** dangerous   **c.** mean   **d.** companions

_____ **3.** In many traditional tales, snakes _____ anyone who trusts them.
  a. are violent toward   **b.** are trusting of   **c.** are disloyal to   **d.** make friends with

_____ **4.** Most people never bother to _____ the positive aspects of these creatures.
  a. get to know   **b.** worry about   **c.** stay away from   **d.** react to

_____ **5.** They are _____ creatures who leave their burrows, caves, or trees only for warmth and food.
  a. nocturnal   **b.** ferocious   **c.** shy   **d.** social

_____ **6.** For the most part, they lead _____ lives.
     a. unsociable   **b.** friendly   **c.** dangerous   **d.** disloyal

_____ **7.** Experienced pet owners often help their _____ learn about the snakes' diet.
     a. relatives   **b.** trainees   **c.** dogs   **d.** owners

_____ **8.** Some believe that snakes' lack of affection makes them less than _____ pets.
     a. fearsome   **b.** perfect   **c.** easy   **d.** messy

_____ **9.** Many snake owners, however, don't mind their pets' _____.
     a. danger   **b.** friendliness   **c.** responsiveness   **d.** lack of affection

_____ **10.** Some even say that their snakes show signs of _____!
     a. hatred   **b.** loyalty   **c.** intelligence   **d.** friendliness

Indicate whether the statements below are TRUE or FALSE according to the passage.

_____ **1.** Doctors have no use for snake venom.

_____ **2.** Snakes are most dangerous in their natural habitat.

_____ **3.** Historically, snakes have often been viewed as treacherous creatures.

FINISH THE THOUGHT

Complete each sentence so that it shows the meaning of the italicized word.

1. The *aloof* woman _____

_____

2. I would like to better *acquaint* myself with _____

_____

WRITE THE DERIVATIVE

Complete the sentence by writing the correct form of the word shown in parentheses. You may not need to change the form that is given.

_____ **1.** Her _____ vacation would be on a warm, sandy beach. (*idealize*)

_____ **2.** The traitor was guilty of _____ of the worst kind. (*treacherous*)

_____ **3.** Her _____ is often misinterpreted as hostility. (*aloof*)

_____ **4.** Lai's strongest traits are her sense of humor and her _____. (*amiable*)

_____ **5.** The manager took the intern under his wing as a _____. (*protégé*)

_____ **6.** Sven enjoys a few moments of _____ every now and then. (*solitary*)

_____ **7.** Have you made any new _____ this year? (*acquaint*)

_____ **8.** The monks lived a _____ lifestyle. *(recluse)*

_____ **9.** The _____ between the feuding families grew stronger. *(enmity)*

_____ **10.** I was hurt by your utter _____ of our friendship. *(betray)*

FIND THE EXAMPLE

Choose the answer that best describes the action or situation.

_____ **1.** Something a *reclusive* person might do
    a. attend a party   **b.** play team soccer   **c.** go fishing alone   **d.** skate with friends

_____ **2.** Something an *amiable* person is likely to do
    a. insult you   **b.** greet you warmly   **c.** betray you   **d.** avoid social contact

_____ **3.** A characteristic of a *treacherous* ski slope
    a. icy   **b.** flat   **c.** fun   **d.** easy

_____ **4.** An *aloof* gesture
    a. pat on the back   **b.** grin   **c.** shrug   **d.** punch

_____ **5.** One way someone could *betray* you
    a. eat too much   **b.** beat you in chess   **c.** buy you a gift   **d.** lie about you

_____ **6.** A *protégé* of an artist
    a. sculpture   **b.** opera   **c.** young painter   **d.** paintbrush

_____ **7.** An effect of *enmity* between two countries
    a. a peace treaty   **b.** a war   **c.** economic trade   **d.** open elections

_____ **8.** Something best described as an *acquaintance*
    a. classmate   **b.** coin   **c.** snake   **d.** parent

_____ **9.** *Ideal* weather for a picnic
    a. snowy and foggy   **b.** sweltering   **c.** sunny and mild   **d.** rainy and cold

_____ **10.** Someone who leads a *solitary* existence
    a. a political leader   **b.** a teacher   **c.** a rock star   **d.** a shepherd

Necessities and Extras

WORD LIST

accessory	auxiliary	entail	essence	excess
frivolous	imperative	notable	pertinent	significant

What is a necessity and what is an extra? The bare necessities of life are clean water, food, and shelter. Yet life is often enriched by the extras we can add to it. We enjoy living in heated homes with indoor plumbing and electricity. Although we could survive on a diet of little more than bread and water, we can choose to eat a varied diet that both keeps us healthy and tastes good. The words in this lesson give you many ways to describe the necessities and the extras in our lives.

1. accessory (ăk-sĕs´ə-rē) *noun*
   a. Something extra that adds attractiveness or usefulness
   • A basket was the only **accessory** on the new bicycle.
   b. Someone who aides a lawbreaker, but who was not present at the crime
   • If you hide a criminal, you become an **accessory** to the crime.

   accessorize *verb* Many people **accessorize** outfits with scarves, jewelry, and matching shoes.

2. auxiliary (ôg-zĭl´yə-rē)
   a. *adjective* Providing extra help or support
   • The truck's **auxiliary** gas tank enabled it to travel extra miles without refueling.
   b. *noun* A helper; an organization of helpers
   • An **auxiliary** of volunteers helped the hospital staff.

3. entail (ĕn-tāl´) *verb*
   To require or involve
   • The plan to build a new school **entails** raising property taxes.

4. essence (ĕs´əns) *noun*
   a. The most necessary and basic part
   • Freedom to vote is the **essence** of democracy.
   b. The concentrated liquid taken from a plant for perfume or flavoring
   • Bakers use the **essence** of the vanilla plant to flavor cakes.

5. excess (ĕk´sĕs´) *noun*
   An extra amount
   • The restaurant served so much food that we took home the **excess.**

   excessive *adjective* **Excessive** exercise may make your muscles sore.

accessorize

Entail also means "to limit the inheritance of property to certain people," usually the eldest sons.

6. frivolous (frĭv´ə-ləs) *adjective*
Not worth serious attention; trivial; silly
• Games may be **frivolous** pastimes, but they are fun!

frivolity *noun* Don't waste your money on **frivolities**!

7. imperative (ĭm-pĕr´ə-tĭv)
a. *adjective* Necessary; commanded
• It's **imperative** that we have a good map before we head out into the desert.
b. *noun* Something that is necessary or commanded
• Helping poor people is a moral **imperative**.

8. notable (nō´tə-bəl)
a. *adjective* Worth attention or notice; important
• Winning an Olympic gold medal is a **notable** achievement.
b. *noun* A famous or an important person
• The mayor, the head of the city council, and other **notables** were honored at the dinner.

Remember that *notable* things are *worth noting*.

9. pertinent (pûr´tn-ənt) *adjective*
Relevant; related to what is being discussed
• The points you make in an essay should all be **pertinent** to the topic.

pertinence *noun* The topic of making a home safe for babies is of great **pertinence** to new parents.

pertain *verb* We have uncovered additional evidence that **pertains** to the unsolved mystery.

10. significant (sĭg-nĭf´ĭ-kənt) *adjective*
Important; meaningful
• Oranges are a **significant** source of vitamin C.

significance *noun* The telephone was an invention of great **significance**.

The opposite of *significant* is *insignificant,* which means "not important." *In-* often means "not."

WORD ENRICHMENT

Changing *y* to *i* when adding endings

Accessory and *auxiliary* are just two of the many words that end with the letter *y*. When changing the form of a word that ends in *y* by adding an ending, remember to change the *y* to an *i* if the *y* comes after a consonant, as in *accessories, accessorize,* and *auxiliaries.*

a notable achievement

WRITE THE CORRECT WORD

Write the correct word in the space next to each definition.

_____ 1. worthy of attention

_____ 2. the most basic part

_____ 3. relevant

_____ 4. helper

_____ 5. something that adds attractiveness

_____ 6. important

_____ 7. to require

_____ 8. necessary

_____ 9. silly; trivial

_____ 10. extra amount

COMPLETE THE SENTENCE

Write the letter for the word that best completes each sentence.

_____ 1. _____, such as presidents and prime ministers, attended the international presentation on global warming.
   a. Excesses   b. Accessories   c. Notables   d. Auxiliaries

_____ 2. Most hospitals have _____ power systems that provide electricity if the main system fails.
   a. pertinent   b. auxiliary   c. imperative   d. accessory

_____ 3. Preparing to run a marathon _____ many hours of training.
   a. accessorizes   b. excesses   c. pertains   d. entails

_____ 4. Justice and equality are the _____ of a fair legal system.
   a. notables   b. accessories   c. essence   d. significance

_____ 5. Noel works hard all week, but he spends his weekends on _____ pastimes.
   a. frivolous   b. pertinent   c. notable   d. essential

_____ 6. It is _____ that all airplane passengers pass through a security check.
   a. imperative   b. notable   c. auxiliary   d. frivolous

_____ 7. The speech was poorly received because it was not _____ to the topic.
   a. notable   b. pertinent   c. frivolous   d. excessive

_____ 8. A person who drives a getaway car for a robber is a(n) _____ to the crime.
   a. essence   b. notable   c. entailment   d. accessory

_____ 9. The tailor measured the fabric and cut away the _____.
   a. frivolity   b. essence   c. imperative   d. excess

_____ 10. Einstein's theory of relativity was a(n) _____ scientific breakthrough.
   a. accessorized   b. entailed   c. significant   d. imperative

Challenge: Because the fire was huge and spreading, it was _____ that the _____ firefighters came to help put it out.

_____   a. pertinent...notable   b. imperative...auxiliary   c. excessive...frivolous

Robot Power: From Science Fiction to Surgery

The word *robot* immediately makes most of us think of science-fiction movies. But modern robots are far from fictional. They help us with household tasks, space exploration, and treating disease.

A remote-controlled robot can now mow your lawn. Another can vacuum your carpet while you lie on the couch. **(1)** This robot is based on *significant* scientific breakthroughs; it uses a system that was originally developed for robotic minesweepers. Similar robots have explored underwater shipwrecks, volcano tops, and the planet Mars.

Robots are also used in medicine. **(2)** With humans needed for more important tasks, robots serve as *auxiliaries* that deliver medication and supplies. The HelpMate, a sort of moving cabinet carries medicine and supplies around the hospital. **(3)** It includes safety features and *accessories* such as flashing lights and turn signals. The machine "speaks" both English and Spanish, using polite phrases, such as "please" and "thank you." To avoid bumping into things, it is programmed with detailed maps of the hospital and sensors that tell it when people are near. Its wireless radio systems open automatic doors. **(4)** To make sure there is no *excess* weight, it will not enter an elevator if anyone else is riding on it. The HelpMate does its job well, but some people still have trouble getting used to a flashing cabinet moving on its own!

(5) Robots are also making *notable* contributions in the operating room. **(6)** All surgery *entails* risk, but heart surgery is particularly dangerous. **(7)** It is *imperative* that surgeons be highly trained and experienced, and that they have the best help available— even if that help is a machine. **(8)** Robotic arms can achieve the precision that is the *essence* of successful surgery. These machines can eliminate the risks posed by the slight shaking of a doctor's hand. Tiny robotic "fingers" can also fit into places too small for human hands.

Using a robot, Dr. Chand Ramaiah was able to do major heart surgery by making only a tiny incision, or surgical cut, into the patient's body. The little fingers of the robot were inserted, and a tiny camera gave the surgeon a full view of what was happening inside the patient. **(9)** Using this picture and other *pertinent* information, Dr. Ramaiah directed the robot as it performed the operation.

To honor advances in robot science, Carnegie Mellon University has established a Robot Hall of Fame. Each year, a panel of robot experts chooses five of our best mechanical friends. **(10)** Some winners are chosen for their abilities to do *frivolous* but entertaining activities such as dancing. Others are space explorers, like the Sojourner that went to Mars.

Today's robots have entertained us in movies, explored for us in space, and fit into tiny spaces in human hearts. We can only guess what the future holds!

Each sentence below refers to a numbered sentence in the passage. Write the letter of the choice that gives the sentence a meaning that is closest to the original sentence.

_____ **1.** This robot is based on _____ scientific breakthroughs.
   a. supportive   **b.** important   **c.** outdated   **d.** technological

_____ **2.** Robots serve as _____ that deliver medication and supplies.
   a. doctors   **b.** cabinets   **c.** nurses   **d.** helpers

_____ **3.** It includes safety features and _____ such as flashing lights and turn signals.
   a. high-tech buttons   **b.** matching jewelry   **c.** extra features   **d.** warning alarms

_____ **4.** To make sure there is no _____ weight, it will not enter an elevator if anyone
else is riding on it.
    a. extra   **b.** robotic   **c.** ordinary   **d.** absence of

_____ **5.** Robots are also making _____ contributions in the operating room.
    a. insignificant   **b.** additional   **c.** medical   **d.** important

_____ **6.** All surgery _____ risk, but heart surgery is particularly dangerous.
    a. supports   **b.** adds   **c.** implies   **d.** involves

_____ **7.** It is _____ that surgeons be highly trained and experienced.
    a. necessary   **b.** safe   **c.** helpful   **d.** forbidden

_____ **8.** Robotic arms can achieve the precision that is the _____ of successful surgery.
    a. new idea   **b.** basic quality   **c.** helper   **d.** importance

_____ **9.** Using _____ information, Dr. Ramaiah directed the robot as it performed the
operation.
    a. limited   **b.** relevant   **c.** researched   **d.** technological

_____ **10.** Some winners are chosen for their abilities to do _____ but entertaining
activities such as dancing.
    a. essential   **b.** energetic and fun   **c.** not so important   **d.** surgery

Indicate whether the statements below are TRUE or FALSE according to the passage.

_____ **1.** Robots are designed to perform both serious and frivolous tasks.

_____ **2.** Some robots can help with housework.

_____ **3.** A doctor would never trust a robot to help with surgery.

WRITING EXTENDED RESPONSES

Imagine you have an urgent problem. How might a robot help you
solve it? Write a narrative essay in which you use a robot. Remember to
describe the problem, the robot's abilities that help you, and the final
solution. Your narrative piece should be at least three paragraphs long.
Use at least three lesson words in your essay and underline them.

WRITE THE DERIVATIVE

Complete the sentence by writing the correct form of the word shown in
parentheses. You may not need to change the form that is given.

_____ **1.** The education of a brain surgeon, which _____ a medical residency
of five years, is rigorous. *(entail)*

_____ **2.** _____ an outfit can often improve one's appearance. *(accessory)*

_____ **3.** Some think that jewelry, while attractive, is _____ . *(frivolous)*

_____ **4.** Albert Einstein, Neils Bohr, and Enrico Fermi were _____ in the field of physics. *(notable)*

_____ **5.** The National Guard can act as an _____ police force. *(auxiliary)*

_____ **6.** The athlete seemed _____ nervous before the game, so the coach tried to calm him. *(excessive)*

_____ **7.** The judge decided that the new evidence had no _____ to the case. *(pertinent)*

_____ **8.** It is _____ that you answer the question honestly. *(imperative)*

_____ **9.** The king's decree had much _____. *(significant)*

_____ **10.** _____ of lemon flavored the pie. *(essence)*

FIND THE EXAMPLE

Choose the answer that best describes the action or situation.

_____ **1.** The *essence* of comedy
  a. theater   **b.** hopefulness   **c.** sadness   **d.** humor

_____ **2.** An example of a *notable* achievement
  a. finishing a chore   **b.** winning an award   **c.** taking a test   **d.** playing a sport

_____ **3.** This is most likely to be *pertinent* in court
  a. evidence   **b.** musical ability   **c.** tasty food   **d.** batting average

_____ **4.** A *frivolous* concern for a presidential candidate
  a. education   **b.** the economy   **c.** health care   **d.** fashion trends

_____ **5.** Something that is *significant* to your academic career
  a. your pets   **b.** your study skills **c.** your clothes   **d.** your friends

_____ **6.** An *accessory* on a car
  a. the engine   **b.** the brake pedal   **c.** the radio   **d.** the wheels

_____ **7.** Cleaning a house might *entail* doing this
  a. gardening   **b.** ironing   **c.** sweeping   **d.** cooking

_____ **8.** The best thing to do with *excess* cake batter
  a. build a car   **b.** make cupcakes   **c.** make a fire   **d.** wear it

_____ **9.** Something that performs an *auxiliary* function
  a. airplane wing **b.** brain   **c.** heart   **d.** spare tire

_____ **10.** Something that is *imperative* for living things to have access to
  a. money   **b.** happiness   **c.** water   **d.** a job

Activity and Inactivity

WORD LIST

dormant	frenetic	industrious	loiter	lull
restless	sluggish	spry	strenuous	vigor

Both motion and rest are a natural part of the rhythm of life. People work or play, and then rest. Many animals actively look for food in warm seasons and hibernate during cold ones. After centuries of inactivity, a volcano can erupt unexpectedly. Each word in this lesson describes a degree of activity or inactivity. As you study the words, try to picture the actions.

1. **dormant** (dôr´mənt) *adjective*
   Temporarily inactive
   • After more than 400 years of being **dormant,** Costa Rica's Arenal volcano erupted in 1968.

   dormancy *noun* During its **dormancy,** a bear sleeps in its den.

2. **frenetic** (frə-nĕt´ĭk) *adjective*
   Wildly active; frantic; frenzied
   • I had to work at a **frenetic** pace to finish the project by the deadline.

3. **industrious** (ĭn-dŭs´trē-əs) *adjective*
   Hardworking
   • The **industrious** students wrote their skit ahead of schedule and had extra time to make props and costumes.

   industriousness *noun* The girls showed great **industriousness** in packing food for flood victims.

4. **loiter** (loi´tər) *verb*
   To stand around doing nothing; to linger
   • The principal told the students not to **loiter** in the school parking lot.

5. **lull** (lŭl)
   a. *noun* A temporary stopping or lessening of activity or noise
   • There was a **lull** in the storm.
   b. *verb* To calm
   • Mom **lulled** the baby to sleep by singing a lullaby.

> *Frenetically* is the adverb form of *frenetic.*

loiter

6. **restless** (rĕst´lĭs) *adjective*
Not able to relax or rest
 • Helen spent a **restless** night tossing and turning in bed.

restlessness *noun* Because of his **restlessness**, Ken had problems sitting still in class.

> *Restlessness* often involves physical movement.

7. **sluggish** (slŭg´ĭsh) *adjective*
Slow; lacking energy
 • Very hot weather makes people **sluggish**.

sluggishness *noun* **Sluggishness** is one sign of illness.

> Slugs are small, slimy, slow-moving creatures similar to snails but with little or no shell. Remember that *slugs* are *sluggish*.

8. **spry** (sprī) *adjective*
Active; energetic; lively
 • "I hope I am as **spry** as Grandmother when I am eighty!" said Dad.

spryness *noun* The old dog had such **spryness** that it raced out the door before we could catch it.

9. **strenuous** (strĕn´yōō-əs) *adjective*
Requiring great effort
 • Moving a grand piano is a **strenuous** task.

strenuousness *noun* We were tired from the **strenuousness** of our run.

> *Strenuous* is related to the word *strain*. A person must *strain* to do something *strenuous*.

10. **vigor** (vĭg´ər) *noun*
Strength or physical energy; intense activity
 • The tennis champion played the game with **vigor**.

vigorous *adjective* The coach raised **vigorous** objections to the umpire's call.

WORD ENRICHMENT

The suffix *-less*

The suffix *-less*, meaning "without," appears in words like *restless*, *noiseless*, *clueless*, *meaningless*, and *painless*. A *restless* person cannot rest. Something *noiseless* makes no sound. If people are *clueless*, they haven't got a clue—they just don't understand.

clueless

WRITE THE CORRECT WORD

Write the correct word in the space next to each definition.

_____ **1.** active or lively

_____ **2.** inactive temporarily

_____ **3.** strength and energy

_____ **4.** to stand around

_____ **5.** a slowing down or stopping of activity

_____ **6.** unable to relax

_____ **7.** hardworking

_____ **8.** without energy; slow

_____ **9.** requiring great effort

_____ **10.** wildly active

COMPLETE THE SENTENCE

Write the letter for the word that best completes each sentence.

_____ **1.** The singers' passion and the dancers' _____ made the performance exciting.
   a. dormancy   **b.** lull   **c.** loitering   **d.** vigor

_____ **2.** When I awoke with a fever, my body ached and I felt _____.
   a. sluggish   **b.** frenetic   **c.** industrious   **d.** spry

_____ **3.** The people in the town were _____ and quickly cleaned up after the hurricane.
   a. strenuous   **b.** sluggish   **c.** industrious   **d.** dormant

_____ **4.** The new gym teacher had us do a long and _____ workout.
   a. sluggish   **b.** lulling   **c.** strenuous   **d.** restless

_____ **5.** Her _____ desire to become an actress was awakened when she saw the play.
   a. spry   **b.** dormant   **c.** frenetic   **d.** restless

_____ **6.** They brought the boat into the harbor during a(n) _____ in the storm.
   a. lull   **b.** industriousness   **c.** vigor   **d.** strenuousness

_____ **7.** The doctor said that Mr. Lin is incredibly healthy and _____ for a ninety-year-old.
   a. sluggish   **b.** spry   **c.** dormant   **d.** strenuous

_____ **8.** The sign reads: "No _____ in the park after dusk."
   a. vigor   **b.** industriousness   **c.** lulling   **d.** loitering

_____ **9.** The _____ contestants raced to be the first to finish the obstacle course.
   a. strenuous   **b.** dormant   **c.** frenetic   **d.** loitering

_____ **10.** After being stuck in their house for three days, the children grew _____.
   a. restless   **b.** vigorous   **c.** spry   **d.** strenuous

Challenge: During the _____ work of building the shed, we all appreciated each other's _____.
_____   **a.** sluggish…lull   **b.** strenuous…vigor   **c.** industrious…sluggishness

The Oryx: A Laid-Back Survivor

If you see an animal that looks like an antelope, you would probably expect it to be quick, alert, and fast. **(1)** But the Arabian oryx is an antelope that doesn't behave like its speedy and *vigorous* cousins.

(2) In contrast to *spry* African antelopes, the oryx seems laid-back—almost lazy. **(3)** It moves slowly and spends hours *loitering* under acacia trees. **(4)** The apparent *sluggishness* of the Arabian oryx actually helps it survive in its desert environment. Its slow-paced habits allow the oryx to conserve water and energy. **(5)** Lots of *strenuous* activity would weaken the animal in the broiling desert sun.

The oryx is smaller than the common antelope, and its coat is almost pure white so that it absorbs a minimum of heat. Because it is usually only three to four feet tall, it can fit easily in the shade of a small bush, and it needs only a small amount of food. As a result, the oryx can handle the constant shortages of food, water, and shade in the desert.

The desert is home to a wide array of animals. **(6)** Many of these animals *frenetically* search for food at night. **(7)** Calm during the day, the desert is often a picture of *restlessness* after sunset. **(8)** Ending their daytime *dormancy*, snakes, mice, and other animals pop up from their burrows to eat (or be eaten). **(9)** Most desert creatures work *industriously* in the night hours. **(10)** There is barely a *lull* in the constant activity. But in the midst of all this frenzy, you will see the patient oryx relaxing lazily and biding its time, quietly observing the activity of other animals.

The oryx's relaxed lifestyle has resulted in some negative consequences, however. Its slowness has made it an easy target for hunters. By 1972, hunters had killed off almost the entire oryx population. A conservation effort called Operation Oryx arose in response to the need to protect these passive creatures. Today, herds of Arabian oryx once again can live their gentle lives in the desert sands.

Each sentence below refers to a numbered sentence in the passage. Write the letter of the choice that gives the sentence a meaning that is closest to the original sentence.

_____ **1.** The Arabian oryx is an antelope that doesn't behave like its speedy and _____ cousins.

    a. social   **b.** relaxed   **c.** energetic   **d.** lazy

_____ **2.** In contrast to _____ African antelopes, the oryx seems laid-back—almost lazy.

    a. quiet   **b.** active   **c.** beautiful   **d.** slow

_____ **3.** It moves slowly and spends hours _____ under acacia trees.

    a. standing   **b.** running   **c.** hunting   **d.** digging

_____ **4.** The apparent _____ of the Arabian oryx actually helps it survive in its desert environment.

    a. lack of instinct   **b.** illness   **c.** gracefulness   **d.** lack of energy

_____ **5.** Lots of _____ activity would weaken the animal in the broiling desert sun.

    a. healthy   **b.** leisurely   **c.** energetic   **d.** hunting

_____ **6.** Many of these animals _____ search for food at night.
      a. carefully   **b.** secretly   **c.** frantically   **d.** quietly

_____ **7.** Calm during the day, the desert is often a picture of _____ after sunset.
      a. happy playing   **b.** calm feasting   **c.** nervous activity   **d.** quiet sleep

_____ **8.** Ending their daytime _____, snakes, mice, and other animals pop up from their burrows.
      a. hunt   **b.** play   **c.** fear   **d.** rest

_____ **9.** Most desert creatures work _____ in the night hours.
      a. hard   **b.** together   **c.** gracefully   **d.** slowly

_____ **10.** There is barely a _____ in the constant activity.
      a. sound   **b.** break   **c.** snack   **d.** song

Indicate whether the statements below are TRUE or FALSE according to the passage.

_____ **1.** The Arabian oryx is energetic at night.

_____ **2.** The oryx needs to conserve energy because of the harshness of the climate where it lives.

_____ **3.** Today, the oryx is extinct.

FINISH THE THOUGHT

Complete each sentence so that it shows the meaning of the italicized word.

1. When I am feeling *sluggish* _____

_____

2. My *spry* grandmother _____

_____

WRITE THE DERIVATIVE

Complete the sentence by writing the correct form of the word shown in parentheses. You may not need to change the form that is given.

_____ **1.** Jill gave the dog a _____ brushing. (*vigor*)

_____ **2.** Ants are known for their _____. (*industrious*)

_____ **3.** The lion paced _____ in its cage. (*restless*)

_____ **4.** Great-Aunt Rose's _____ amazed everyone. (*spry*)

_____ **5.** She worked _____ because there was much to do and little time. (*frenetic*)

_____ **6.** The construction team worked _____ all day long. (*strenuous*)

_____ **7.** The team's _____ annoyed the coach. *(sluggish)*

_____ **8.** The sound of crickets always _____ me to sleep. *(lull)*

_____ **9.** The police officer told us not to _____ in front of the school. *(loiter)*

_____ **10.** Seeds often remain in a state of _____ until they sprout. *(dormant)*

FIND THE EXAMPLE

Choose the answer that best describes the action or situation.

_____ **1.** Something a *restless* person might do
    a. pace the floor   **b.** take a nap   **c.** calmly listen   **d.** quietly watch

_____ **2.** A sound most likely to *lull* you to sleep
    a. a power drill   **b.** ocean waves   **c.** loud music   **d.** police siren

_____ **3.** Something you might want to do on a day you feel *sluggish*
    a. run ten miles   **b.** write an essay   **c.** take a rest   **d.** build a shed

_____ **4.** An animal that is *dormant* in the winter
    a. bear   **b.** cow   **c.** human   **d.** cat

_____ **5.** Something you do when you *loiter*
    a. read a book   **b.** swim laps   **c.** stand around   **d.** ride a bike

_____ **6.** A *strenuous* activity
    a. walking a cat   **b.** humming a tune   **c.** eating a snack   **d.** lifting weights

_____ **7.** Something an *industrious* person would do
    a. waste time   **b.** gossip for hours   **c.** watch TV   **d.** work extra hours

_____ **8.** A way to demonstrate *spryness*
    a. sneezing loudly   **b.** lying by the pool   **c.** doing a back-flip   **d.** cooking dinner

_____ **9.** How a person might show *vigor*
    a. sleeping   **b.** watching TV   **c.** playing basketball   **d.** hiding in a crowd

_____ **10.** How you would most likely feel while working at a *frenetic* pace
    a. rushed   **b.** relaxed   **c.** lazy   **d.** stuffed

Reading and Reasoning

Context Clues

When people read, they commonly meet unfamiliar words. Using *context clues* is a strategy that can help you to figure out the meaning of these words. As you learned in Lesson 1, *context* refers to the words and sentences that surround a word. When you use context clues, you use the words surrounding an unfamiliar word to help you make an intelligent guess about the meaning of that word.

Using Context Clues in Reading

You probably use context clues already, although you may not realize it. Context clues are also the only way to choose the correct meaning for words that have more than one meaning. Look at the three sentences below and answer the questions.

1. A cough and sneezing are signs of a *cold*.

2. Why did he act so *cold* to me?

3. Arctic winters are very *cold*.

Write the number of the sentence that matches each definition below.

1. an illness _____

2. having a low temperature _____

3. unfriendly _____

Context clues allow you to use your common sense. They also enable you to keep reading without stopping. However, context clues do not always give an exact definition. For this reason, it is wise to check a dictionary to see whether the information you get from using these clues is accurate.

Strategies

Here are some strategies for using context clues:

1. Read the sentence completely. Information about meaning is given both before and after a word.

2. Use the other words in the sentence as clues to the meaning of the word you don't know.

3. Make an intelligent guess about the meaning of a word.

4. After you have made this guess, reread the sentence to see if your definition makes sense.

5. Check your definition by looking up the word in a dictionary.

Practice

Each of the sentences below contains a difficult word that has been italicized. Read each sentence and use context clues to make an intelligent guess about the meaning. Write your definition. Then look up the word in the dictionary and write the formal definition. (Remember to choose the definition that best matches the use of the word.)

1. Injuries to two players had a *deleterious* effect on the team.

   My definition _____

   Dictionary definition _____

2. The concert hall was a large and beautiful *edifice*.

   My definition _____

   Dictionary definition _____

3. The *parsimonious* millionaire refused to give any money to charity.

   My definition _____

   Dictionary definition _____

4. During storms, the rocky islands are a *menace* to ships.

   My definition _____

   Dictionary definition _____

5. After the *armistice*, the two armies stopped fighting for a while.

   My definition _____

   Dictionary definition _____

6. We appreciate the fact that you *comply* with the rules of the class.

   My definition _____

   Dictionary definition _____

7. Her *condescending* attitude made me feel that I was not as good as she was.

   My definition _____

   Dictionary definition _____

8. The iceberg was nearly split in two by a *crevice*.

   My definition _____

   Dictionary definition _____

9. The woodcutter's progress through the forest was *hampered* by the thick growth of trees and bushes.

   My definition _____

   Dictionary definition _____

10. With our *paltry* funds, we could not afford to eat at restaurants.

    My definition _____

    Dictionary definition _____

Appearance and Texture

WORD LIST

blunt	coarse	dense	dingy	iridescent
opaque	radiant	sheen	tinge	transparent

We experience the world through our senses. Imagine, for example, the sight of the vast ocean, the sound of the crashing waves, the smell of the salt water, and the feel of the hot sand on your toes. The words in this lesson focus on the senses of sight and touch. As you read the words, think about objects you have seen or touched that have each quality.

1. **blunt** (blŭnt)
   a. *adjective* Dull-edged; not sharp or pointed
   - The knife was too **blunt** to slice tomatoes.
   b. *adjective* Rude or rudely spoken, or spoken with hurtful honesty
   - My brother's **blunt** comments made me wonder if my new jacket was ugly.
   c. *verb* To make less intense, effective, or sharp
   - The barriers **blunted** the effect of the storm.

   bluntness *noun* The **bluntness** of the sword's tip helped prevent accidents during fencing lessons.

2. **coarse** (kôrs) *adjective*
   a. Rough in texture
   - Do you want medium-grade or **coarse** sandpaper?
   b. Not having good manners; rude
   - He showed his **coarse** manners by slurping his soup.

   coarseness *noun* Many people object to the increasing **coarseness** of language on the radio.

3. **dense** (dĕns) *adjective*
   Tightly crowded together; thick
   - Hikers in a **dense** forest will need a compass.

   density *noun* Cities have a higher **density** of people than rural areas do.

dense jungle

4. dingy (dǐn´jē) *adjective*
Dirty and discolored
• A thorough cleaning improved the appearance of the **dingy** statue.

dinginess *noun* Despite the **dinginess** of his blanket, the toddler
carried it with him wherever he went.

5. iridescent (ĭr´ĭ-dĕs´ənt) *adjective*
Having shiny, rainbowlike colors
• Many butterflies have jewel-like, **iridescent** wings.

iridescence *noun* The beautiful fish's scales gleamed with **iridescence.**

In ancient Greek mythology,
Iris was the goddess of
rainbows.

6. opaque (ō-pāk´) *adjective*
  a. Completely blocking light
   • The thick window shades were **opaque.**
  b. Not understood
   • The reasons for his opinion were completely **opaque** to me.

opacity *noun* The **opacity** of the material made it a good choice for
window panes.

7. radiant (rā´dē-ənt) *adjective*
  a. Giving out light or heat
   • Lamps, heaters, and the sun are **radiant** objects.
  b. Shining with happiness
   • Mary looked **radiant** after she won the spelling bee.

radiance *noun* The coals in the hearth gave off a soft **radiance.**

radiate *verb* Enough heat **radiates** from the fireplace to warm the
entire room.

8. sheen (shēn) *noun*
Shine, brightness
• Danielle polished her car until it had a glossy **sheen.**

9. tinge (tǐnj)
  a. *noun* A hint or small amount of color
   • Liam's hair was brown with a **tinge** of red.
  b. *noun* A hint or small amount of a feeling
   • David felt a **tinge** of jealousy when his younger brother beat him
    in tennis.
  c. *verb* To give a small amount of color to
   • Autumn frost **tinged** the grass with white.

10. transparent (trăns-pâr´ənt) *adjective*
  a. Letting light through, so that objects on the other side can be seen
   • Window glass and plastic wrap are **transparent.**
  b. Clearly understood; obvious
   • His nervous gestures made it **transparent** that he was hiding
    something.

transparency *noun* The **transparency** of the wedding veil allowed all
to see Helen's smiling face.

Transparent is the opposite
of *opaque. Trans-* means
"through." A *transparent*
material lets light or
information through.

WRITE THE CORRECT WORD

Write the correct word in the space next to each definition.

_____ **1.** dirty

_____ **2.** a polish or shine

_____ **3.** not sharp or pointed

_____ **4.** letting light through

_____ **5.** giving out heat

_____ **6.** shimmering colors

_____ **7.** tightly packed together

_____ **8.** not letting light through

_____ **9.** a small amount of color

_____ **10.** rough in texture

COMPLETE THE SENTENCE

Write the letter for the word that best completes each sentence.

_____ **1.** For safety, scissors meant for young children often have _____ ends.
a. blunt **b.** opaque **c.** coarse **d.** dense

_____ **2.** The skin of some sharks is so _____ that it can scrape your own skin.
a. radiant **b.** coarse **c.** dingy **d.** blunt

_____ **3.** The window was so dirty it was practically _____!
a. radiant **b.** transparent **c.** blunt **d.** opaque

_____ **4.** The ad for the new shampoo promised to give your hair a healthy _____.
a. dense **b.** coarse **c.** sheen **d.** tinge

_____ **5.** The roses were white with a(n) _____ of pink.
a. density **b.** transparency **c.** tinge **d.** opacity

_____ **6.** The child's lie was _____; he was obviously not telling the truth.
a. transparent **b.** iridescent **c.** radiant **d.** coarse

_____ **7.** We knew that Lakshmi was happy because her face was _____.
a. opaque **b.** blunt **c.** tinged **d.** radiant

_____ **8.** The peacock's shimmering, _____ feathers delighted the children.
a. blunt **b.** iridescent **c.** coarse **d.** dingy

_____ **9.** The _____ house hadn't been cleaned in years.
a. opaque **b.** dingy **c.** blunt **d.** dense

_____ **10.** It was hard to find a walking path in the _____ woods.
a. coarse **b.** dense **c.** transparent **d.** radiant

Challenge: His _____ comments revealed his _____ manners.

_____ **a.** dense…radiant **b.** opaque…transparent **c.** blunt…coarse

The Invention of Velcro®

About fifty years ago, sticky, prickly burrs in a forest inspired the creation of the stuff that we call Velcro®. These burrs made a creative person stop and think.

George de Mestral was an engineer with an annoying and common problem. **(1)** When he walked his dogs in the *dense* forest, he often needed to spend time picking the burrs out of their fur. **(2)** He wondered why burrs stuck so tightly to *coarse* materials. **(3)** He also noticed that the burrs stuck to wool clothes but not to smooth-surfaced fabrics that had a *sheen,* such as certain athletic or rainproof gear. **(4)** As a scientist, de Mestral knew that investigation often revealed the reasons for things that had once seemed *opaque.*

De Mestral decided to examine some burrs more closely. There were many different types. **(5)** Most were medium brown with a *tinge* of tan. **(6)** Some were a *dingy* dark brown. **(7)** Others were shiny, almost *iridescent.* De Mestral studied all the burrs under a microscope and found that they had one thing in common. Each was covered with hundreds of tiny, sharp hooks.

Next, de Mestral studied fabrics under the microscope. He could see that woolly or terry cloth fabrics had tiny loops on the surface. He suspected that the coats of animals with long or curly fur that acted like loops picked up the most burrs.

(8) Suddenly the process became *transparent.* The burrs had little hooks, and they stuck to material with loops. So if there were two materials, one with hooks and another with loops, they would stick together tightly.

De Mestral realized materials that could do this would have many uses, so he took his idea to fabric experts in France. **(9)** Some *bluntly* expressed the opinion that the idea would never work. One weaver, however, showed an interest. He carefully wove two strips, one with hooks and one with loops. When pressed together, they stuck fast.

(10) *Radiant* and energized with the success of his idea, de Mestral started to manufacture the fasteners we now call Velcro®. Every day, people all over the world use this and similar products to fasten sneakers, gloves, boots, jackets, and raincoats. Velcro® also has some unexpected uses. It helped hold a heart together for the first artificial-heart surgery. Velcro® is even used to keep equipment from floating around during space missions. De Mestral's creative mind took an idea from nature and turned it into something that helps people on Earth and beyond.

Each sentence below refers to a numbered sentence in the passage. Write the letter of the choice that gives the sentence a meaning that is closest to the original sentence.

_____ 1. When he walked his dogs in the _____ forest, he spent time picking the burrs out of their fur.
     a. thick   **b.** empty   **c.** nearby   **d.** rainy

_____ 2. He wondered why burrs stuck so tightly to _____ materials.
     a. sleek   **b.** wet   **c.** rough   **d.** dirty

_____ 3. He also noticed that the burrs stuck to wool clothes but not to fabrics that had a _____.
     a. pattern   **b.** roughness   **c.** shine   **d.** material

_____ 4. De Mestral knew that investigation often revealed the reasons for things that had once seemed _____.
     a. an invention   **b.** a game   **c.** an adventure   **d.** a mystery

_____ **5.** Most were medium brown with a _____ of tan.
    a. stripe   **b.** hint   **c.** burr   **d.** darkness

_____ **6.** Some were a _____ dark brown.
    a. dirty-looking   **b.** bright and shiny   **c.** hard-to-see   **d.** see-through

_____ **7.** Others were shiny, almost _____.
    a. purple   **b.** black   **c.** rainbowlike   **d.** smooth

_____ **8.** Suddenly the process became _____.
    a. light   **b.** confusing   **c.** unknown   **d.** understood

_____ **9.** Some _____ expressed the opinion that the idea would never work.
    a. kindly   **b.** insensitively   **c.** colorfully   **d.** happily

_____ **10.** _____ and energized with the success of his idea, de Mestral started to manufacture the fasteners we now call Velcro®.
    a. Apparent   **b.** Textured   **c.** Joyful   **d.** Hardworking

Indicate whether the statements below are TRUE or FALSE according to the passage.

_____ **1.** Examining everyday problems can lead to great innovations.

_____ **2.** Velcro® was invented by accident.

_____ **3.** Burrs stick to glass.

WRITING EXTENDED RESPONSES

Velcro® can be used to fasten clothes. Think about a favorite costume that you have seen or worn. Describe exactly how that costume looked and why it was especially good for the occasion. Your descriptive piece should be at least two paragraphs long. Use at least three lesson words in your essay and underline them.

WRITE THE DERIVATIVE

Complete the sentence by writing the correct form of the word shown in parentheses. You may not need to change the form that is given.

_____ **1.** "I don't like that song," she said _____. (*blunt*)

_____ **2.** His coat was even _____ than his old shoes. (*dingy*)

_____ **3.** The _____ of the full moon cast shadows on the sidewalk. (*radiant*)

_____ **4.** A _____ of dew sparkled on the grass. (*sheen*)

_____ **5.** Her eyes were brown _____ with green. (*tinge*)

_____ **6.** The bus was _____ packed with tourists. (*dense*)

_____ **7.** I love the _____ of dragonfly wings. (*iridescent*)

_____ 8. Because of the _____ of that fabric, you need to line it with something. (transparent)

_____ 9. The _____ of his language shocked the audience. (coarse)

_____ 10. Painting the glass black will make it _____. (opaque)

FIND THE EXAMPLE

Choose the answer that best describes the action or situation.

_____ 1. Something that is *iridescent*
a. a window pane   **b.** a thick fabric   **c.** a butterfly wing   **d.** a brick wall

_____ 2. A *blunt* comment
a. "You look awful."   **b.** "What a nice hat."   **c.** "How are you?"   **d.** "You're nice."

_____ 3. Something that has a *sheen*
a. a satin gown   **b.** a sidewalk   **c.** a wool coat   **d.** flannel pajamas

_____ 4. Another word to describe a *densely* packed elevator
a. light   **b.** crowded   **c.** empty   **d.** visible

_____ 5. Something that might give you just a *tinge* of happiness
a. a black eye   **b.** a million dollars   **c.** a compliment   **d.** a broken pen

_____ 6. How a *radiant* person might act
a. crying   **b.** sighing   **c.** thinking   **d.** smiling

_____ 7. An example of *coarse* behavior
a. humming a tune   **b.** baking a pie   **c.** washing clothes   **d.** pushing in line

_____ 8. Something that is *transparent*
a. a stone   **b.** a window   **c.** a butterfly   **d.** a mirror

_____ 9. Something you would probably do to your dress shoes if they were *dingy*
a. polish them   **b.** repair them   **c.** run in them   **d.** break them in

_____ 10. Something that is *opaque*
a. fishbowl   **b.** air   **c.** velvet cape   **d.** pair of eyeglasses

Stops and Delays

WORD LIST

adjourn	cease	decisive	detain	hinder
prolong	repel	shackle	tarry	undermine

Have you ever waited for rain to stop? Did you ever want a long trip to be over? Have you ever heard people telling children to wait and look before they cross a street? Were you ever behind schedule in your homework? Stops and delays are part of everyday life. By learning the words in this lesson, you can refine your expression and understanding of these common times.

adjourned

1. adjourn (ə-jûrn´) *verb*
  a. To stop or end a meeting
    • The meeting wasn't **adjourned** until noon, an hour later than scheduled.
  b. To go to another place
    • After lunch in the dining room, the guests **adjourned** to the living room to continue socializing.

  adjournment *noun* After the meeting's **adjournment,** we went home.

2. cease (sēs) *verb*
  To end; to stop
    • The parrot **ceased** talking after we covered its cage.

3. decisive (dĭ-sī´sĭv) *adjective*
  a. Settled in a final way; firm
    • The Battle of Waterloo in 1815 was a **decisive** victory for the English over the French.
  b. Able to make up one's mind
    • **Decisive** people usually make decisions quickly.

  decisiveness *noun* **Decisiveness** is an important trait for an executive to have.

> A meeting may be *adjourned* for a recess and then start again. Or the meeting may be *adjourned* until the next session.

> *Decisive* comes from the word *decide.*

4. **detain** (dĭ-tān´) *verb*
   a. To delay
   - Flight 131 has been **detained** by bad weather in Chicago.
   b. To hold or arrest
   - The immigrant was **detained** at the border while officials checked his passport.

   detention *noun* The suspect was arrested and held in **detention**.

5. **hinder** (hĭn´dər) *verb*
   To make more difficult; to interfere with
   - Not studying will **hinder** your chances of getting a scholarship.

   hindrance *noun* His heavy backpack was a **hindrance** to his progress up the hill.

6. **prolong** (prə-lông´) *verb*
   To lengthen in time
   - The new school schedule **prolonged** each semester by two weeks.

7. **repel** (rĭ-pĕl´) *verb*
   a. To drive away
   - The army **repelled** the enemy's charge.
   b. To cause a feeling of disgust
   - Though many people around the world enjoy them, the thought of eating frog's legs **repelled** her.

   repellent *adjective* The odor of sewage is **repellent**.

   repellent *noun* Our insect **repellent** protected us from mosquito bites.

8. **shackle** (shăk´əl)
   a. *noun* A metal chain put around the ankle or wrist and attached to another chain
   - Prisoners were sometimes put in **shackles.**
   b. *noun* Something that limits or causes difficulties
   - Without education, it is difficult to escape from the **shackles** of superstition.
   c. *verb* To put a chain around an ankle or a wrist
   - Prisoners on chain gangs were once **shackled** to each other.

9. **tarry** (tăr´ē) *verb*
   To stay for a while; to delay in coming or going
   - She **tarried** in the garden before leaving her house for the last time.

10. **undermine** (ŭn´dər-mīn´) *verb*
    To weaken or affect negatively
    - Vicious gossip can **undermine** a person's good reputation.

WORD ENRICHMENT

Words from Old English

Modern English is partly based on Old English, spoken in England before the year 1100. Old English would probably not make sense to you if you heard it today. You wouldn't be able to read Old English either, even though many of our simplest and most useful words come from it, including *fly, food, line, light, mine,* and *under.*

NAME ______________________ DATE ______________

WRITE THE CORRECT WORD

Write the correct word in the space next to each definition.

________ **1.** to weaken or affect negatively

________ **2.** to drive away

________ **3.** to stop or end

________ **4.** to interfere with

________ **5.** settled in a final way

________ **6.** to lengthen in time

________ **7.** to hold or arrest

________ **8.** to stay for a while

________ **9.** a metal chain

________ **10.** to move to another place

COMPLETE THE SENTENCE

Write the letter for the word that best completes each sentence.

____ **1.** It would be unkind to ______ a dog to a tree.
a. undermine **b.** shackle **c.** repel **d.** hinder

____ **2.** Even after she ______ studying, Caitlin couldn't help thinking about the test.
a. repelled **b.** hindered **c.** ceased **d.** tarried

____ **3.** The band ______ the concert by performing three additional songs.
a. prolonged **b.** detained **c.** ceased **d.** tarried

____ **4.** Eating an unbalanced diet with lots of junk food ______ a person's health.
a. ceases **b.** prolongs **c.** repels **d.** undermines

____ **5.** Before we ______ the meeting, I have another issue to address.
a. adjourn **b.** prolong **c.** shackle **d.** undermine

____ **6.** The karate class was canceled because the teacher was ______ by a traffic jam.
a. ceased **b.** adjourned **c.** detained **d.** prolonged

____ **7.** Jason's quest to reach the peak of the mountain was ______ by bad weather.
a. shackled **b.** tarried **c.** hindered **d.** adjourned

____ **8.** If you use this spray on your boots, they will ______ water more effectively.
a. repel **b.** undermine **c.** adjourn **d.** shackle

____ **9.** Please don't ______ in front of the mirror when we are running late!
a. hinder **b.** tarry **c.** cease **d.** adjourn

____ **10.** After the ______ third round, we knew who would win.
a. ceased **b.** adjourned **c.** undermined **d.** decisive

Challenge: After the chairwoman broke the tie with a(n) ______ vote, the meeting was ______.
____ **a.** hindered...prolonged **b.** decisive...adjourned **c.** undermined...ceased

Nelson Mandela: Architect of Freedom

A rebel, a prisoner, a leader of a nation—all of these describe Nelson Mandela. **(1)** Without *ceasing*, Mandela fought for justice and human rights in South Africa.

When Mandela was young, the South African laws of apartheid guaranteed discrimination against blacks. They were not allowed to vote or to own land in white areas. **(2)** Their freedom of movement was *undermined* because they had to carry "passes" wherever they went. **(3)** Lack of educational opportunities *hindered* their futures.

When Mandela protested apartheid laws, he was suspended from college. Unwilling to be denied an education, he finished school by mail and became a lawyer. He opened an office and dedicated himself to fighting for blacks.

(4) Convinced that South Africa should be freed from the *shackles* of apartheid, Mandela became active in the African National Congress. He helped blacks to resist through peaceful means. In response, white government officials tried to make Mandela stop practicing law. Later, they refused to let him make speeches. Finally, after Mandela decided to lead a general strike, he felt he had to "go underground." Disguised as a servant, he hid with white friends.

After several months, he snuck out of the country so that he could speak from abroad. **(5)** Though it might have kept him safe and out of jail, he refused to *tarry* outside South Africa. **(6)** When he returned, he was *detained*, put on trial, and sentenced to five years in prison. **(7)** While in prison, his sentence was *prolonged* to life. Mandela spent the next fourteen years on an island, living in a small cell with no running water. He worked as a common laborer, building roads under the harsh sun. Even as a prisoner, though, Mandela was a protest leader. **(8)** *Repelled* by the lack of respect the guards showed him, Mandela refused to obey many orders. He inspired other prisoners by starting an educational program. The prison soon became known as "Island University."

After many years, Mandela was transferred to another jail. Although still not free, he began meetings with the white leader F. W. de Klerk. **(9)** By the time the last meeting *adjourned*, Mandela was scheduled to be released. **(10)** Even more important, *decisive* steps were being taken to end apartheid.

The years that followed Mandela's twenty-seven-year prison term brought him fame and honor. Mandela was elected the first black president of South Africa. He and de Klerk together received the 1993 Nobel Peace Prize. Throughout his life, Mandela has remained faithful to his vision, saying, "I have cherished the ideal of a democratic and free society in which all persons live together in harmony and with equal opportunities."

Each sentence below refers to a numbered sentence in the passage. Write the letter of the choice that gives the sentence a meaning that is closest to the original sentence.

_____ **1.** Without _____, Mandela fought for justice and human rights in South Africa.
    a. working   **b.** thinking   **c.** stopping   **d.** speaking

_____ **2.** Their freedom of movement was _____ because they had to carry "passes" wherever they went.
    a. allowed   **b.** lessened   **c.** lengthened   **d.** increased

_____ **3.** Lack of educational opportunities _____ their futures.
    a. limited   **b.** advanced   **c.** lost   **d.** fostered

_____ **4.** He thought South Africa should be freed from the _____ of apartheid.
    a. liberty   **b.** adjournments   **c.** justice   **d.** hardships

_____ **5.** He refused to _____ outside South Africa.
   a. fight his people   **b.** wait or delay   **c.** serve or bow   **d.** eat healthily

_____ **6.** When he returned, he was _____, put on trial, and sentenced to five years in prison.
   a. famous   **b.** delayed   **c.** arrested   **d.** sued

_____ **7.** While in prison, his sentence was _____ to life.
   a. extended   **b.** punished   **c.** ended   **d.** shortened

_____ **8.** _____ by the lack of respect the guards showed him, Mandela refused to obey many orders.
   a. Surprised   **b.** Disgusted   **c.** Jailed   **d.** Saddened

_____ **9.** By the time the last meeting _____, Mandela was scheduled to be released.
   a. happened   **b.** finished   **c.** discussed   **d.** began

_____ **10.** _____ steps were being taken to end apartheid.
   a. Several   **b.** Political   **c.** Firm   **d.** Weak

Indicate whether the statements below are TRUE or FALSE according to the passage.

_____ **1.** Nelson Mandela spent years in a jail cell with no running water.

_____ **2.** Nelson Mandela's hardships caused him to give up hope.

_____ **3.** Nelson Mandela fought for the right of all people to have equal opportunities.

FINISH THE THOUGHT

Complete each sentence so that it shows the meaning of the italicized word.

1. If we *tarry* much longer _____

_____

2. One thing I am *repelled* by is _____

_____

WRITE THE DERIVATIVE

Complete the sentence by writing the correct form of the word shown in parentheses. You may not need to change the form that is given.

_____ **1.** Many people are _____ by skunks. *(repel)*

_____ **2.** Jamie _____ in the hall, waiting for no good reason. *(tarry)*

_____ **3.** Strong gusts _____ the blimp's ability to fly in a straight line. *(hinder)*

_____ **4.** The student who chewed gum in class received afterschool _____. *(detain)*

_____ **5.** After the meeting's _____, we all had lunch together. *(adjourn)*

_____ **6.** That loud music is a _____ to my studying. _(hinder)_

_____ **7.** _____ is important in coaching. _(decisive)_

_____ **8.** The hostages were _____ to each other. _(shackle)_

_____ **9.** The dog _____ its barking when its owner came home. _(cease)_

_____ **10.** Avoid _____ exposure to the sun. _(prolong)_

FIND THE EXAMPLE

Choose the answer that best describes the action or situation.

_____ **1.** An example of something that _undermines_ driving safety
    a. traffic lights   **b.** bad roads   **c.** speed limits   **d.** construction signs

_____ **2.** A place where you would be most likely to _tarry_
    a. on a highway   **b.** in a swamp   **c.** in a park   **d.** by a garbage dump

_____ **3.** Something many people find _repellent_
    a. a puppy   **b.** a rainbow   **c.** a pizza   **d.** a spider

_____ **4.** The most _decisive_ margin of victory in a local election
    a. 3,000 votes   **b.** 3 votes   **c.** 30 votes   **d.** 300 votes

_____ **5.** Something you might want to _prolong_
    a. a boring speech   **b.** a fun party   **c.** grueling work   **d.** a horrible day

_____ **6.** Something that would _hinder_ an athlete's performance
    a. strength training   **b.** good nutrition   **c.** regular practice   **d.** muscle cramps

_____ **7.** A person likely to be _detained_
    a. game show host   **b.** housekeeper   **c.** crime suspect   **d.** quiet citizen

_____ **8.** In class, something a teacher would want to _cease_
    a. reading   **b.** participation   **c.** passing notes   **d.** taking notes

_____ **9.** Something most likely to be considered a _shackle_
    a. democracy   **b.** gourmet food   **c.** libraries   **d.** poverty

_____ **10.** Something you might do before _adjourning_ a meeting
    a. welcome everyone   **b.** give a summary   **c.** throw candy   **d.** introduce yourself

Usual and Unusual

WORD LIST

absurd	authentic	bizarre	conventional	exception
exotic	habitual	norm	novel	superlative

As fashions change, so does what we consider usual and unusual. Have you seen anyone wearing a powdered wig lately? A situation also helps us determine what is "normal" and what is out of the ordinary. Wearing a white gown or tuxedo would be normal at a wedding, but would it be usual to see people wearing wedding gowns and tuxedos while jogging in the park? The words in this lesson will help you make your writing more vivid by improving your descriptions of the usual and the unusual.

1. absurd (əb-sûrd´) *adjective*
Ridiculous; not sensible
• We laughed at the **absurd** thought that an ant could hold an elephant up in the air.

absurdity *noun* It is an **absurdity** to think that standing on one foot cures hiccups.

2. authentic (ô-thĕn´tĭk) *adjective*
Not faked or copied; real
• The museum housed **authentic** Stone Age carvings.

authenticate *verb* An expert **authenticated** that the table was an antique from the sixteenth century.

authenticity *noun* The principal called the student's mother to check the **authenticity** of her signature.

"NOW THAT'S BIZARRE"

3. bizarre (bǐ-zär´) *adjective*
Extremely strange or odd
• The man looked **bizarre** dressed in a winter coat on the warm summer day.

Don't confuse *bizarre* with *bazaar*, an open market.

4. conventional (kən-vĕn´shə-nəl) *adjective*
Usual; generally accepted
• White is the **conventional** color for a bride's dress.

convention *noun* It is a **convention** for people to shake hands when they are introduced.

5. exception (ĭk-sĕp´shən) *noun*
A case or an example that does not follow a rule or convention
• Although animals are not allowed in the store, the owners make an **exception** for guide dogs.

exceptional *adjective* Maria has **exceptional** talent in basketball.

6. exotic (ĭg-zŏt´ĭk) *adjective*
Unusual and interesting because of being from another part of the world
• Mrs. John Rolfe, known as the Native American princess Pocahontas, was considered **exotic** by the English people of 1616.

7. habitual (hə-bĭch´o͞o-əl) *adjective*
a. Done on a regular basis
• We found Christopher's **habitual** lateness to be annoying.
b. Established by long use or custom
• She sat in her **habitual** chair.

> *Habitual* comes from the common word *habit*.

8. norm (nôrm) *noun*
A standard, model, or pattern that is typical
• Knowledge of the alphabet is the **norm** for children entering first grade.

normal *adjective* It is **normal** for young people to grow at different rates.

abnormal *adjective* Not normal
• An **abnormal** body temperature is 104 degrees Fahrenheit.

9. novel (nŏv´əl) *adjective*
Unusual because of newness
• Women doctors were a **novel** idea in the early 1900s, but today they are common.

novelty *noun* The first automobiles were considered a useless **novelty**.

> A long work of fiction was first called a *novel* because it was a new type of literature.

10. superlative (so͞o-pûr´lə-tĭv)
a. *adjective* The best or most outstanding; superior
• I suggest that you publish your **superlative** essay.
b. *noun* The form of an adjective or adverb that indicates the most or strongest
• The **superlative** form of the word *good* is *best*.
c. *noun* Adjectives meaning "the best"
• The judge used **superlatives** to describe the outstanding science experiment.

WORD ENRICHMENT

Out of tune

Absurd comes from the Latin word *absurdus*, meaning "out of tune." In a way, something that is *absurd* is "out of tune" with reality.

WRITE THE CORRECT WORD

Write the correct word in the space next to each definition.

_____ 1. something outside a rule or convention

_____ 2. the best; outstanding

_____ 3. the typical standard

_____ 4. generally accepted

_____ 5. foreign; unusual

_____ 6. real; not fake

_____ 7. very strange

_____ 8. ridiculous

_____ 9. new

_____ 10. established by long use

COMPLETE THE SENTENCE

Write the letter for the word that best completes each sentence.

_____ 1. When they were first introduced at the 1893 World's Fair, ice-cream cones were a(n) _____ idea.
a. conventional   b. authentic   c. novel   d. habitual

_____ 2. The storm prevented him from taking his _____ afternoon walk around the neighborhood, so he didn't see the friend he usually met.
a. habitual   b. exotic   c. novel   d. authentic

_____ 3. We were fascinated by her _____ clothing from Morocco.
a. conventional   b. normal   c. habitual   d. exotic

_____ 4. We laughed when we saw the _____ Halloween costume the teacher wore.
a. authentic   b. absurd   c. habitual   d. normal

_____ 5. A(n) _____ Van Gogh painting can be worth millions of dollars.
a. authentic   b. absurd   c. bizarre   d. habitual

_____ 6. Her _____ piano performance won her first place in the contest.
a. conventional   b. habitual   c. superlative   d. bizarre

_____ 7. "Hello" is considered a _____ telephone greeting.
a. novel   b. conventional   c. superlative   d. bizarre

_____ 8. Because the girl was sick, the teacher made a(n) _____ to the homework rule.
a. norm   b. authenticity   c. absurdity   d. exception

_____ 9. It seemed _____ that heavy rain could be falling while the sun was shining brightly.
a. bizarre   b. authentic   c. superlative   d. habitual

_____ 10. A score of 85 on this exam is the _____ for eleven-year-olds.
a. authenticity   b. habitual   c. norm   d. exceptional

Challenge: To some people the _____ food was _____, but others were more familiar with it.
a. exotic…bizarre   b. absurd…habitual   c. superlative…exceptional

Silly Laws

The legislators of our countries, states, and cities have passed many excellent laws that protect us and help us live in an orderly way. **(1)** But occasionally, laws seem to depart from this *norm* because they are outdated or just plain silly. **(2)** These laws, the *exceptions* to the rule, are found throughout the United States. Some are no longer in effect or are not being followed. Still, it is amusing to read about them.

In Massachusetts, for example, it is illegal to cross Boston Common (a large city park) without carrying protection against bears. **(3)** Perhaps, long ago, bears *habitually* roamed the area. But Boston Common has been in the heart of a busy city for at least a hundred years. **(4)** The city of New Orleans has regulations about *exotic* animals. There, it is illegal to tie an alligator to a fire hydrant.

Other laws deal with gifts. In Idaho, if you want to buy candy for your sweetheart, the box must weigh at least fifty pounds. **(5)** Now that seems like a *novel* idea! **(6)** A New York law protects against behavior that seems *bizarre*. It forbids people to walk with ice-cream cones in their pockets, but only on Sunday. **(7)** It seems doubtful that this would be *conventional* behavior on any day of the week!

(8) In other cases, laws seem *absurd* because they try to regulate nature. An Illinois town forbids bees to be within the city limits. Arkansas law does not permit the Arkansas River to rise to the Main Street Bridge in Little Rock.

Certain laws were written to protect birds and animals. In Honolulu, Hawaii, it is illegal to annoy a bird. In Massachusetts, you may not frighten a pigeon. On the other hand, some laws involving animals seem to be aimed at protecting people. In Ohio, owners of tigers have only an hour to notify officials if one escapes. Perhaps these tiger owners should move to Nevada, where it is illegal to leave a gate open.

(9) These relatively useless but entertaining laws are all *authentic*. Their existence has been confirmed by searches of legal records. **(10)** As we laugh at them for their silliness, let's also appreciate the *superlative* wisdom of our legal system, which aims to protect us all.

Each sentence below refers to a numbered sentence in the passage. Write the letter of the choice that gives the sentence a meaning that is closest to the original sentence.

_____ **1.** Occasionally, laws seem to depart from the _____ because they are outdated or just plain silly.
    a. legal system   **b.** usual   **c.** exception   **d.** humorous

_____ **2.** These laws, _____ the rule, are found throughout the United States.
    a. different from   **b.** parallels to   **c.** definitions of   **d.** not faked for

_____ **3.** Perhaps, long ago, bears _____ roamed this area.
    a. joyfully   **b.** unusually   **c.** regularly   **d.** strangely

_____ **4.** The city of New Orleans regulates _____ animals.
    a. exciting   **b.** desert   **c.** fierce   **d.** unusual

_____ **5.** Now that seems like a _____ idea!
    a. funny and happy   **b.** good and silly   **c.** bad and foolish   **d.** new and strange

6. A New York law protects against behavior that seems _____.
 a. overly cruel **b.** good-humored **c.** very strange **d.** antisocial

7. It seems doubtful that this would be _____ behavior on any day of the week!
 a. messy **b.** great **c.** normal **d.** unusual

8. At other times, laws seem _____ because they try to regulate nature.
 a. ridiculous **b.** funny **c.** serious **d.** ordinary

9. These useless but entertaining laws are all _____.
 a. effective **b.** genuine **c.** normal **d.** fake

10. As we laugh at them for their silliness, let's also gratefully appreciate the _____ wisdom of our legal system, which protects our society.
 a. funny **b.** outstanding **c.** odd **d.** ridiculous

Indicate whether the statements below are TRUE or FALSE according to the passage.

1. In general, most laws are useful.

2. Ohio tiger owners have a day to notify authorities if a tiger escapes.

3. Laws that seem silly now might have made sense when they were first written.

WRITING EXTENDED RESPONSES

You have just read about some funny but rather strange laws. Think of a new law or rule that would change your school environment in a positive way. Would it involve clothes? Assignments? Activities? In a persuasive essay, present your rule and argue for it to be passed. You are free to imagine a rule that would make your school experience more fun. In your essay, state the new rule and give at least two reasons that support it. Your persuasive piece should be at least three paragraphs long. Use at least three lesson words in your response and underline them.

WRITE THE DERIVATIVE

Complete the sentence by writing the correct form of the word shown in parentheses. You may not need to change the form that is given.

1. The first airplanes were such a _____ that people would stop and stare at them. (novel)

2. Jerome is _____ early to school. (habitual)

3. With a few _____, mammals live mainly on land. (exception)

4. Many outfits worn at costume parties would look like _____ if worn every day. (absurd)

5. The collector had certificates of _____ for his valuable stamps. (authentic)

_____ 6. The _____ flowers attracted lots of attention. *(exotic)*

_____ 7. *Greatest*, *wisest*, and *prettiest* are examples of _____. *(superlative)*

_____ 8. His scar was _____; it was shaped like a star! *(bizarre)*

_____ 9. A forty-hour workweek is the _____ in this company. *(norm)*

_____ 10. People who work in this industry _____ wear business suits. *(conventional)*

FIND THE EXAMPLE

Choose the answer that best describes the action or situation.

_____ 1. An *absurd* thing for your teacher to say if you failed a quiz
    a. "Did you study?"   **b.** "Try harder."   **c.** "I'm proud of you."   **d.** "I'm disappointed."

_____ 2. A *superlative*
    a. ugliest   **b.** wiser   **c.** better   **d.** beautiful

_____ 3. A *bizarre* food combination
    a. butter and toast   **b.** cereal and milk   **c.** pickles and honey   **d.** crackers and cheese

_____ 4. A *novel* type of vacuum cleaner
    a. efficient   **b.** small   **c.** powerful   **d.** talking

_____ 5. A *conventional* thing to say when you first meet someone
    a. "I like eggs."   **b.** "My name is . . ."   **c.** "You stink!"   **d.** "Do you like my hat?"

_____ 6. A person who *habitually* wears face paint and floppy shoes
    a. an athlete   **b.** a student   **c.** a clown   **d.** a businessperson

_____ 7. An *exotic* pet
    a. boa constrictor   **b.** dog   **c.** cat   **d.** goldfish

_____ 8. A creature that is an *exception*
    a. a swimming fish   **b.** a talking human   **c.** a flightless bird   **d.** a barking dog

_____ 9. Where *authentic* famous paintings are most likely to be found
    a. supermarket   **b.** flea market   **c.** aquarium   **d.** museum

_____ 10. An article of clothing that is the *norm* at the beach
    a. snow pants   **b.** necktie   **c.** gown   **d.** bathing suit

Taking Tests

Synonym Tests

Vocabulary tests often include a section on identifying *synonyms*—words that have the same or nearly the same meaning. Because these tests generally present words in a sentence or paragraph, you can use *context clues* to help figure out meanings. Here are seven helpful strategies for taking synonym tests.

Strategies

1. *Read the sentence and all of the choices before selecting an answer.* If you do not read all of the choices, you will not be able to choose the best answer effectively.

2. *Imagine a possible answer.* You need to have a possible answer in mind to check against the choices the test presents.

3. *Narrow your choice by eliminating answers that are clearly incorrect.* Here is an example.

   Despite the bravery of the firefighters, all efforts to save the forest proved *futile.*
   a. successful   **b.** strange   **c.** useless   **d.** assistance

   Assistance can be eliminated because it is the wrong part of speech. An adjective, rather than a noun such as *assistance,* is needed in the sentence.

4. *Do not let an antonym in the answer choices confuse you.* In the sentence about the firefighters, the word *despite* gives us a clue that the forest was not saved. For this reason, *successful* can also be eliminated. A synonym is needed, not an antonym like *successful.* The answer is *c,* useless.

5. *Watch for choices that have been added to confuse you.* Sometimes words that sound like the correct choice are added.

   The musicians gave a benefit performance to show their *compassion* for the earthquake victims.
   a. fear   **b.** sympathy   **c.** confidence   **d.** belief

   Even though *confidence* sounds a bit like *compassion,* it is not correct. Chances are that it was added to confuse you. The answer is *b,* sympathy.

6. *Use context clues to study the sentence and figure out the correct meaning.*

   He watched the pelican *plummet* from the sky to catch the fish.
   a. swim   **b.** dive   **c.** go   **d.** climb

   The sentence states that the pelican plummets *from* the sky *to* the water. *Swim* and *climb* would not go from the sky to the water, so they cannot be correct.

7. *When two answers fit, remember to choose the best one.* In the sentence about the pelican, the choices *go* and *dive* would both fit. However, *dive* is more specific and descriptive than *go.* Therefore, *dive* is the answer.

Practice

Use the strategies given in this skill feature to identify synonyms in context. In each sentence, choose the synonym of the italicized word. Write the letter of your choice on the answer line.

_____ 1. Although they studied the evidence carefully, the jury members came to an *erroneous* conclusion.
   a. surprising   **b.** unclear   **c.** incorrect   **d.** correct

_____ 2. The private investigator's document was placed in the *confidential* files.
   a. secret   **b.** appropriate   **c.** short-term   **d.** correct

_____ 3. Because of poor grades, Calvin's name was *deleted* from the list of students eligible for the team.
   a. kept   **b.** chosen   **c.** erased   **d.** lost

_____ 4. Because time for the meeting was limited, Ms. Murphy gave a *succinct* account of the conference she had attended.
   a. interesting   **b.** long   **c.** brief   **d.** illustrated

_____ 5. Genevieve tried to sneak a *furtive* glance at the hiding place.
   a. secret   **b.** angry   **c.** gloom   **d.** merry

_____ 6. On their last night together, the campers sang with *gusto*.
   a. tune   **b.** taste   **c.** enthusiasm   **d.** eager

_____ 7. The unkind remark *disconcerted* Meredith.
   a. bothered   **b.** amused   **c.** helped   **d.** self-conscious

_____ 8. Tamara was *commended* for her prize-winning science project.
   a. outstanding   **b.** worried   **c.** criticized   **d.** praised

_____ 9. Since the club members come from all over the world, their backgrounds are *diverse*.
   a. strong   **b.** different   **c.** similar   **d.** intelligent

_____ 10. Nearly everyone agrees that health care is an issue of *primary* importance.
   a. greater   **b.** less   **c.** little   **d.** most

_____ 11. We were fortunate enough to get *gratis* tickets to the rock concert.
   a. nearby   **b.** free   **c.** easily   **d.** expensive

_____ 12. The judge's *judicious* decision was fair to all.
   a. nasty   **b.** humorous   **c.** happy   **d.** wise

_____ 13. The man's *haggard* appearance shocked his friends.
   a. exhausted   **b.** nice   **c.** happy   **d.** neat

_____ 14. The committee did a *prodigious* amount of work on the project.
   a. huge   **b.** immerse   **c.** noticeably   **d.** poor

_____ 15. We watched the mountain goats *ascend* the steep slope.
   a. walk   **b.** sturdy   **c.** climb   **d.** hurdle

Family

ancestor	clan	compatible	domestic	filial
hereditary	kin	lineage	matrimony	spouse

Family members are usually related to one another through ties of blood or marriage. Sometimes we speak of a "nuclear" family—parents and children. In contrast, an "extended" family is a larger unit that includes grandparents, aunts, uncles, and cousins. Even larger family groups are clans or tribes. Family relationships span many generations, from the elderly to the newly born. In this lesson, you will explore some of the types of family ties that link human beings together.

1. **ancestor** (ăn´sĕs´tər) *noun*
   a. A person whom someone is descended from
   • In 1860, Ching's **ancestors** came from China to the United States.
   b. An idea or a thing that something is descended from
   • The harpsichord is the **ancestor** of the piano.

   ancestral *adjective* The ancient vase was found near his **ancestral** home in Italy.

   ancestry *noun* Adopted at birth, he longed to know more about his **ancestry**.

2. **clan** (klăn) *noun*
   A group that has a common ancestor or background
   • The McIntyre **clan** has its origins in the Scottish Highlands.

   clannish *adjective* Tending to stick together; not welcoming outsiders
   • The **clannish** townspeople did not welcome the newcomers.

3. **compatible** (kəm-păt´ə-bəl) *adjective*
   Getting along or working well together
   • I was happy that the new software was **compatible** with my computer.

   compatibility *noun* Because of their **compatibility**, the two cousins often played together.

4. **domestic** (də-mĕs´tĭk) *adjective*
   a. Relating to the family or household
   • Taking out the garbage was one of Erik's **domestic** chores.
   b. Not wild; tame
   • My dog Ruby is a **domestic** animal.
   c. Not foreign; produced in one's own country
   • Our **domestic** oil supply is decreasing rapidly.

   domesticate *verb* It is difficult to **domesticate** jungle animals.

> Although *clan* may refer to relatives, it can also simply refer to people who have a close association.

a Scottish clan

5. filial (fĭl´ē-əl) *adjective*
Relating to a son or daughter
• She showed her **filial** devotion by taking care of her elderly father.

6. hereditary (hə-rĕd´ĭ-tĕr´ē) *adjective*
  a. Passed from parent to child by means of genes
    • Eye color is a **hereditary** trait.
  b. Passed down from parent to child
    • In English society, *Lord* and *Lady* are **hereditary** titles.

  heredity *noun* **Heredity** is important in determining one's height.

7. kin (kĭn) *noun*
A person's relatives; family
• The **kin** of many immigrants were left in their native land.

  kinship *noun* Maya and Anna felt a **kinship** because they were the only foreign-born students in the class.

  kindred *adjective* My lab partner and I were **kindred** spirits.

8. lineage (lĭn´ē-ĭj) *noun*
Direct descent from a particular ancestor
• She was able to date her **lineage** to the 1620 voyage of the Mayflower.

9. matrimony (măt´rə-mō´nē) *noun*
Marriage
• A **matrimony** unites two people as a family unit.

  matrimonial *adjective* It is a **matrimonial** custom for the bride to walk down the aisle.

10. spouse (spous) *noun*
A wife or husband
• Marla and her **spouse** went on a honeymoon.

> *Kindred* and *kinship* can indicate feelings of closeness rather than family ties.

> A person's *lineage* is his or her *line* of ancestors.

WORD ENRICHMENT

Spouses

The word *spouse* comes from the Latin word *spondere*, meaning "to pledge." In the days of the ancient Romans, married couples pledged vows to each other, a custom that continues today. In contrast, *husband* comes from the Old Norse word *husbondi*. *Hus* meant house. A *bondi* was an owner of land and livestock. *To husband* still means to manage well and conserve, as one might *husband* the resources of a good farm. The word *wife* comes from the Old English word for *woman*, spelled *wif*. When Norse invaders settled in Anglo Saxon England (roughly between the years 400 and 1000), they often married English women. This may be why *husband* comes from Old Norse, but *wife* comes from Old English.

WRITE THE CORRECT WORD

Write the correct word in the space next to each definition.

_____   **1.** working well together

_____   **2.** not wild; tame

_____   **3.** a person's relatives

_____   **4.** direct descent from a particular ancestor

_____   **5.** a person from whom one is descended

_____   **6.** passed down through genes

_____   **7.** a group that shares a common background

_____   **8.** wife or husband

_____   **9.** marriage

_____   **10.** relating to a son or daughter

COMPLETE THE SENTENCE

Write the letter for the word that best completes each sentence.

_____ **1.** A lot of high-quality furniture is manufactured _____.
   a. compatibly   **b.** hereditarily   **c.** ancestrally   **d.** domestically

_____ **2.** _____ arranged by young peoples' parents is still common in some countries.
   a. Ancestry   **b.** Matrimony   **c.** Lineage   **d.** Heredity

_____ **3.** Miklos drew a family tree to trace his _____.
   a. compatibility   **b.** matrimony   **c.** ancestry   **d.** domesticity

_____ **4.** The poor farm girl was surprised to learn of her royal _____.
   a. domesticity   **b.** lineage   **c.** compatibility   **d.** spouse

_____ **5.** Only close _____ were invited to the wedding.
   a. kin   **b.** matrimonies   **c.** spouses   **d.** lineage

_____ **6.** Many diseases, such as diabetes and heart disease, are _____.
   a. hereditary   **b.** clannish   **c.** spousal   **d.** filial

_____ **7.** Jan glowed with _____ pride when her father received the award.
   a. compatible   **b.** ancestral   **c.** matrimonial   **d.** filial

_____ **8.** The _____ worked together to build a large fortress around their settlement.
   a. ancestor   **b.** lineage   **c.** clan   **d.** spouses

_____ **9.** In more than half of American families, both _____ work.
   a. spouses   **b.** ancestors   **c.** clans   **d.** heredities

_____ **10.** That phone line is not _____ with the computer hookup.
   a. matrimonial   **b.** compatible   **c.** ancestral   **d.** filial

Challenge: The _____ between the children of the leaders of the warring _____ led to peace between the two groups.
_____   **a.** matrimony...clans   **b.** kinship...ancestry   **c.** lineage...kin

Traditions of the Hopi

(1) The Hopi Indians are a group of Native Americans, whose customs and *ancestry* date back several thousand years. Today, many Hopi live in Arizona, in an area of small villages and high mesas. They call themselves *Hopitu*—the peaceable people. **(2)** Evidence suggests that their *lineage* can be traced to the Aztec Indians of Mexico. Hopi migration to present-day Arizona took place between five and ten thousand years ago.

(3) The Hopi are *kin* to a group of southwestern people called the Pueblo. Like the Pueblo, the Hopi are rather small and muscular in build. **(4)** Other common *hereditary* traits include reddish brown skin, high cheekbones, and straight black hair.

(5) In traditional Hopi life, there were special *matrimonial* customs. **(6)** A Hopi bride ground corn for three days at the home of her future *spouse* to show that she had the skills necessary to be a good wife. The groom and his male relatives wove the bride's wedding clothes. **(7)** In their *domestic* life, the women and men each had specific duties to perform. Women cooked and wove baskets. Men planted and harvested, wove cloth, and performed ceremonies. After marriage, a Hopi husband moved in with his wife's family. Women owned the land and the house.

(8) *Filial* ties were strong among traditional Hopi. Children were taught to respect their parents and elders at a very early age. **(9)** Adults performed rituals to welcome new babies into their *clan*. In Hopi culture, when children were born, they received a special blanket and a perfect ear of corn. On the twentieth day of their lives, babies were taken to the mesa cliff and held facing the rising sun. When the sun shone on the child, the baby was given a name.

The Hopi recognized several gods, which they called *kachinas*. Numerous religious ceremonies were performed at times that were determined by the position of the rising sun or by the moon. The religious and ceremonial life centered in the *kiva*, which was a room, wholly or partly below ground.

(10) Today, the Hopi have managed to follow some traditional practices while living in ways that are *compatible* with modern times. They love their traditions, arts, and land, but also appreciate many aspects of modern American culture. There are currently twelve Hopi villages in Arizona. Each one presents its own balance between traditional and modern-day culture.

Each sentence below refers to a numbered sentence in the passage. Write the letter of the choice that gives the sentence a meaning that is closest to the original sentence.

_____ **1.** The Hopi Indians are a group of Native Americans, whose customs and _____ date back several thousand years.
   a. art and pottery   **b.** line of descent   **c.** religious beliefs   **d.** arranged marriages

_____ **2.** Evidence suggests that their _____ can be traced to the Aztec Indians of Mexico.
   a. land   **b.** enemies   **c.** art   **d.** ancestry

_____ **3.** The Hopi are also _____ to a group of southwestern people called the Pueblo.
   a. related   **b.** married   **c.** settled   **d.** grateful

_____ **4.** Other common _____ traits include reddish brown skin, high cheekbones, and straight black hair.
   a. physical   **b.** medical   **c.** genetic   **d.** unusual

_____ **5.** In traditional Hopi life, there were special _____ customs.
   a. birth   **b.** funeral   **c.** wedding   **d.** ritual

_____ **6.** A Hopi bride ground corn for three days at the home of her future _____ to
show that she had the skills necessary to be a good wife.
    a. father   **b.** husband   **c.** daughter   **d.** life

_____ **7.** In their _____ life, the women and men each had specific duties to perform.
    a. tame   **b.** calm   **c.** uncivilized   **d.** household

_____ **8.** _____ ties were strong among traditional Hopi.
    a. Newborn babies'   **b.** Religious leaders'   **c.** Marriage   **d.** Children's

_____ **9.** Adults performed rituals to welcome new babies into their _____.
    a. group   **b.** religion   **c.** ancestors   **d.** childhood

_____ **10.** Today, the Hopi have managed to follow some traditional practices while living
in ways that are _____ with modern times.
    a. harmonious   **b.** in conflict   **c.** struggling   **d.** avoiding

Indicate whether the statements below are TRUE or FALSE according to the passage.

_____ **1.** In traditional Hopi society, men and women had different domestic roles.

_____ **2.** The Hopi Indians have ancestry that links them to other tribes.

_____ **3.** There are no longer any Hopi settlements in the United States.

FINISH THE THOUGHT

Complete each sentence so that it shows the meaning of the italicized word.

1. When friends are *compatible* _____

_____

2. My *lineage* includes people who _____

_____

WRITE THE DERIVATIVE

**Complete the sentence by writing the correct form of the word shown in
parentheses. You may not need to change the form that is given.**

_____ **1.** I'd like you to meet Pat, my _____. (*spouse*)

_____ **2.** Based on her _____, she was likely to have beautiful skin. (*hereditary*)

_____ **3.** Dogs were some of the first animals to be _____. (*domestic*)

_____ **4.** Jared always felt a _____ with other poets. (*kin*)

_____ **5.** Many species of animals are _____, not allowing other animals into their
group. (*clan*)

_____ **6.** Respecting your parents' rules is a part of your _____ responsibility. (*filial*)

_____ 7. In the Jewish _____ ceremony, seven blessings are given to the bride and groom. *(matrimony)*

_____ 8. Our team always wins; some say it's because of our _____. *(compatible)*

_____ 9. He traced his _____ back to Spain in the fifteenth century. *(lineage)*

_____ 10. There is a common _____ between birds and dinosaurs. *(ancestor)*

FIND THE EXAMPLE

Choose the answer that best describes the action or situation.

_____ 1. A *filial* thing to do
    a. play solitaire   **b.** hug your mom   **c.** visit a grandma   **d.** hang out with friends

_____ 2. A person most likely to perform a *matrimony*
    a. minister   **b.** firefighter   **c.** historian   **d.** construction worker

_____ 3. Close *kin*
    a. a third cousin   **b.** a sister   **c.** a best friend   **d.** a neighbor

_____ 4. A *domestic* task
    a. doing homework   **b.** setting up a tent   **c.** eating out   **d.** washing the dishes

_____ 5. The most likely *spouse* of Mrs. Frieda Jameson Curtis
    a. Mr. Morris Lei   **b.** Mr. James Freed   **c.** Mr. Fred Clark   **d.** Mr. Jon Curtis

_____ 6. Something that could help someone learn about his or her *ancestors*
    a. old diary   **b.** video game   **c.** telescope   **d.** scale

_____ 7. What the members of a *clan* would most probably do
    a. dress identically   **b.** share customs   **c.** stay angry   **d.** live far apart

_____ 8. Most likely to be *compatible* with a television
    a. walkie-talkie   **b.** microwave oven   **c.** DVD player   **d.** printer

_____ 9. Someone in your direct *lineage*
    a. favorite teacher   **b.** best friend   **c.** nephew   **d.** great-grandfather

_____ 10. A position based on *heredity*
    a. president   **b.** diplomat   **c.** king   **d.** manager

Music and Sound

WORD LIST

ballad	choral	lyrics	opera	resonant
rhythmically	serenade	shrill	symphony	vocal

What kind of music do you like? What rhythms make you want to get up and dance? What song *lyrics* make you stop and think about life? This lesson is based on words related to music and sound. Some words describe aspects of music or groups of music makers. Others deal with qualities of sound. You will find that some of the words have meanings that go beyond music.

1. **ballad** (băl´əd) *noun*
   A poem, often set to music, that tells a story; a romantic popular song
   • The knight sang a **ballad** to his fair lady.

2. **choral** (kôr´əl) *adjective*
   Relating to music that is sung by a group of singers or choir
   • The director gave copies of the **choral** music to each choir member.

3. **lyrics** (lĭr´ĭks) *noun*
   The words to a song
   • Francis Scott Key wrote the **lyrics** to "The Star-Spangled Banner."

   lyrical *adjective* Expressing deep personal feelings or thoughts
   • The poem was a **lyrical** description of her first love.

> Long ago, singers traveled throughout the countryside singing *ballads* of heroic deeds.

> In ancient Greece, the *lyre* was a harp-like instrument that accompanied a singer or storyteller.

opera

4. **opera** (ŏp´ər-ə) *noun*
   A theatrical performance in which the words of a play are sung with an orchestra as accompaniment
   • Verdi's **opera** *Aida* includes a cast of more than fifty singers.

   operatic *adjective* **Operatic** performances are often sung in Italian.

5. **resonant** (rĕz´ə-nənt) *adjective*
   Having a strong, deep sound
   • A **resonant** voice is a quality valued in radio announcers.

   resonate *verb* Her booming voice **resonated** throughout the house.

   resonance *noun* The cello's **resonance** makes it a powerful instrument.

6. rhythmically (rĭth´mĭ-kə-lē) *adverb*

  a. Having movement or sound that recurs in a regular sequence
    • The waves danced **rhythmically** to shore.
  b. Relating to the beat or time pattern of music
    • The **rhythmically** complex music alternated fast and slow notes.

7. serenade (sĕr´ə-nād´)

  a. *noun* A musical piece expressing love or the desire to honor
  someone
    • He sang a **serenade** to his beloved, who listened from the balcony.
  b. *verb* To sing in a romantic manner
    • The singer **serenaded** the audience with "The Very Thought
    of You."

> While a *ballad* often tells a story, a *serenade* simply expresses emotions.

8. shrill (shrĭl) *adjective*
High-pitched and piercing
  • The **shrill** wail of the siren warned swimmers to get out of the water.

shrillness *noun* The **shrillness** of the monkey's cries sent shivers
down my spine.

9. symphony (sĭm´fə-nē) *noun*
A long piece of music written for an orchestra
  • The Detroit Symphony Orchestra performed Beethoven's Fifth
  Symphony.

symphonic *adjective* The musician spent years completing
his **symphonic** masterpiece.

10. vocal (vō´kəl) *adjective*

  a. Relating to the voice
    • We use our **vocal** cords when we speak.
  b. Expressing one's opinions often and openly
    • Parents were **vocal** in their fight for more traffic lights near
    the school.

vocalize *verb* The workers **vocalized** their concerns to their boss.

vocalization *noun* Marine biologists study the **vocalizations**
of dolphins.

WORD ENRICHMENT

Having a ball with ballads

    Before television and movies, people often amused themselves by
listening to *ballads.* Experts think that these poems and stories set to music
first became popular in medieval France.
    People probably danced to early *ballads.* The Latin word *ballare* means
"to dance." That Latin word is also the root of *ballet,* and of *ball,* which can
mean "a formal dance party." *Bailar,* which means "to dance" in Spanish,
also comes from this root.

WRITE THE CORRECT WORD

Write the correct word in the space next to each definition.

_____ 1. having a deep sound

_____ 2. relating to the voice

_____ 3. high-pitched; piercing

_____ 4. relating to music sung by a choir

_____ 5. a love song

_____ 6. a type of musical theater

_____ 7. with a regular beat

_____ 8. a long piece for an orchestra

_____ 9. a song that tells a story

_____ 10. the words to a song

COMPLETE THE SENTENCE

Write the letter for the word that best completes each sentence.

_____ 1. He sang a _____ about a farm boy whose wisdom won him a kingdom.
a. ballad   b. chorus   c. symphony   d. resonance

_____ 2. Bertha didn't know that Elmer was in love with her until he _____ her.
a. vocalized   b. serenaded   c. resonated   d. lyrical

_____ 3. It's so frustrating that I keep forgetting the _____ to that song!
a. ballads   b. operas   c. lyrics   d. serenades

_____ 4. I could feel the sleeping puppy's heart beat _____ as I held him.
a. lyrically   b. rhythmically   c. chorally   d. vocally

_____ 5. The _____ sound of the fire engine's siren frightened the children.
a. lyrical   b. symphonic   c. operatic   d. shrill

_____ 6. The tuba's deep sound _____ in the empty concert hall.
a. resonated   b. shrilled   c. serenaded   d. vocalized

_____ 7. His costume for the _____ took several weeks to sew.
a. resonance   b. ballad   c. opera   d. vocal

_____ 8. Because of her incredible voice, Karen got a solo in the _____ performance.
a. shrill   b. choral   c. symphonic   d. resonant

_____ 9. Fifty violinists auditioned for a seat in the _____.
a. ballad   b. chorus   c. lyric   d. symphony

_____ 10. No one could ignore Vera; she was very _____ about how she felt.
a. vocal   b. choral   c. rhythmic   d. lyrical

Challenge: The _____ ability of the lead singer in the _____ was unmatched.

_____ a. vocal...opera   b. choral...symphony   c. operatic...resonance

Andrea Bocelli—Popera Star

Very few people have what it takes to become a music star. Even fewer achieve success as stars if they have a serious disability, such as blindness. But Italian tenor Andrea Bocelli has succeeded because of his tremendous talent, as well as his determination and belief in himself.

A soccer accident at age twelve left Bocelli blind, but this did not stop him from pursuing his passion for music. As a child, he studied piano, flute, and saxophone. **(1)** His *vocal* talents also won him many prizes.

In 1992, he won a contest to record a song written by Bono of the rock band U2. Bocelli performed the song with world-famous opera singer Luciano Pavarotti and continued singing in concert with other famous artists. **(2)** His *resonant* voice thrilled his audiences. The popularity of Bocelli's singing led him to produce several albums. *Sogno,* his fifth album, sold more than ten million copies and won a Golden Globe Award. Bocelli was also nominated for a Grammy as "best new artist."

(3) As a pop star, Bocelli has *serenaded* audiences with slow, romantic tunes. **(4)** He has performed many *ballads* that were made famous by Frank Sinatra. Tickets to his appearances are often high-priced, yet he continues to fill huge concert halls.

Bocelli has loved opera since he was a child. Listening to opera recordings calmed him when he was upset. Knowing this, relatives gave him gifts of opera records. He used these to study great operatic voices. **(5)** The poor quality of the old recordings sometimes made singers of the past sound *shrill.* But as Bocelli studied them more closely, he began to appreciate their artistry. He never lost his ambition to sing opera. Even as a successful pop star, he vowed to return to classical music. "Pop music is easier," he explains, "but classical music can change you." **(6)** Bocelli enjoys all forms of classical music, from *symphonies* to operas.

An opera is a drama set to music. **(7)** A full *opera* is much more difficult to perform than a popular music concert. **(8)** Bocelli needs to learn pages and pages of notes and *lyrics.* To act in a believable manner on stage, he has to memorize the layout of the set and every movement he will make. He acts in dramas with singers he cannot see. **(9)** Because he cannot observe the conductor, he must perfectly memorize the flow of the melodies so that his singing is *rhythmically* correct. **(10)** And, of course, while on stage, he needs to listen to the cues of solo and *choral* parts. Bocelli has risen to the challenge. As the lead in the opera *Werther,* he even rode a white horse onto the stage!

His mastery of so many types of music has earned Bocelli the label "popera" star. "Popera" is a combination of "pop" (short for "popular music") and "opera." Bocelli has overcome tremendous odds in his musical career. As he says, "My parents' influence has taught me never to accept life's difficulties in a passive way, but rather to draw strength from them."

Each sentence below refers to a numbered sentence in the passage. Write the letter of the choice that gives the sentence a meaning that is closest to the original sentence.

_____ **1.** His _____ talents won him many prizes for singing.
  a. soccer-related **b.** piano-related **c.** voice-related **d.** blindness-related

_____ **2.** His _____ voice thrilled his audiences.
  a. regular **b.** strong **c.** high **d.** musical

_____ **3.** As a pop star, Bocelli has _____ audiences with slow, romantic tunes.
  a. bored **b.** played softly to **c.** sung lovingly to **d.** danced with

_____ **4.** He has performed many _____ that were made famous by Frank Sinatra.
  a. rap hits **b.** opera arias **c.** poems and prose **d.** romantic songs

_____ **5.** The poor quality of the old recordings sometimes made singers of the
past sound _____.
    a. high pitched   **b.** extraordinary   **c.** operatic   **d.** vocal

_____ **6.** Bocelli enjoys all forms of classical music, from _____ to operas.
    a. orchestra pieces   **b.** string quartets   **c.** romantic songs   **d.** pop songs

_____ **7.** A full _____ is much more difficult to perform than a popular music concert.
    a. love song   **b.** musical play   **c.** Italian song   **d.** resonance

_____ **8.** Bocelli needs to learn pages and pages of notes and _____.
    a. piano pieces   **b.** foreign languages   **c.** words to songs   **d.** stage directions

_____ **9.** Because he cannot observe the conductor, he must perfectly memorize the flow
of the melodies so that his singing _____.
    a. is on key   **b.** is harmonious   **c.** is audible   **d.** goes with the timing

_____ **10.** While on stage, he needs to listen to the cues of solo and _____ parts.
    a. group singing   **b.** instrumental   **c.** percussion   **d.** dramatic

Indicate whether the statements below are TRUE or FALSE according to the passage.

_____ **1.** "Popera" is a word that combines "popular music" and "opera."

_____ **2.** Andrea Bocelli enjoyed opera as a child.

_____ **3.** Bocelli believes that opera is a more difficult to perform than popular music.

WRITING EXTENDED RESPONSES

When it comes to music, we all have our favorite styles and artists. Write
a letter to a parent or another adult, explaining why you like your favorite
musical artist or your favorite type of music. Give convincing reasons
why this music is worth listening to. Provide at least two general reasons
for your claim. In addition, for each reason, provide a specific example.
Your letter should be at least three paragraphs long. Remember to use
proper letter form. Use at least three lesson words in your letter and
underline them.

WRITE THE DERIVATIVE

Complete the sentence by writing the correct form of the word shown in
parentheses. You may not need to change the form that is given.

_____ **1.** The _____ sound of the rain lulled me to sleep. (*rhythmically*)

_____ **2.** You need to _____ your opinions if you want people to know how you feel.
(*vocal*)

_____ **3.** Her poem was so _____ that it made the whole class cry. (*lyrics*)

_____ **4.** Our _____ director insisted that we rest our voices when not singing. (*choral*)

_____ 5. With much practice and training, one can attain _____ success. (opera)

_____ 6. Horatio stood beneath his love's window and _____ her. (serenade)

_____ 7. The _____ of the birds' cries hurt my ears. (shrill)

_____ 8. The _____ piece was written for string, wind, and percussion instruments. (symphony)

_____ 9. In the Middle Ages, people told about historical events by singing _____. (ballad)

_____ 10. The _____ of his voice made him a good candidate to be a stage actor. (resonant)

FIND THE EXAMPLE

Choose the answer that best describes the action or situation.

_____ 1. An example of *lyrics* to a children's song
  a. ballad   **b.** popular music   **c.** "soprano and tenor"   **d.** "Mary had a little lamb"

_____ 2. Type of music that most often includes *symphonies*
  a. classical   **b.** blues   **c.** salsa   **d.** metal

_____ 3. Of the following, the most likely title for a *serenade*
  a. World Peace   **b.** My Country   **c.** I Love You   **d.** Big Bad Ben

_____ 4. Something that makes a *shrill* sound
  a. whistle   **b.** tuba   **c.** piano   **d.** cello

_____ 5. Something a *rhythmic* song has
  a. a changing beat   **b.** no beat   **c.** a regular beat   **d.** an irregular beat

_____ 6. Something an *opera* singer might NOT need
  a. musical talent   **b.** good memory   **c.** acting ability   **d.** writing ability

_____ 7. A *resonant* sound
  a. cricket chirp   **b.** thunder   **c.** squeaky hinge   **d.** cat's meow

_____ 8. Someone who would perform in a *choral* production
  a. violinist   **b.** singer   **c.** drummer   **d.** French-horn player

_____ 9. What a *vocal* person would be most likely to do
  a. nothing   **b.** whisper "O.K."   **c.** shout "No way!"   **d.** bow silently

_____ 10. Most likely to be the title of a *ballad*
  a. Happy Birthday   **b.** Midnight Blues   **c.** Spaghetti Again   **d.** The Story of Noble Joan

Literature

autobiography	biography	flashback	folklore	genre
metaphor	onomatopoeia	prose	proverb	simile

Do you remember your favorite childhood books? Did you identify with characters? Whether we are six or sixty, literature brings us adventure. By reading, we can travel around the world—or beyond. We can understand our own problems through the eyes of a character. These are just a few of the reasons why literature has fascinated people for thousands of years. The words in this lesson will help you understand and discuss literature in its many forms.

1. autobiography (ô´tō-bī-ŏg´rə-fē) *noun*
The story of a person's life, written by that person
• Former president Bill Clinton's **autobiography** is entitled *My Life.*

autobiographical *adjective* The world-famous scientist told **autobiographical** stories during his speech.

2. biography (bī-ŏg´rə-fē) *noun*
The story of a person's life, written by someone else
• James Boswell wrote a famous **biography** of dictionary maker Samuel Johnson.

biographical *adjective* The reporter met with the movie star's family to gather some **biographical** details about her.

biographer *noun* The **biographer** spent years researching his subject's life.

3. flashback (flăsh´băk´) *noun*
A scene that is set at a time earlier than the main events of the story
• The film opened with a car chase, followed by a **flashback** to the hero's childhood.

4. folklore (fōk´lôr´) *noun*
The traditional tales and beliefs of a people
• Paul Bunyan is a figure from American **folklore.**

folkloric *adjective* **Folkloric** stories are often told to young people in order to pass along cultural customs.

a flashback

5. **genre** (zhän´rə) *noun*
A type of literature or art
• **Genres** of literature include fiction, nonfiction, poetry, and drama.

> The *genre* of fiction includes fantasy, science fiction, historical fiction, and realistic fiction. Nonfiction includes biographies, articles, and essays.

6. **metaphor** (mĕt´ə-fôr´) *noun*
A figure of speech in which one thing is described as if it were another
• The **metaphor** "The moon was a ribbon of darkness" appears in *The Highway Man.*

metaphoric *adjective* The words "ship of state" are a **metaphoric** way to refer to government.

7. **onomatopoeia** (ŏn´ə-măt´ə-pē´ə) *noun*
The use of words that imitate the sounds that they stand for
• Some examples of **onomatopoeia** are *meow, whoosh,* and *pop.*

onomatopoeic *adjective* The **onomatopoeic** name *pop* for "soda" imitates the sound of a can being opened.

8. **prose** (prōz) *noun*
Ordinary speech or writing that does not have a regular rhythm
• Although most ancient stories were rhymed to aid memory, most modern stories are in **prose.**

prosaic *adjective* Commonplace, dull, unimaginative
• Julio decided his story was too **prosaic,** so he threw it away and started over.

9. **proverb** (prŏv´ûrb´) *noun*
A short saying that expresses a truth or gives advice
• Dad's response to our hurried job was the **proverb** "Haste makes waste."

> A *proverb* (also known as an *adage*) usually expresses folk wisdom, or wisdom from the people.

proverbial *adjective* Widely or often referred to; commonly known
• John really did have the **proverbial** "bird in the hand worth two in the bush" when he caught the valuable parrot.

10. **simile** (sĭm´ə-lē) *noun*
A figure of speech that uses *like* or *as* to compare two things that are not alike
• One **simile** written by Shakespeare is "My love is like a red, red rose."

WORD ENRICHMENT

A word of the people

The English word *folk,* which is part of the word *folklore,* means "people." *Folk* has been in our language for more than 1,000 years. At one time, it meant "the troops of an army." Today, a word containing *folk* usually refers to common, regular, or traditional people. A *folktale* is a traditional story passed down through the ages. A *folksinger* performs tunes also handed down through generations. *Folk art* is created according to the traditions of the common people. Something *folksy* is simple and informal.

WRITE THE CORRECT WORD

Write the correct word in the space next to each definition.

_____ 1. ordinary writing

_____ 2. type of literature or art

_____ 3. a comparison using the words *like* or *as*

_____ 4. a description of something as if it were another

_____ 5. a story of someone's life, by that person

_____ 6. traditional stories

_____ 7. a short saying

_____ 8. the use of words that imitate sounds

_____ 9. a story of someone's life, written by another person

_____ 10. a scene set at an earlier time

COMPLETE THE SENTENCE

Write the letter for the word that best completes each sentence.

_____ 1. The book is set in 2006 but includes a ———— to 2000.
    a. folklore   **b.** genre   **c.** simile   **d.** flashback

_____ 2. "Her tears were an ocean" is an example of a(n) ————.
    a. metaphor   **b.** simile   **c.** biography   **d.** onomatopoeia

_____ 3. "A stitch in time saves nine" is an example of a ————.
    a. proverb   **b.** genre   **c.** simile   **d.** prose

_____ 4. In his ————, Benjamin Franklin gave the details of his childhood.
    a. proverb   **b.** autobiography   **c.** folklore   **d.** biography

_____ 5. The word *plop* is an example of ————.
    a. prose   **b.** flashback   **c.** genre   **d.** onomatopoeia

_____ 6. Because it can take a lifetime to master just one type of writing, writers often specialize in one ————.
    a. metaphor   **b.** biography   **c.** genre   **d.** proverb

_____ 7. When you are writing ————, try to vary the length of your sentences.
    a. prose   **b.** similes   **c.** proverbs   **d.** metaphors

_____ 8. Much ———— has been passed down orally from generation to generation.
    a. folklore   **b.** biography   **c.** proverb   **d.** onomatopoeia

_____ 9. "Fit as a fiddle" is an example of a ————.
    a. genre   **b.** simile   **c.** metaphor   **d.** proverb

_____ 10. I enjoyed reading the ———— of Thomas Jefferson by R. B. Bernstein.
    a. onomatopoeia   **b.** flashback   **c.** biography   **d.** metaphor

Challenge: In her ————, Helen Keller uses several ———— to describe what it is like growing up blind, deaf, and mute.
_____   **a.** metaphors…flashbacks   **b.** biography…genres   **c.** autobiography…metaphors

The Grimm Brothers' Tales

Do the names Cinderella, Rapunzel, or Snow White sound familiar to you? If they do, you can thank the Grimm brothers, Jacob and Wilhelm. **(1)** These brothers turned their enthusiasm for German *folklore* into the world's most famous collection of fairy tales.

(2) There are several good *biographies* of the Grimm brothers, but here is a brief summary of their story: They were born in Germany in the 1780s. Their father died when they were boys, and the family was left with little money. Fortunately, they attended a good school and proved themselves by studying and reading. When their mother passed away, the Grimm brothers worked at a library to help support their younger siblings. **(3)** There, they read books of all types, including *autobiographies,* history, and literature. **(4)** In the course of their reading, the brothers became fascinated with the *genre* of folklore.

They then devoted themselves to listening to more than forty people who told traditional tales. The brothers published these tales in a series of books. At first, the books sold only a few hundred copies a year. In 1812, when the collections were first published, the Grimms were so poor that they could afford only one meal each day!

But the tales have an appeal that has lasted for more than two hundred years. What is it about these tales that keeps generations of children —and adults—so intrigued? **(5)** For many adults, the stories provide a *flashback* to their own childhood, when they sat at bedtime, listening to these amazing tales. Some of the settings of the Grimm fairy tales can also explain their appeal. Many of the stories include the dark forest beyond the village, where a big, bad wolf awaits his victims. **(6)** These elements seem to be *metaphors* for the fear of the unknown.

The original tales were violent and filled with prejudice. When it became clear how much they appealed to children, however, the brothers decided to edit them. They toned down the violence and cruelty. **(7)** They also improved the *prose,* turning the tales from simple stories into sophisticated works of art. **(8)** Sometimes the Grimm brothers added *proverbs* at the beginning or the end of the tale. **(9)** *Onomatopoeia* also brought the stories to life. For example, readers can almost hear the spinning wheel in Rumpelstiltskin in the line: "Whirr, whirr, whirr, three turns, and the reel was full, then he put another on, and whirr, whirr, whirr." **(10)** The Grimm brothers also used *similes,* such as "The white pebbles glittered like real silver pennies." These words help readers imagine the road that Hansel and Gretel took to the witch's house.

The brothers later became respected language scholars and even started a dictionary. But they are best remembered for the magical tales of witches, princes, stepmothers, and wolves that now line the shelves of children's libraries.

Each sentence below refers to a numbered sentence in the passage. Write the letter of the choice that gives the sentence a meaning that is closest to the original sentence.

_____ **1.** These brothers turned their enthusiasm for German _____ into the world's most famous collection of fairy tales.
  a. life stories   **b.** dictionaries   **c.** figures of speech   **d.** traditional stories

_____ **2.** There are several good _____ of the Grimm brothers.
  a. life stories   **b.** traditional tales   **c.** fairy tales   **d.** short sayings

_____ **3.** There, they read books of all types, including _____, history, and literature.
  a. traditional tales   **b.** poems and plays   **c.** fantasy stories   **d.** first-person life stories

_____ **4.** The brothers became fascinated with the _____ of folklore.
  a. dramatic writings   **b.** narrative poems   **c.** type of literature   **d.** oral tradition

_____ **5.** For many adults, the stories provide a ———— to their own childhood.
   a. short saying   **b.** jump back   **c.** diary   **d.** life story

_____ **6.** These elements seem to be ———— for the fear of the unknown.
   a. figures of speech   **b.** characteristics   **c.** short sayings   **d.** ordinary writing

_____ **7.** They improved the ————, turning the tales from simple stories into sophisticated works of art.
   a. writing   **b.** stories   **c.** characters   **d.** traditions

_____ **8.** Sometimes the Grimm brothers added ———— at the beginning or the end of the tale.
   a. ordinary writing   **b.** new translations   **c.** truthful sayings   **d.** first-hand sources

_____ **9.** ———— also brought the stories to life.
   a. Ordinary writing   **b.** Poetic language   **c.** Comparisons   **d.** Words imitating sounds

_____ **10.** The Grimm brothers also used ————, such as "The white pebbles glittered like real silver pennies."
   a. ordinary writing   **b.** short sayings   **c.** advice   **d.** comparisons

Indicate whether the statements below are TRUE or FALSE according to the passage.

_____ **1.** German folklore was based on true stories.

_____ **2.** The work of the Grimm brothers has been popular for hundreds of years.

_____ **3.** The Grimm brothers revised the tales to include many literary techniques.

FINISH THE THOUGHT

Complete each sentence so that it shows the meaning of the italicized word.

1. The *genres* I most like to read are _____

_____

2. One *proverb* that I have heard is _____

WRITE THE DERIVATIVE

Complete the sentence by writing the correct form of the word shown in parentheses. You may not need to change the form that is given.

_____ **1.** The ———— spent years researching President Lyndon Johnson. (*biography*)

_____ **2.** Realism, Impressionism, and Cubism are different ———— of painting. (*genre*)

_____ **3.** The short story was ————. (*autobiography*)

_____ **4.** There are many ———— references to beauty in poetry and in prose. (*metaphor*)

_____ **5.** There are often magical creatures in _____ literature. *(folklore)*

_____ **6.** The American South's hospitality is _____. *(proverb)*

_____ **7.** _____ in novels often give us background and help us better understand the main characters. *(flashback)*

_____ **8.** Poets use _____ to paint vivid pictures in their readers' imaginations. *(simile)*

_____ **9.** What do you prefer to write, poetry or _____? *(prose)*

_____ **10.** Children often enjoy poems that use _____ language. *(onomatopoeia)*

FIND THE EXAMPLE

Choose the answer that best describes the action or situation.

_____ **1.** A good title for an *autobiography*
   a. How I Lived   **b.** The President   **c.** History of Food   **d.** Science Today

_____ **2.** Examples of *onomatopoeia*
   a. yesterday, today   **b.** paper, papyrus   **c.** hiss, clang   **d.** fiction, poetry

_____ **3.** Something usually written in *prose*
   a. sign language   **b.** music   **c.** poetry   **d.** science fiction

_____ **4.** A *simile* that describes a busy person
   a. a busy person   **b.** woosh!   **c.** busy as a bee   **d.** frenetic

_____ **5.** A *proverb*
   a. sly as a fox   **b.** the dancing sun   **c.** splashing puddles   **d.** practice makes perfect

_____ **6.** A *biography* title
   a. Physics Theory   **b.** Harry S. Truman   **c.** My Success   **d.** National Landmarks

_____ **7.** A *genre* of literature
   a. opera   **b.** drama   **c.** rhyme   **d.** comparison

_____ **8.** A character most likely to be found in *folklore*
   a. a talking spider   **b.** an athlete   **c.** a movie star   **d.** a businessperson

_____ **9.** A likely opening for a *flashback*
   a. Today…   **b.** Tomorrow…   **c.** A year before…   **d.** In the future…

_____ **10.** The best *metaphor* for true love
   a. a sharp needle   **b.** an off-key piano   **c.** an old shoe   **d.** a perfect rose

Taking Tests

Antonym Tests

In the last skill feature, you learned about taking tests that ask you to identify a synonym. This skill feature teaches you strategies for identifying *antonyms* on a test. In Lesson 1, you learned that an *antonym* is a word that means the opposite of another word. The words *good* and *bad* are *antonyms*.

Since these tests generally present words in a sentence or paragraph, you can use *context clues* to help figure out meanings. Here are seven helpful strategies for taking antonym tests.

Strategies

1. *Read the sentence and all of the choices before selecting an answer.* If you do not read all of the choices, you will not be able to choose the best answer effectively.

2. *Imagine a possible answer.* You need to have a possible answer in mind to check against the choices the test presents.

3. *Narrow your choice by eliminating answers that are clearly incorrect.* Here is an example.

   The dirt road was *barred* for hours by a fallen tree.
   a. suddenly   **b.** opposed   **c.** blocked   **d.** opened

   Suddenly can be eliminated because it is the wrong part of speech. An adjective, not an adverb like *suddenly,* is needed in the sentence.

4. *Do not let a synonym in the answer choices confuse you.* In the sentence about the dirt road, *blocked* is a synonym for *barred.* Remember that the directions call for an antonym.

5. *Watch for choices that have been added to confuse you.* The choices for the sentence about the dirt road include both *opposed* and *opened.* Of course, these words sound very much alike. The correct choice is *opened.* If you read too fast, however, you may get confused and choose *opposed.*

6. *Use context clues to study the sentence and figure out the correct meaning.*

   The *minute* computer chip can fit on a person's fingertip.
   a. tiny   **b.** invisible   **c.** large   **d.** whole

   Since the chip fits on a fingertip, it must be very *small.* The opposite of *small* is *large. Large* is the correct answer.

7. *When two answers fit, remember to choose the best one.*

   Working outdoors in the *broiling* sun, we soon tired.
   a. cool   **b.** hot   **c.** misty   **d.** freezing

   In this item, both *cool* and *freezing* are opposites of broiling. But the word used in the sentence, *broiling,* suggests a great degree of heat. Therefore, we must look for an antonym with an equally great degree of cold. *Cool* suggests only a limited degree of cold, but *freezing* refers to a high degree. Therefore, the answer is *freezing.*

Practice

Use the strategies given in this skill feature to identify antonyms in context. In each sentence, choose the antonym of the italicized word. Write the letter of your choice on the answer line.

_____ 1. After it was taken over by another firm, the James Company *relinquished* control of the design of its products.
    a. exercised   **b.** lost   **c.** strengthened   **d.** regained

_____ 2. The television program about the candidate was considered *controversial* by many viewers.
    a. agreeable   **b.** shocking   **c.** interesting   **d.** boring

_____ 3. Famous in the world of sports, the *coveted* trophy is awarded annually.
    a. polished   **b.** admired   **c.** unwanted   **d.** valuable

_____ 4. The cell phones of today may seem *obsolete* in the future.
    a. uninteresting   **b.** strange   **c.** up-to-date   **d.** old

_____ 5. The actress *declined* to give an interview to the press.
    a. refused   **b.** argued   **c.** wished   **d.** agreed

_____ 6. The beautiful day made me feel *lighthearted*.
    a. old   **b.** uninterested   **c.** depressing   **d.** worried

_____ 7. I wish I could hear what Savanah was *murmuring*.
    a. gesturing   **b.** intending   **c.** shouting   **d.** muttering

_____ 8. Brianna spoke *candidly* about her reasons for quitting the team.
    a. popularly   **b.** dishonestly   **c.** much   **d.** hastily

_____ 9. A *novice* skier should first learn how to come to a stop.
    a. expert   **b.** brave   **c.** young   **d.** beginner

_____ 10. Unfortunately, the runner *fumbled* the ball.
    a. kicked   **b.** grasped   **c.** saw   **d.** rubbed

_____ 11. The winner's happiness was *evident* to everyone.
    a. silly   **b.** hideous   **c.** hidden   **d.** obvious

_____ 12. Manuel's *lucid* explanation helped me to understand the math problem.
    a. confusing   **b.** first   **c.** quiet   **d.** long

_____ 13. The *arduous* work exhausted the entire crew.
    a. difficult   **b.** easy   **c.** busy   **d.** abrupt

_____ 14. *Murky* waters hid the sunken ship.
    a. northern   **b.** calm   **c.** chilly   **d.** clear

_____ 15. The plane flew upward to get over the *lofty* peak.
    a. low   **b.** distant   **c.** jagged   **d.** steep

Certainty and Uncertainty

WORD LIST

approximate	assumption	certify	contend	hypothesis
illusion	inevitable	inquire	presume	vague

Have you ever made a decision and then felt unsure about whether it was the best choice? The words in this lesson deal with certainty and uncertainty. Since degrees of certainty or uncertainty are a large part of everyday life, these words will help you to better describe many common situations.

1. **approximate**
   a. *adjective* (ə-prŏk´sə-mĭt) Almost exact or correct
      • The **approximate** size of my bedroom is ten feet by twelve feet.
   b. *verb* (ə-prŏk´sə-māt) To come close to; to be nearly the same as
      • The sugar substitute **approximated** the taste of real sugar.

   approximation *noun* The statue was barely an **approximation** of the queen's beauty.

2. **assumption** (ə-sŭmp´shən) *noun*
   a. Something that is accepted as true without proof
      • The **assumption** that toads cause warts is false.
   b. The act of taking on or taking over
      • A grand ceremony marked the **assumption** of power by the new king.

   assume *verb* I **assume** you will wear a coat in this cold weather.

3. **certify** (sûr´tə-fī´) *verb*
   a. To guarantee or confirm to be true, accurate, or genuine
      • The building inspector **certified** that the apartment met city requirements.
   b. To issue a license or certificate indicating that certain standards have been met
      • The state board of education **certifies** teachers.

   certification *noun* The **certification** test for accountants involves math.

certify

4. **contend** (kən-tĕnd´) *verb*
   a. To struggle against difficulties
      • Every day, the ill patient must **contend** with his disease.
   b. To compete
      • The two teams **contended** for the debate championship.
   c. To claim
      • The man on trial **contended** that he was innocent.

   contention *noun* The expert's **contention** was that the work of art is not by Mir.

   contender *noun* Three **contenders** competed for the prize.

> The related word *contentious* means "involving conflict," as in "a *contentious* meeting."

5. hypothesis (hī-pŏth´ĭ-sĭs) *noun*
A theory; an educated guess than can be tested by further investigation
• The results of the experiments supported the scientist's **hypothesis.**

hypothesize *verb* Physicists **hypothesized** that there were undiscovered particles within atoms.

6. illusion (ĭ-lōō´zhən) *noun*
   a. An image that is not real
      • Is that puddle in the road ahead real, or is it just an **illusion?**
   b. An idea that is mistaken or false
      • The karate student soon got over the **illusion** that he could defeat his teacher in a contest.

illusory *adjective* Although we remain hopeful, world peace has so far proved **illusory.**

> Don't confuse *illusion* with *allusion*. An *allusion* is a reference to something.

7. inevitable (ĭn-ĕv´ĭ-tə-bəl) *adjective*
Impossible to avoid or prevent
• Growing older is **inevitable.**

inevitability *noun* Disagreement between people is an **inevitability.**

8. inquire (ĭn-kwīr´) *verb*
To ask; to request information
• We called the hotel to **inquire** about the rates.

inquiry *noun* The personnel office made **inquiries** about his recent job performance.

> *Inquire about* is a common phrase. *Inquire* can also be spelled *enquire.*

9. presume (prĭ-zōōm´) *verb*
To take for granted as being true without having proof
• We **presumed** there would be no word problems on the math test, but we were mistaken.

presumption *noun* In U.S. trials, there is a **presumption** of innocence until guilt is proven.

> *Presume to* is a common phrase, as in "I don't *presume to* know who is in charge." This means "I don't *claim* to know who is in charge."

10. vague (vāg) *adjective*
   a. Not specific; not clear
      • Because of Cal's **vague** directions, we got lost.
   b. Lacking definite form
      • I saw the **vague** shadow of an animal through the fog.

vagueness *noun* Because of the **vagueness** of the directions, we got lost.

WORD ENRICHMENT

Sound changes

The *u* in *presume* is pronounced "oo," but in *presumption,* it is pronounced the same way as the *u* in "bug." The same sound change occurs with *assume* and *assumption.* Similarly, the *i* in *hypothesis* is short, as in *sit,* but in *hypothesize* it is long, as in *size.*

WRITE THE CORRECT WORD

Write the correct word in the space next to each definition.

_____ **1.** unclear

_____ **2.** a theory

_____ **3.** to ask for information

_____ **4.** a mistaken idea or belief

_____ **5.** to claim

_____ **6.** to come close to

_____ **7.** impossible to prevent

_____ **8.** something accepted as true

_____ **9.** to take for granted

_____ **10.** to guarantee

COMPLETE THE SENTENCE

Write the letter for the word that best completes each sentence.

_____ **1.** The noble prince _____ with the fierce dragon.
    a. presumed   **b.** contended   **c.** inquired   **d.** certified

_____ **2.** Marie _____ about the price of this necklace.
    a. contended   **b.** inquired   **c.** certified   **d.** assumed

_____ **3.** Janine took a course in order to be _____ as a lifeguard.
    a. hypothesized   **b.** inquired   **c.** presumed   **d.** certified

_____ **4.** What is the _____ number of people who will be at the surprise party?
    a. illusory   **b.** contended   **c.** approximate   **d.** vague

_____ **5.** It was _____ that you would be grounded after disobeying your father's rules!
    a. inevitable   **b.** approximated   **c.** illusory   **d.** contended

_____ **6.** The scientist tested her _____ with a number of experiments.
    a. hypothesis   **b.** certification   **c.** illusion   **d.** inevitability

_____ **7.** Wearing vertical stripes gives the _____ that you are taller than you actually are.
    a. vagueness   **b.** contention   **c.** illusion   **d.** assumption

_____ **8.** I _____ that the man at the hospital wearing a white coat was a physician.
    a. certified   **b.** assumed   **c.** inquired   **d.** approximated

_____ **9.** I wouldn't _____ to have all of the answers!
    a. certify   **b.** presume   **c.** inquire   **d.** hypothesize

_____ **10.** Jason had a(n) _____ memory of his great-grandfather, who passed away when Jason was four.
    a. vague   **b.** contentious   **c.** assumed   **d.** approximate

Challenge: Sometimes people _____ that their _____ are real.

_____   **a.** certify…inquiries   **b.** inquire…assumptions   **c.** presume… illusions

Dactyloscopy: The Science of Fingerprints

(1) A police *inquiry,* an eyewitness, or a security camera can all help to catch a criminal. **(2)** But experts *contend* that one of the key elements to fighting crime is dactyloscopy, the identification of the criminal's fingerprints.

(3) When a crime such as a burglary takes place, it is almost *inevitable* that the crime scene will be dusted for fingerprints. **(4)** Witnesses, if there are any, may only be able to give a *vague* description of the criminal. **(5)** Sometimes they may even make false *assumptions* about what happened and who the guilty person might be. **(6)** Research shows that investigators should not *presume* that witness accounts are accurate. The identification of fingerprints, on the other hand, allows

criminals to be identified with far more certainty. **(7)** Because no two people in the world have the exact same prints, a *hypothesis* about who committed the crime can often be confirmed.

When photographs of a set of fingerprints are sent to a crime laboratory for identification, specialists identify the general pattern of the prints first. The prints are then checked to determine if their unique combination of whorls, arches, or loops matches those in any set of prints on file with the authorities. Then, there must be further matching. The one-of-a-kind spacing of the ridges and the number of tiny holes along them must be examined. These tiny holes are the final proof. **(8)** They make it possible for a fingerprint expert to *certify* a set of prints as an exact match with another set.

In the past, fingerprints were identified through visual inspection. **(9)** At times, especially when working with only a part of a print, the identifications were only *approximate.*

(10) Today, however, a criminal whose fingerprints are on file can have few *illusions* about remaining unidentified if he or she has left even traces of prints at the scene of a crime. Modern technology, including computers and lasers, can build whole prints from mere traces. New advances can even help lift fingerprints from the inside of a glove. Using all the tools of dactyloscopy, an expert can quickly match a pair of prints from a crime scene with a single set drawn from the millions on file.

Each sentence below refers to a numbered sentence in the passage. Write the letter of the choice that gives the sentence a meaning that is closest to the original sentence.

_____ 1. A police _____, an eyewitness, or a security camera can all help to catch a criminal.
   a. questioning   **b.** record   **c.** arrest   **d.** fingerprint

_____ 2. But experts _____ that one of the key elements to fighting crime is dactyloscopy.
   a. claim   **b.** guess   **c.** disagree   **d.** fight

_____ 3. When a crime such as a burglary takes place, it is almost _____ that the crime scene will be dusted for fingerprints.
   a. lucky   **b.** never   **c.** immediate   **d.** certain

_____ 4. Witnesses may only be able to give a(n) _____ description of the criminal.
   a. complete   **b.** inaccurate   **c.** detailed   **d.** entertaining

_____ 5. Sometimes they may even form false _____ about what happened and who the guilty person might be.
   a. facts   **b.** stories   **c.** ideas   **d.** criminals

_____ **6.** Research shows that we should never _____ that witness accounts are accurate.
    a. pretend   **b.** take a guess   **c.** take for granted   **d.** agree

_____ **7.** Because no two people in the world have the exact same prints, a _____ about who committed the crime can often be confirmed.
    a. knowledge   **b.** theory   **c.** suspicion   **d.** report

_____ **8.** They make it possible for a fingerprint expert to _____ a set of prints as an exact match with another set.
    a. build   **b.** accept   **c.** match   **d.** confirm

_____ **9.** At times, especially when working with part of a print, the identifications were only _____.
    a. imaginary   **b.** genuine   **c.** uncertain   **d.** dusted

_____ **10.** Today, a criminal whose fingerprints are on file can have few _____ about remaining unidentified if he or she has left even traces of prints at the scene of a crime.
    a. questions   **b.** false ideas   **c.** struggles   **d.** guarantees

Indicate whether the statements below are TRUE or FALSE according to the passage.

_____ **1.** Fingerprinting is accurate less than 50 percent of the time.

_____ **2.** Computers can help rebuild a full fingerprint image from a small section of one.

_____ **3.** Eyewitness accounts of a crime are always accurate.

WRITING EXTENDED RESPONSES

Imagine you are a detective trying to solve a case of theft. Think about what was taken, the place it was taken from, who might have taken it and why. Then, tell how you would successfully solve the crime and capture the criminal. You might use clues, witnesses, or both. Write a narrative essay describing the robbery and how you solve it. Remember that you are the detective, so use the first person. Your narrative piece should be at least three paragraphs long. Use at least three lesson words in your piece and underline them.

WRITE THE DERIVATIVE

Complete the sentence by writing the correct form of the word shown in parentheses. You may not need to change the form that is given.

_____ **1.** My dog _____ barks when I open the front door. (inevitable)

_____ **2.** Charlotte made some _____ to learn about her potential roommate. (inquire)

_____ **3.** The _____ of her reply made me wonder if she was telling the truth. (vague)

4. The teacher's aide _____ the role of lead teacher once she got her teaching certificate. (*assumption*)

5. Our _____ was that the hike would be easy. (*presume*)

6. An expert _____ that my coin collection is authentic. (*certify*)

7. _____ 70 percent of the earth's surface is covered with water. (*approximate*)

8. Magicians rely on many optical _____ to trick their audiences. (*illusion*)

9. The scientist _____ that the bacteria was actually helpful. (*hypothesis*)

10. It is my _____ that people in the United States need to use energy more efficiently. (*contend*)

FIND THE EXAMPLE

Choose the answer that best describes the action or situation.

_____ **1.** How a *vague* outline of a person might appear
    a. blurry   **b.** sharp   **c.** colorful   **d.** definite

_____ **2.** A person who is most likely to form *hypotheses*
    a. an artist   **b.** a biologist   **c.** a musician   **d.** a typist

_____ **3.** The *approximate* weight of an elephant
    a. 2 tons   **b.** 2 pounds   **c.** 2 ounces   **d.** 2 acres

_____ **4.** A question that someone who is *inquiring* about concert tickets might ask
    a. What's up?   **b.** I love this music!   **c.** How are you?   **d.** Are any seats left?

_____ **5.** Something that will *inevitably* happen to ice cream left out in the hot sun
    a. It will sing.   **b.** It will stiffen.   **c.** It will melt.   **d.** It will grow.

_____ **6.** A logical *assumption* from the facts that your sandwich has disappeared and your dog is licking his chops
    a. He's loyal.   **b.** A friend took it.   **c.** He ate it.   **d.** He gave it to charity.

_____ **7.** Something early settlers in Canada had to *contend* with
    a. sleep   **b.** cold winters   **c.** bad TV   **d.** pollution

_____ **8.** Something that would be used to *certify* a dentist
    a. an exam   **b.** a race   **c.** an experiment   **d.** a yardstick

_____ **9.** One who is *presumed* to be physically fit
    a. a baby   **b.** a scientist   **c.** an accountant   **d.** a pro athlete

_____ **10.** A likely response to someone's *illusion*
    a. You're right.   **b.** You're mistaken.   **c.** You're happy.   **d.** You're welcome.

Limiting and Releasing

WORD LIST

compress	concise	eject	exclusion	expulsion
liberate	propel	regulate	restrain	restriction

This lesson presents words that express the everyday ideas of holding and letting go, or limiting and releasing. Studying this vocabulary will enable you to use words like *regulate* and *restriction* to give the sense of controlling or limiting something. Other words, like *eject* and *expel*, signal releasing something or pushing it away.

1. **compress** (kəm-prĕs´) *verb*
   To make smaller by pressing together
   • The compactor will **compress** the old cartons into a tight package.

   compression *noun* We sat on our overflowing suitcase, hoping that **compression** would allow us to zip it up.

2. **concise** (kən-sīs´) *adjective*
   Expressing a lot in few words; short and clear
   • I shortened the letter to state my point in a more **concise** way.

   conciseness *noun* We appreciated the **conciseness** of the mayor's speech.

3. **eject** (ĭ-jĕkt´) *verb*
   To push out by force
   • Please **eject** the disk from the DVD player.

   ejection *noun* Seconds before the plane crashed, an automatic **ejection** device allowed the pilot to escape.

eject

> *Eject* generally means "to force out physically." *Expel* has the broader meaning of forcing out by nonphysical means.

4. **exclusion** (ĭk-sklōō´zhən) *noun*
   The act of keeping out or shutting out
   • **Exclusion** based on race is illegal.

   exclude *verb* The choir had to **exclude** anyone who could not read music.

   exclusive *adjective* The **exclusive** club was open only to champion golfers.

> *Exclusive* often means "snobbish or having very high standards."

5. **expulsion** (ĭk-spŭl´shən) *noun*
   The act of forcing out or driving out
   • After his **expulsion** from school, he wandered around during the day and got into even more trouble.

   expel *verb* If you break the rules, you may be **expelled** from the organization.

6. **liberate** (lĭb´ə-rāt´) *verb*
   To set free; release
   • After a new trial, the wrongly convicted men were **liberated**
     from prison.

   liberator *noun* Abraham Lincoln was called the Great **Liberator.**

   liberation *noun* The captives were thankful for their **liberation** from
   enemy forces.

7. **propel** (prə-pĕl´) *verb*
   To cause to move forward or onward
   • Sailboats are **propelled** by the wind.

   propeller *noun* The speedboat's **propeller** spun so fast I couldn't
   see the blades.

   propulsion *noun* A squid achieves **propulsion** by squirting water
   out of a special tube.

8. **regulate** (rĕg´yə-lāt´) *verb*
   To control with rules
   • The traffic department **regulates** parking along the streets.

   regulation *noun* A state **regulation** requires that drivers carry
   their licenses.

   regulator *noun* Federal **regulators** monitor pollution.

9. **restrain** (rĭ-strān´) *verb*
   To hold back, keep in check, or deprive of freedom
   • A good rider knows when to **restrain** a horse and when to let
     it gallop.

   restraint *noun* She showed real **restraint** by not raising her voice.

> Someone may be put in
> *restraints,* such as handcuffs.

10. **restriction** (rĭ-strĭk´shən) *noun*
    A limit or limitation
    • Because of the shortage, our town put **restrictions** on water use.

    restrict *verb* Mom **restricted** the amount of television we watch
    each day.

    restrictive *adjective* Due to recent accidents, the swimming pool rules
    have become more **restrictive.**

WORD ENRICHMENT

Cutting words

The word *concise* comes from the Latin verb *caedere,* meaning "to cut."
We may think of *concise* writing and speech as "cut" to make it short. The
words *scissors* and *chisel* (a tool used to cut stone) also come from this root.
So does *cement,* which was once made from cut-up limestone. (Today,
cement is made from a mixture of limestone, clay, and water.)

The verb *caedere* also means "to kill." This meaning appears as *-cide* in
insecticide, a compound that kills insects.

WRITE THE CORRECT WORD

Write the correct word in the space next to each definition.

_____ **1.** to cause to move forward

_____ **2.** limit or limitation

_____ **3.** the act of keeping out

_____ **4.** to press together

_____ **5.** to release or set free

_____ **6.** using few words

_____ **7.** forcing or driving out

_____ **8.** to push out by force

_____ **9.** to hold back

_____ **10.** to control with rules

COMPLETE THE SENTENCE

Write the letter for the word that best completes each sentence.

_____ **1.** I hope the toaster _____ the bread before it starts burning.
a. regulates **b.** restrains **c.** ejects **d.** compresses

_____ **2.** A(n) _____ manual will help people who are in a hurry.
a. propelled **b.** ejected **c.** concise **d.** regulated

_____ **3.** Was the country club guilty of illegal _____?
a. exclusion **b.** ejection **c.** compression **d.** restraint

_____ **4.** The punishment for breaking that rule is automatic _____.
a. expulsion **b.** regulation **c.** propulsion **d.** compression

_____ **5.** We _____ our wedding guests to close family members.
a. expelled **b.** restricted **c.** excluded **d.** ejected

_____ **6.** The software _____ large computer files so that they take up less storage space.
a. restrains **b.** compresses **c.** ejects **d.** liberates

_____ **7.** County laws _____ the use of snowmobiles in the park.
a. eject **b.** compress **c.** liberate **d.** regulate

_____ **8.** A motor _____ a car.
a. liberates **b.** ejects **c.** propels **d.** restrains

_____ **9.** The soldiers _____ the prisoners from their captors.
a. liberated **b.** restrained **c.** ejected **d.** regulated

_____ **10.** State laws require parents to _____ small children in car seats.
a. propel **b.** compress **c.** expel **d.** restrain

Challenge: Do laws _____ us by limiting our behavior, or do they _____ us by creating a safe place to be free?
_____ **a.** propel…compress **b.** regulate…eject **c.** restrain…liberate

Lesson 20 **129**

Escaping Our Limits

Most of us have gazed with envy at a soaring hawk or flock of seagulls. **(1)** Can you imagine yourself spreading your arms and rising upward, your feet *liberated* from the grip of the earth?

According to an ancient Greek myth, Icarus made wings of wax and flew . . . at least for a time. Soaring higher and higher, he came too near the sun. His beautiful wings began to melt, and he plunged downward, his glorious experiment ending in tragedy. Still, he is celebrated in legend and memorialized in the name of the Greek island Icaros.

By the 1400s, a few inventors and other dreamers believed we would fly one day. The genius Leonardo da Vinci even made drawings of aircraft similar to today's gliders and helicopters.

At last, in 1903, the Wright brothers flew their wobbly, creaking "Flyer" at Kitty Hawk, North Carolina. They had designed the airplane in their bicycle shop in Ohio after carefully studying the records of other flying experiments. **(2)** They *excluded* ideas that did not work from their final design, but they had learned even from others' failures. **(3)** Their flight was the first to use a motor to *propel* the plane.

Since then, we have flown farther and faster with each passing year. By World War I, planes were advanced enough to be used as fighters. The original Red Baron flew one. **(4)** We can picture him zooming through the sky, *restrained* only by the limits of his plane.

Between the two world wars, passenger planes appeared. At first, they were without comforts. Today, heated and air-conditioned cabins have leather seats. But as with any flying machine, safety is a concern.

(5) Flight attendants give *concise* instructions to passengers about emergency procedures.

(6) With thousands of flights in the air at once, *regulations* are needed to control the planes. **(7)** A list of *restrictions,* including no-fly zones, is given to pilots and air-traffic controllers every day.

Planes are now so speedy that some move faster than sound. At the nation's testing grounds, scientists and military officers watch closely as experimental planes soar. Flights are timed and new records are set. **(8)** Pilots also test new ways to *eject* themselves from planes. **(9)** One method is like a catapult that tosses the pilot outward, using *compressed* gas. **(10)** Timely *expulsion* can be the difference between life and death.

Since the Wright Brothers, flying has taken us around the world and beyond. Our rocket-propelled flights have even reached space. As we read or watch science fiction, it is easy to imagine ourselves flying across the galaxy someday.

Each sentence below refers to a numbered sentence in the passage. Fill in the letter of the choice that gives the sentence a meaning that is closest to the original sentence.

_____ **1.** Can you imagine rising upward, your feet _____ the grip of the earth?
  a. pressed into   **b.** kicked out of   **c.** limited by   **d.** freed from

_____ **2.** They _____ ideas that did not work from their design.
  a. easily powered   **b.** left out   **c.** tried to improve   **d.** often limited

_____ **3.** Their flight was the first to use a motor to _____ the plane.
  a. weaken   **b.** charge   **c.** move   **d.** slow

_____ **4.** The Red Baron was _____ only by the limits of his plane.
  a. held back   **b.** boosted up   **c.** erased   **d.** tossed around

_____ **5.** Flight attendants give _____ instructions about emergency procedures.
  a. wordy and silly   **b.** quick and clear   **c.** helpful and slow   **d.** loud and odd

6. With thousands of flights in the air, _____ are needed to control the planes.
a. rules   b. hurdles   c. observers   d. experts

7. A list of _____ is given to pilots and air-traffic controllers every day.
a. expressions   b. rejections   c. limitations   d. pressures

8. Pilots also test new ways to _____ themselves from planes.
a. keep   b. press   c. avoid   d. push

9. One method is like a catapult that tosses the pilot outward, using _____ gas.
a. free   b. unleaded   c. released   d. pressurized

10. Timely _____ can be the difference between life and death.
a. codes   b. forcing out   c. clarity   d. holding back

Indicate whether the statements below are TRUE or FALSE according to the passage.

1. Leonardo da Vinci designed and built a working, gas-powered helicopter.

2. The Wright brothers did most of their preflight work in Ohio.

3. Passenger planes came on the scene about ten years after World War II.

FINISH THE THOUGHT

Complete each sentence so that it shows the meaning of the italicized word.

1. She was *excluded* from playing in the championship game because _____

_____

2. My *concise* paper _____

_____

WRITE THE DERIVATIVE

Complete the sentence by writing the correct form of the word shown in parentheses. You may not need to change the form that is given.

_____ **1.** The rules are much more _____ in the indoor league. *(restriction)*

_____ **2.** She was _____ after the incident in the cafeteria. *(expulsion)*

_____ **3.** The prisoner struggled against his _____. *(restrain)*

_____ **4.** Current _____ do not allow children to vote. *(regulate)*

_____ **5.** _____ Norma, no one finished the assignment. *(exclusion)*

_____ **6.** With its _____ bent beyond recognition, the ship was helpless. *(propel)*

_____ **7.** I appreciate _____ in graduation speeches. *(concise)*

_____ 8. Arguing with the referee caused the basketball player's _____ from the game. (*eject*)

_____ 9. Certain kinds of pumps use _____ to do amazing things. (*compress*)

_____ 10. After the revolution, the citizens celebrated their _____ from tyranny. (*liberate*)

FIND THE EXAMPLE

Choose the answer that best describes the action or situation.

_____ 1. Something that creates *propulsion*
    a. a brake   **b.** an agency   **c.** a pencil   **d.** a sail

_____ 2. Something many people consider to be the ultimate *liberator*
    a. clothing   **b.** knowledge   **c.** soap   **d.** gravity

_____ 3. Something an *ejected* pilot needs
    a. parachute   **b.** book   **c.** sandwich   **d.** car

_____ 4. A situation when being *concise* might be especially important
    a. thinking out loud   **b.** thinking silently   **c.** having little time   **d.** no microphone

_____ 5. An event that might make someone feel *excluded*
    a. admitted to college   **b.** freed from jail   **c.** cut from a team   **d.** honored in song

_____ 6. Something that *compresses* items
    a. trash compactor   **b.** notebook   **c.** lunch box   **d.** dishwasher

_____ 7. A situation in which having emotional *restraint* would most likely be helpful
    a. dreaming   **b.** sleeping   **c.** watching a ball game   **d.** debating an issue

_____ 8. Something that, for safety reasons, is subject to many government *regulations*
    a. political thoughts   **b.** water purification   **c.** stormy weather   **d.** taking walks

_____ 9. Something most likely to get a student *expelled* from school
    a. studying   **b.** fighting   **c.** whispering   **d.** coughing

_____ 10. The goal of laws that *restrict* inexperienced drivers
    a. safety   **b.** employment   **c.** happiness   **d.** frustration

Attack and Defense

WORD LIST

battalion	casualty	corps	encampment	formidable
garrison	infiltrate	provoke	sentry	siege

This lesson deals with "fighting words." Their meanings center around war-related situations involving attack and defense. Many of the words, however, can also be applied to everyday life. We can attack a problem as well as an enemy. We can defend our rights and our opinions as well as our country. As you learn these words, think of the different ways they can be used.

1. battalion (bə-tăl´yən) *noun*
  a. A large unit of soldiers, usually made up of many smaller units
   • The **battalion** commander ordered the leader of each company to report to him immediately.
  b. Any large group that acts as one
   • A **battalion** of ants invaded the kitchen.

> A *regiment* is an even larger unit of soldiers, formed from at least two *battalions*.

2. casualty (kăzh´o͞o-əl-tē) *noun*
  a. A soldier who is injured, killed, captured, or otherwise made unable to take part in battle
   • Lieutenant Todd had the sad duty of reporting **casualties**.
  b. A person who has been killed in an accident or a disaster
   • The police officer raced toward the scene after being notified of a **casualty**.

3. corps (kôr) *noun*
  a. A branch or department of the armed forces, with a specialized function
   • The Kramer's eldest son joined an elite **corps** of soldiers whose mission was top secret.
  b. A group of people acting together under the same leadership
   • A **corps** of engineers built the bridge in record time.

> The plural of *corps* is spelled the same way as the singular form, but pronounced kôrz.

4. encampment (ĕn-kămp´mənt) *noun*
  A campsite; a place where people set up camp temporarily
  • Snow fell as men throughout the **encampment** huddled around small fires, trying to stay warm.

  encamp *verb* Once they were **encamped**, the tourists decided to do some fishing.

> Typically, people in *encampments* are housed in tents, cabins, or other rough shelters.

encampment

5. formidable (fôr´mĭ-də-bəl) *adjective*
   a. Inspiring fear or awe; fearsome
   • In World War II, the Allies defeated **formidable** foes.
   b. Difficult to undertake or achieve
   • Climbing Mount Everest presents a **formidable** challenge.

6. garrison (găr´ĭ-sən)
   a. *noun* A protected place where soldiers are stationed or live while
   on duty
   • Before the Revolutionary War, British troops used colonists' homes
   as **garrisons.**
   b. *verb* To station soldiers in a place in order to defend it
   • During the Civil War, after Union soldiers captured Memphis, they
   were **garrisoned** there to control the Mississippi River.

7. infiltrate (ĭn´fĭl-trāt´) *verb*
   a. To enter secretly, so as to surprise
   • Spies **infiltrated** the general's headquarters.
   b. To pass into through small gaps and fill space
   • Smoke from the fire next door **infiltrated** the neighbors'
   apartments.

   infiltration *noun* **Infiltration** of the enemy camp was key to
   their plan.

8. provoke (prə-vōk´) *verb*
   a. To upset or to cause an angry response
   • The player tried to **provoke** her opponent into committing a foul.
   b. To inspire or cause to act
   • The professor's lecture **provoked** much discussion.

   provocation *noun* He threw the first punch without **provocation.**

   provoking *adjective* Her comments about the story were
   thought-**provoking.**

9. sentry (sĕn´trē) *noun*
   A guard, particularly a soldier, posted at a certain spot to keep watch
   • The **sentries** were alarmed by a sudden noise.

10. siege (sēj) *noun*
   a. The act of soldiers surrounding a place and cutting off its supplies
   in an attempt to capture it
   • Expecting a **siege,** the soldiers at the fort had piled up supplies.
   b. A long period of distress or unpleasantness
   • The **siege** of cold weather finally ended.

> In the 900-day *siege* of
> Leningrad, Russia (now
> Saint Petersburg), Nazi forces
> tried to starve the town into
> surrendering. The people's
> refusal to give in was critical
> in winning World War II.

WORD ENRICHMENT

Sitting it out
The word *siege* comes from the Latin verb *sedere,* meaning "to sit."

WRITE THE CORRECT WORD

Write the correct word in the space next to each definition.

_____ **1.** a guard

_____ **2.** a group with a specialized function

_____ **3.** inspiring fear

_____ **4.** the act of surrounding a place

_____ **5.** to enter secretly

_____ **6.** a campsite

_____ **7.** a place where soldiers are stationed

_____ **8.** to cause to act

_____ **9.** a soldier who is injured or killed

_____ **10.** a large unit of soldiers

COMPLETE THE SENTENCE

Write the letter for the word that best completes each sentence.

_____ **1.** The company hired a _____ of computer scientists to update its operating system.
a. siege   **b.** casualty   **c.** corps   **d.** sentry

_____ **2.** The first _____ of the war was injured while repairing a damaged tank.
a. casualty   **b.** sentry   **c.** battalion   **d.** siege

_____ **3.** Some Native American warriors painted their faces before battle so that they would seem more _____.
a. encamped   **b.** garrisoned   **c.** infiltrated   **d.** formidable

_____ **4.** The lieutenant reported that he had lost two companies from his _____.
a. sentry   **b.** battalion   **c.** siege   **d.** casualty

_____ **5.** _____ were placed on the rooftops to keep an eye out for enemy troops.
a. Battalions   **b.** Corps   **c.** Sentries   **d.** Encampments

_____ **6.** The general _____ an attack north of the city in order to keep enemy troops busy while civilians escaped to the south.
a. infiltrated   **b.** provoked   **c.** encamped   **d.** garrisoned

_____ **7.** Colonist Nathan Hale _____ a British camp to find out their troop locations.
a. provoked   **b.** garrisoned   **c.** encamped   **d.** infiltrated

_____ **8.** The _____ was weakened when enemy soldiers broke through one of the walls.
a. garrison   **b.** sentry   **c.** provocation   **d.** casualty

_____ **9.** The medical _____ was set up less than a mile from the battlefield.
a. siege   **b.** casualty   **c.** encampment   **d.** sentry

_____ **10.** The _____ of the city of Troy by the Greeks lasted for ten years.
a. sentry   **b.** siege   **c.** encampment   **d.** corps

Challenge: The spies managed to _____ the _____ by posing as a traveling circus act.
_____ **a.** siege…battalion   **b.** provoke…casualty   **c.** infiltrate…encampment

Minutemen: American Heroes

It was 1775 in the British colony of Massachusetts. Tensions were rising between the American colonists and their rulers. **(1)** The British government had *provoked* the colonists almost to the point of open rebellion. At the Boston Tea Party, colonists protested a tax on tea by dumping it into the water of Boston Harbor.

The British struck back. **(2)** They shut the port of Boston and sent *battalions* of highly trained soldiers to the city. **(3)** There, the British soldiers were *garrisoned* in colonists' homes. **(4)** Citizens began to feel that their city was under *siege*.

minuteman

(5) Massachusetts patriots—men who wanted independence from British rule—organized a *corps* of citizen volunteers called Minutemen. These were ordinary citizens who were ready to fight "in a minute." Unlike the well-equipped British soldiers, the Minutemen had no uniforms. **(6)** They received little training and lived at home, rather than in *encampments*. As the situation grew worse, Minutemen began to store arms to fight the British.

By April, rumors were flying that the British would march on the towns around Boston. The colonists watched and listened closely for movement. On April 18, the British general Gage ordered 700 of his troops to go to the town of Lexington, seize the weapons stored there, and arrest colonial leaders John Hancock and Samuel Adams.

The British tried hard to keep their plans secret, but this proved extremely difficult because they were living in the homes of Bostonians. **(7)** The network of Boston patriots, including stable boys, homemakers, and businessmen, found it easy to *infiltrate* the British information system.

As soon as they heard that the British were on the move, Paul Revere and a comrade set out on separate paths toward Lexington, to warn the Minutemen there. Thanks to their alerts, Hancock and Adams escaped. On the morning of April 19, the Minutemen of Lexington gathered to protect their arms and homes.

"Don't fire unless fired upon. But if they want a war let it begin here," said their commander John Parker. Suddenly a shot was heard, and the fighting began! The outnumbered Minutemen could not fend off the British attack. **(8)** In the end, the colonists suffered eighteen *casualties*, eight dead and ten wounded.

As the British soldiers pressed on toward Concord, more Minutemen poured in to protect the town. **(9)** Warned by *sentries*, the colonists met the British at the North Bridge. Against the odds, the Minutemen won the battle!

Defeated, the British fled back to Boston, but the colonists followed. Hiding behind trees and shrubs, small bands of Minutemen were easily able to pick off the fleeing British soldiers in their bright red coats. **(10)** The once *formidable* British troops were reduced to frightened targets.

The American Revolution had begun. Poet Ralph Waldo Emerson called the first shot at Lexington "the shot heard 'round the world." The British would hold Boston for another year, but in the end, the United States of America would become an independent country.

Each sentence below refers to a numbered sentence in the passage. Write the letter of the choice that gives the sentence a meaning that is closest to the original sentence.

_____ **1.** The British government had _____ the colonists.
     a. guarded   **b.** upset   **c.** captured   **d.** surrounded

_____ **2.** They sent _____ of highly trained soldiers to the city.
     a. large units   **b.** campsites   **c.** protected stations   **d.** guards

_____ **3.** There, the British soldiers were _____ in colonists' homes.
     a. surrounded   **b.** injured   **c.** stationed   **d.** inspired

_____ **4.** Citizens began to feel that their city was _____.
   a. inspiring fear   **b.** being protected   **c.** causing anger   **d.** being surrounded

_____ **5.** Massachusetts patriots organized a _____ of citizen volunteers.
   a. group   **b.** leader   **c.** capture   **d.** station

_____ **6.** They received little training and lived at home, rather than in _____.
   a. stations   **b.** companies   **c.** hotels   **d.** camps

_____ **7.** The network of Boston patriots found it easy to _____ the British information system.
   a. protect   **b.** accidentally kill   **c.** secretly enter   **d.** guard

_____ **8.** In the end, the colonists suffered eighteen _____.
   a. wounded or dead   **b.** burned camps   **c.** posted guards   **d.** defeats

_____ **9.** Warned by _____, the colonists met the British at the North Bridge.
   a. units   **b.** branches   **c.** guards   **d.** stations

_____ **10.** The once _____ British troops were reduced to frightened targets.
   a. specialized   **b.** fearsome   **c.** angry   **d.** guarded

Indicate whether the statements below are TRUE or FALSE according to the passage.

_____ **1.** John Hancock and Samuel Adams were leaders in the American Revolution.

_____ **2.** Minutemen were volunteers who fought for American independence.

_____ **3.** "The shot heard 'round the world" was fired in Concord, Massachusetts.

WRITING EXTENDED RESPONSES

Many of the military terms used today have been used for hundreds of
years. Select five words taught in this lesson. List them on the left side
of a sheet of paper, allowing space under each word. Next, interview an
adult about a war or another military action that he or she remembers.
Ask about each word that you have chosen. For example, what do you
remember about battalions in that war? Who provoked whom and
why? Write the responses on the lines beneath each word. Share your
information with a classmate.

WRITE THE DERIVATIVE

Complete the sentence by writing the correct form of the word shown in
parentheses. You may not need to change the form that is given.

_____ **1.** There had been so many _____ at the intersection that the town finally
   decided to install a stoplight. *(casualty)*

_____ **2.** Protesters were _____ on the Washington Mall, awaiting the rally.
   (encampment)

3. A _____ of explosion specialists was sent in to diffuse the bomb. *(corps)*

_____ **4.** The _____ of water into the underground safe destroyed the important documents. *(infiltrate)*

_____ **5.** There was no way to get past the armed _____ who were posted by each entrance. *(sentry)*

_____ **6.** "He attacked my client without _____," the lawyer said. *(provoke)*

_____ **7.** _____ of protesters marched against the new city regulations. *(battalion)*

_____ **8.** The JV team proved to be more _____ than expected. *(formidable)*

_____ **9.** The _____ of flu outbreaks finally ended in the spring. *(siege)*

_____ **10.** The _____ along the coast were the first to fall to the enemy. *(garrison)*

FIND THE EXAMPLE

Choose the answer that best describes the action or situation.

_____ **1.** Something a *formidable* enemy would inspire
   a. fear   **b.** anger   **c.** boredom   **d.** hope

_____ **2.** A likely result of *provoking* a wild animal
   a. playing catch   **b.** getting licked   **c.** getting bitten   **d.** playing tag

_____ **3.** A place where you are likely to find a *sentry*
   a. movie theater   **b.** river boat   **c.** military base   **d.** hotel lounge

_____ **4.** Something you are likely to find at an *encampment*
   a. televisions   **b.** tents   **c.** toys   **d.** top hats

_____ **5.** A piece of clothing that water cannot *infiltrate*
   a. jeans   **b.** T-shirt   **c.** sweatshirt   **d.** raincoat

_____ **6.** What you are likely to find at a *garrison*
   a. football players   **b.** bicycles   **c.** soldiers   **d.** red clothing

_____ **7.** What the people in a *corps* share
   a. a home   **b.** a leader   **c.** a parent   **d.** a surprise

_____ **8.** The length of a *siege* of cold weather
   a. many months   **b.** a few hours   **c.** several seconds   **d.** a few minutes

_____ **9.** A place where you are LEAST likely to find a *casualty* of war
   a. hospital   **b.** home   **c.** front lines   **d.** POW camp

_____ **10.** The best way to describe a *battalion*
   a. a small force   **b.** a large group   **c.** a few good men   **d.** a special department

Prefixes, Roots, and Suffixes

Identifying Prefixes, Roots, and Suffixes

If you encounter an unknown word, you can use clues both outside and inside the word to figure out the meaning. Clues that are found outside the word are called context clues. The clues that are found inside the word are known as *word part* clues. The three word parts are called *prefixes*, *suffixes*, and *roots*.

A *prefix* is added to the beginning of a word. *Re-*, *sub-*, and *im-* are all prefixes. The hyphen shows where they attach to other word parts. A *root* is the main part of a word. A *suffix* is added to the end of a word. A hyphen before a *suffix (-ing)* when it stands alone shows where it attaches to the root. The meaning of the root word may be changed by the addition of prefixes and suffixes.

The words *rewinding* and *impatiently* are formed from a *prefix, root,* and *suffix.*

Prefix	Root	Suffix	Word
re-	wind	-ing	rewinding
im-	patient	-ly	impatiently

Some words, like *misstep* and *container,* only contain two parts.

Prefix	Root	Suffix	Word
mis-	step		misstep
	contain	-er	container

At other times, the spelling of a root may change when a prefix or suffix is added. For example, the word *united* drops one *e* when *ed* is added. The word *strain* changes to *stren* and adds a *u* when *-ous* is added.

Root	Suffix	Word
unite	-ed	united
strain	-ous	strenuous

Can you identify the word parts in the words below?

	Prefix	Root	Suffix
unfriendly	_____	_____	_____
unfeeling	_____	_____	_____
supersaturated	_____	_____	_____

(There is a spelling change for the last one.)

Prefixes, roots, and suffixes all affect the meaning of a word. The **root** is the main part of a word. It gives most of the meaning. However, there are two types of roots. Some roots can stand alone as words. The words *wind, patient,* and *step* are used as roots in the words *unwind, impatient,* and *stepped.*

Other roots cannot stand alone as English words. This type of root is derived from words in other languages, and they no longer are words in English. Still, they can be roots. In order to form English words, they must combine with a *prefix* or *suffix*, or they must have a spelling change.

In Lesson 24, you will learn about the root *mit* (or *mis*), which means "to send." When *mit* is combined with different prefixes, it changes meaning. Notice that this root can be spelled in different ways when it appears in English.

Prefix-Meaning	Root-Meaning	Word-Meaning
dis-, away	*mis*, send	*dismiss*, to send away
e-, out	*mit*, send	*emit*, to send out

As you can see, a **prefix** attached to the beginning of a root changes the meaning.

A **suffix** is attached to the end of a root. Some suffixes change meaning. For example, in the word *odometer,* the root *odo,* meaning "distance," combines with *-meter.* Together they form the word *odometer,* which is an instrument used to measure distance. You will learn this word in Lesson 23.

Other *suffixes* simply change the part of speech of a root word. That is, they form derivatives. For example, *infiltrate* is a verb. If we add the suffix *-ation*, we get the noun *infiltration.* Some suffixes change the tense or number of a root word. If we add an *-ed* to the end of *play* we get the past tense, *played.*

If you learn how to use prefixes, roots, and suffixes as word clues, you will have very useful ways to unlock word meaning.

Practice

You can combine the use of context clues and word parts to help you figure out unknown words. Using both sets of clues, try to figure out the meaning of each word. Write the meaning of each word on the line below, then write out the word parts. Finally, look up the word in the dictionary and write the formal definition.

1. She was very *unskilled* at juggling, and she always dropped the balls.

   Prefix, root, suffix _____ _____ _____

   My definition _____

   Dictionary definition _____

2. I am *reworking* the rough draft of my essay.

   Prefix, root, suffix _____ _____ _____

   My definition _____

   Dictionary definition _____

3. The *mishandled* suitcase arrived damaged.

   Prefix, root, suffix _____ _____ _____

   My definition _____

   Dictionary definition _____

The Suffix -logy

| anthropology | archaeology | biology | criminology | geology |
| paleontology | physiology | sociology | technology | theology |

In this lesson, you will study the suffix *-logy*, which means "the study of." It comes from the ancient Greek word *logi*, or "study." *Paleontology, physiology, anthropology,* and many other subjects studied in universities end in *-logy*. *-Logy* also combines with other ancient Greek roots. For example, *bio* means "life," so *biology* is the study of living things.

1. **anthropology** (ăn´thrə-pŏl´ə-jē) *noun* from Greek *anthropos,* "human being" + *-logy,* "study of"
The study of human culture, beliefs, and physical history
• **Anthropology** has documented the many ways that different cultures mark a person's passage from childhood to adulthood.

anthropological *adjective* The **anthropological** study sheds light on how the tribe uses resources in the rain forest.

anthropologist *noun* **Anthropologist** Margaret Mead studied life in Samoa.

archaeological evidence

2. **archaeology** (är´kē-ŏl´ə-jē) *noun* from Greek *arkhaio,* "old" + *-logy,* "study of"
The study of past human life by examination of physical evidence
• **Archaeology** has revealed that humans used stone and then forged bronze to make tools.

archaeological *adjective* **Archaeological** findings confirm that the first human beings lived in Africa.

archaeologist *noun* **Archaeologists** explored the ancient tomb.

3. **biology** (bī-ŏl´ə-jē) *noun* from Greek *bio,* "life" + *-logy,* "study of"
The study of living things
• Marine **biology** is the study of plants and animals that live in the ocean.

biological *adjective* The **biological** study investigated the role of wolves in the northern forest ecosystem.

biologist *noun* The **biologist** researched carbon dioxide intake by trees.

4. **criminology** (krĭm´ə-nŏl´ə-jē) *noun* from Latin *crimin,* "accusation" + *-logy,* "study of"
The study of crime and criminals
• **Criminology** can lead to better ways of policing neighborhoods.

criminologist *noun* The **criminologist** explored the reasons behind weather-related crime trends.

5. **geology** (jē-ŏl´ə-jē) *noun* from Greek *geo,* "earth" + *-logy,* "study of"
The study of the earth's structure and physical history
• **Geology** shows that the collision of tectonic plates causes earthquakes.

geological *adjective* **Geological** studies show that there have been many ice ages.

geologist *noun* The **geologist** studied the volcanic ash.

6. **paleontology** (pā´lē-ŏn-tŏl´ə-jē) *noun* from Greek *palai,* "long ago" + *-logy,* "study of"
The study of ancient life by the examination of fossils
• The **paleontology** museum displays fossils of the archaeopteryx, believed to be the world's first bird.

paleontologist *noun* The **paleontologist** studied the dinosaur teeth.

7. **physiology** (fĭz´ē-ŏl´ə-jē) *noun* from Greek *phusis,* "nature" + *-logy,* "study of"
The study of the organs and parts of living things, and how they function
• **Physiology** has helped to explain how animals take in oxygen.

physiological *adjective* **Physiological** studies researched how plants regulate glucose.

physiologist *noun* The **physiologist** studied the long-term effects of emotional stress on strength and endurance.

Physiology is a specialty within *biology.*

8. **sociology** (sō´sē-ŏl´ə-jē) *noun* from French *socio,* "companion" + *-logy,* "study of"
The study of human social behavior
• **Sociology** shows that human beings tend to live in family groups.

sociological *adjective* **Sociological** studies show that many people define themselves mainly as members of certain groups.

sociologist *noun* The **sociologist** compared two communities.

9. **technology** (tĕk-nŏl´ə-jē) *noun* from Greek *tekhne,* "skill" + *-logy,* "study of"
The application of science to practical uses
• Developments in **technology** have given us e-mail and text messaging.

technological *adjective* **Technological** advances enable robots to assemble car parts.

10. **theology** (thē-ŏl´ə-jē) *noun* from Greek *theo,* "god" + *-logy,* "study of"
The study of religious questions
• Science, philosophy, and **theology** each try to answer the question "What is the universe, really?"

theological *adjective* Professors debated the meaning of Biblical passages and other **theological** questions.

WRITE THE CORRECT WORD

Write the correct word in the space next to each definition.

_____ 1. the study of fossils

_____ 2. the study of past human life

_____ 3. the study of human social behavior

_____ 4. the study of religious questions

_____ 5. the study of humans

_____ 6. science applied to practical uses

_____ 7. the study of the organs of a living thing

_____ 8. the study of living things

_____ 9. the study of crime

_____ 10. the study of the earth's structure

COMPLETE THE SENTENCE

Write the letter for the word that best completes each sentence.

_____ 1. Findings from _____ help us understand how plants and animals live.
   a. archaeology   **b.** anthropology   **c.** sociology   **d.** biology

_____ 2. Because of breakthroughs in _____, bookkeeping is now done by computer.
   a. technology   **b.** geology   **c.** theology   **d.** physiology

_____ 3. _____ confirm that volcanic rock can be found across the continent.
   a. Archaeologists   **b.** Biologists   **c.** Geologists   **d.** Anthropologists

_____ 4. The professor of _____ made the Bible his lifelong study.
   a. geology   **b.** physiology   **c.** theology   **d.** sociology

_____ 5. _____ enables us to understand how groups of families interact.
   a. Physiology   **b.** Sociology   **c.** Archaeology   **d.** Criminology

_____ 6. _____ understand that people around the world have many different customs.
   a. Anthropologists   **b.** Paleontologists   **c.** Physiologists   **d.** Geologists

_____ 7. A _____ would be most likely to have a theory about why the dinosaurs vanished.
   a. physiologist   **b.** paleontologist   **c.** criminologist   **d.** technologist

_____ 8. According to _____, areas with high unemployment often have high crime rates.
   a. criminologists   **b.** physiologists   **c.** geologists   **d.** archaeologists

_____ 9. The _____ of gills is similar in some ways to that of the lungs.
   a. geology   **b.** sociology   **c.** physiology   **d.** paleontology

_____ 10. _____ often study the pottery that ancient humans used.
   a. Biologists   **b.** Criminologists   **c.** Physiologists   **d.** Archaeologists

Challenge: _____ and _____ overlap because religious beliefs often affect group behavior.
_____   **a.** Archaeology…geology   **b.** Physiology…biology   **c.** Theology…sociology

Scanning for Knowledge

Would you like to see inside a mummy? Or find out what is going on inside a brain, without doing surgery? You can do these things and more with a CT scan.

Computerized Axial Tomography, better known as a CT scan or "cat scan," is solving problems in many fields. **(1)** In this *technological* breakthrough, x-rays photograph something from many angles. A computer then reconstructs data from the x-rays into three-dimensional images. This means that the inside of an object (or person) can be studied without cutting into it.

In the past, brain surgery was needed to diagnose certain medical conditions. **(2)** Now, CT scans provide images that help us understand problems in brain *physiology*. The areas involved in epileptic seizures, for example, can be precisely pinpointed. **(3)** This tool has also advanced veterinary care and *biology* in similar ways.

(4) CT scans are also useful in *paleontology*. In one case, scientists scanned the fossilized ribs of a duck-billed dinosaur to make a complete image of a bite that it had received. The scan showed that the bite had come from a tyrannosaurus. From this, scientists determined that the tyrannosaurus actually attacked other animals rather than just eating dead animals that it found.

(5) Scans also provide information in *anthropology,* helping to establish relationships among different groups of humans. Ancient human skulls can be scanned without damaging them. Their measurements can shed light on how closely groups of people are related to modern people. This helps us understand the history of human migration.

(6) CT scans can help *archaeologists,* too. Ancient mummies harbor many important secrets, but archaeologists generally do not want to unwrap them. Recently, scientists scanned a 3,000-year-old Egyptian mummy. The results showed a face with a mole on the left side. Such scans can also tell us about the diseases that these ancient people suffered.

Of course, there are other sources of information about ancient Egypt. **(7)** The books and paintings found in Egyptian tombs provide windows into that great society's *theology.* **(8)** Clues found in archaeological digs can help us understand the *sociology* of ancient Egypt, including the various professions and social classes that existed. Now, with CT scans, we can further fill in our picture of who the ancient Egyptians really were.

(9) CT scans even help modern *geologists* by revealing holes inside rock. This sheds light on how liquids flow and how fracturing takes place. Such knowledge can be used to locate water in dry areas. Scans can also lead people to diamonds and other precious stones.

Finally, CT scans don't just help us study natural or ancient things. **(10)** *Criminologists* and homeland security officials have outlined the need for CT scanners that examine the contents of the countless trucks and shipping containers that come into our country every day. These huge new CT scanners might one day save lives.

Each sentence below refers to a numbered sentence in the passage. Write the letter of the choice that gives the sentence a meaning that is closest to the original sentence.

_____ **1.** In this _____ breakthrough, x-rays photograph something from many angles.
    a. complicated   **b.** science-based   **c.** religion-based   **d.** expensive

_____ **2.** CT scans provide images that help us understand problems in brain _____.
    a. function   **b.** weight   **c.** intelligence   **d.** roots

_____ **3.** This tool has advanced veterinary care and _____ in similar ways.
    a. the study of rocks   **b.** tomb building   **c.** crime fighting   **d.** the study of life

_____ **4.** CT scans are also useful in _____.
    a. insect study   **b.** muscle building   **c.** house building   **d.** fossil study

_____   5. Scans also provide information in _____.
      a. religious studies   **b.** crime studies   **c.** study of humans   **d.** study of dinosaurs

_____   6. CT scans can help _____, too.
      a. mummies   **b.** people who steal   **c.** fossils   **d.** people studying the ancients

_____   7. Books and paintings found in Egyptian tombs provide windows into that great society's _____.
      a. religious beliefs   **b.** living things   **c.** sports events   **d.** marriage customs

_____   8. Clues found in archaeological digs can help us understand the _____ of ancient Egyptians.
      a. rock formations   **b.** social interactions   **c.** strategic plans   **d.** crime evidence

_____   9. CT scans even help modern _____ by revealing holes inside rock.
      a. practical uses   **b.** choir singers   **c.** needy farmers   **d.** people studying Earth

_____   10. _____ have outlined the need for CT scanners that examine shipping containers.
      a. Fossil experts   **b.** Crime experts   **c.** Religion experts   **d.** Volcano experts

Indicate whether the statements below are TRUE or FALSE according to the passage.

_____   1. Computerized Axial Tomography is used in many fields.

_____   2. One must cut through a body when making at CT scan.

_____   3. We can learn about the health of ancient people from 3,000-year-old remains.

FINISH THE THOUGHT

Complete each sentence so that it shows the meaning of the italicized word.

1. New *technology* has enabled us to _____

_____

2. The *archaeologist* _____

_____

WRITE THE DERIVATIVE

Complete the sentence by writing the correct form of the word shown in parentheses. You may not need to change the form that is given.

_____   1. Digging in Israel, _____ found artifacts more than 5,000 years old. *(archaeology)*

_____   2. _____ findings show that humans form many types of groups. *(sociology)*

_____ 3. The _____ had a theory about why the suspect always robbed men in their forties. (*criminology*)

_____ 4. A sports _____ could tell you many ways to improve your game. (*physiology*)

_____ 5. Truly, satellite communication is a _____ marvel. (*technology*)

_____ 6. The Koran outlines many Muslim _____ practices. (*theology*)

_____ 7. _____ often search for months before finding fossils. (*paleontology*)

_____ 8. Rocks can be divided into different _____ categories. (*geology*)

_____ 9. The _____ lived in the rain forest, with members of native clans. (*anthropology*)

_____ 10. Some _____ study the effects of heredity on disease. (*biology*)

FIND THE EXAMPLE

Choose the answer that best describes the action or situation.

_____ 1. An object most likely to be studied by a *paleontologist*
   a. a twig   **b.** space   **c.** hair   **d.** a fossil

_____ 2. An organization that employs many *criminologists*
   a. chess club   **b.** motorcycle club   **c.** FBI   **d.** elementary school

_____ 3. Something an *anthropologist* would do
   a. cat-scan a cat   **b.** study rock layers   **c.** measure pulses   **d.** study a culture

_____ 4. A likely area of expertise for a *geologist*
   a. mineral deposits   **b.** mental health   **c.** rain clouds   **d.** religions

_____ 5. Possible subject of a *biological* study
   a. bald eagle   **b.** the Bible   **c.** lava   **d.** government

_____ 6. Something that might be studied by a *sociologist*
   a. bacteria   **b.** sports riots   **c.** yogurt   **d.** ancient tombs

_____ 7. What might be found in an *archaeological* expedition
   a. a new moon   **b.** a skeleton   **c.** a blood vessel   **d.** a spreading attitude

_____ 8. Subjects studied in *physiology*
   a. Greeks and Romans   **b.** soil and sky   **c.** brain and liver   **d.** media and crime

_____ 9. A comparison that might be made in a *theology* class
   a. Bible and Koran   **b.** TV and shopping   **c.** liver and kidneys   **d.** winter and spring

_____ 10. An example of recent *technology*
   a. wheel   **b.** cell-phone camera   **c.** hot-air balloon   **d.** spear

The Suffix -meter

WORD LIST

altimeter	barometer	diameter	geometry	kilometer
metric	metronome	micrometer	odometer	perimeter

This lesson presents the suffix *-meter*, which means "measure." It is taken from the ancient Greek word *metron*. The common word *thermometer* is formed from the root *therm* (Greek for "heat") and *-meter*. Many English words are formed from *-meter*, and more are being invented, especially for use in science.

1. altimeter (ăl-tĭm´ĭ-tər) *noun* from Latin *altus*, "high" + *-meter*, "measure"
An instrument that measures altitude, or height above a certain point
• The **altimeter** showed that the plane was flying at 30,000 feet.

> *Altimeters* usually measure the distance above sea level, not above the ground.

2. barometer (bə-rŏm´ĭ-tər) *noun* from Greek *baros*, "weight" + *-meter*, "measure"
a. An instrument, useful for predicting weather, that meaures atmospheric pressure
• If the **barometer** falls sharply, a storm is probably on the way.
b. Something that registers or shows changes; an indicator
• The stock market is one **barometer** of economic health.

barometric *adjective* **Barometric** pressure often changes as new weather moves in.

3. diameter (dī-ăm´ĭ-tər) *noun* from Greek *dia*, "through" + *-meter*, "measure"
A line through the exact center of a figure, usually a circle or sphere
• The **diameter** of the earth measures almost 8,000 miles.

4. geometry (jē-ŏm´ĭ-trē) *noun* from Greek *geo*, "earth" + *-meter*, "measure"
The branch of mathematics dealing with points, lines, angles, and shapes
• Mario learned how to find the area of a circle in **geometry** class.

> The *geo-* in *geometry* reminds us that *geometry* deals with measuring the different kinds of shapes found on Earth.

geometric *adjective* **Geometric** knowledge is needed both to design a spaceship and to plot a course for the moon.

5. kilometer (kĭ-lŏm´ĭ-tər, kĭl´ə-mē´-tər) *noun* from Greek *kilo*, "thousand" + *-meter*, "measure"
A unit of length equal to 1,000 meters, or about 0.62 miles
• In most of the world, road signs give distances in **kilometers**.

6. metric (mĕt´rĭk) *adjective* from Greek *metron*, "measure"
Referring to the international metric system of measurement
• Grams, milliliters, and centimeters are **metric** units of measurement.

7. **metronome** (mĕt´rə-nōm´) *noun* from Greek *metron*, "measure" + *nomos*, "division" or "rule"
   An instrument that marks time, with ticks or flashes at regular adjustable intervals
   • The **metronome** helped the violin student play in rhythm.

8. **micrometer** *noun* from Greek *micro*, "small" + *-meter*, "measure"
   a. (mī-krŏm´ĭ-tər) An instrument that measures very small distances, objects, or angles
   • The **micrometer** measured the thickness of the metal's plastic coating.
   b. (mī´krō-mē´tər) A unit of length equal to one thousandth of a millimeter, or one millionth of a meter
   • A plant's cell walls measure a few **micrometers** across.

9. **odometer** (ō-dŏm´ĭ-tər) *noun* from Greek *hodos*, "journey" + *-meter*, "measure"
   An instrument that indicates distance traveled by a vehicle
   • The car's **odometer** showed that we had traveled sixty-five miles.

10. **perimeter** (pə-rĭm´ĭ-tər) *noun* from Greek *peri*, "around" + *-meter*, "measure"
    The outer boundary of a shape or an object, or the distance around that boundary
    • To find the length of the **perimeter** of the tabletop, Kian measured all the sides and then added those measurements.

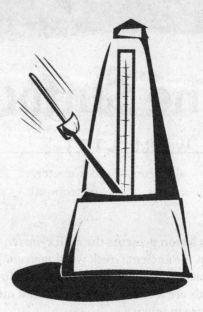

metronome

WORD ENRICHMENT

Big and small

Micro-, a prefix meaning "small," is found in more than one hundred English words. Examples are *micrometer* (a word in this lesson), *microorganism* (a very small living thing), *microfilament* (tiny fibers in cells), and *microsecond* (one millionth of a second), as well as more familiar words like *microwave* and *microscope*. New words using *micro-* are constantly being invented. *Microfiber*, material woven so finely that rain cannot get through it, was first used in 1966.

Macro-, a prefix meaning "big," is the opposite of *micro-*. *Macrofossils* are fossils big enough to be seen without a microscope; *microfossils* may be as small as a single cell. *Macroclimates* refer to weather conditions in a large country or land area. In contrast, a museum might need to create a *microclimate* to make sure that a single valuable object is preserved at the right temperature and humidity.

Strangely enough, *micro-* is found in a very long word that refers to a lung disease. It is *pneumonoultramicroscopicsilicovolcanokoniosis*. The word was deliberately created to be the longest one in English.

WRITE THE CORRECT WORD

Write the correct word in the space next to each definition.

_____ 1. device that measures distance traveled

_____ 2. device that measures height

_____ 3. device that measures very small things

_____ 4. the line or distance across the center

_____ 5. study of points, angles, and shapes

_____ 6. an outer boundary

_____ 7. referring to a measurement system

_____ 8. device that measures atmospheric pressure

_____ 9. 1,000 meters

_____ 10. device marking time, with regular beats

COMPLETE THE SENTENCE

Write the letter for the word that best completes each sentence.

_____ 1. According to the _____, atmospheric pressure was increasing.
a. kilometer   b. barometer   c. perimeter   d. altimeter

_____ 2. She planted flowers along the _____ of the property.
a. micrometer   b. odometer   c. metric   d. perimeter

_____ 3. Since the car's _____ was broken, we didn't know how far we had traveled.
a. odometer   b. diameter   c. kilometer   d. altimeter

_____ 4. Liters are part of the _____ system.
a. kilometer   b. metric   c. altimeter   d. barometer

_____ 5. In _____, we learn to calculate the areas of triangles and squares.
a. perimeter   b. diameter   c. odometer   d. geometry

_____ 6. The metric unit of distance that is closest in length to a mile is a _____.
a. kilometer   b. perimeter   c. diameter   d. micrometer

_____ 7. A(n) _____ divides a circle into two halves.
a. diameter   b. micrometer   c. perimeter   d. altimeter

_____ 8. The _____ showed the blimp's height above sea level.
a. metronome   b. micrometer   c. altimeter   d. barometer

_____ 9. The tiny object was only two _____ long.
a. metronomes   b. perimeters   c. micrometers   d. altimeters

_____ 10. The piano teacher adjusted the _____ so that his student would play faster.
a. diameter   b. metronome   c. barometer   d. geometry

Challenge: She used the car's _____ to measure the _____ of the racetrack.
_____ a. altimeter…geometry   b. barometer…diameter   c. odometer…perimeter

Measurements, Old and New

A thousand years ago, many measurements were based on the human body. A foot was the length of a man's foot; a yard was the distance around a man's waist. The yard was officially changed in the 1100s when King Henry I of England declared it to be the distance from a man's nose to his outstretched hand. Because people were different sizes, the lengths of feet and yards varied greatly. Now, these customary English measurements have been standardized. However, even today, converting from one of these units to another involves using numbers that can be difficult to multiply or divide, like 12 (inches per foot), 3 (feet per yard), or 5,280 (feet per mile).

(1) It is not surprising, then, that European scientists welcomed the *metric* system when it was introduced about 200 years ago. This system is based on multiples of 10, such as 100 and 1,000. **(2)** If you want to know the number of meters in a *kilometer,* just add three zeros to the number of kilometers! **(3)** Scientists have expanded the metric system by adding measurements like *micrometers.*

Other ways to calculate measurements have been unchanged for thousands of years. **(4)** About 2,500 years ago, the ancient Greeks developed *geometric* proofs now taught in schools. **(5)** For example, they figured out the formula for the *perimeter* of a circle. **(6)** Once you know the formula, to calculate the perimeter you need only know the *diameter.*

(7) Vitruvius, a Roman architect and engineer, may have invented the first *odometer* around 15 BC. Like the modern instrument, it included a wheel of known size, and it kept track of how many times the wheel turned. From this, the distance traveled could be calculated. Odometers can be used with wagons, carriages, cars, and trains, but they cannot be used with vehicles that don't have wheels, like airplanes and boats.

Although air is very light, there is a lot of it. As a matter of fact, at sea level, the weight of the atmosphere puts roughly 14.7 pounds of pressure on every square inch of exposed surface! But air pressure, like the weather, changes from minute to minute. **(8)** First invented in the 1600s, *barometers* measure these changes using a column of mercury in a tube. If the air pressure is rising, the mercury is pushed upward in the tube, and the weather is likely to be stable. Falling pressure can mean storms.

(9) An *altimeter* is a special type of barometer. It can tell an airplane's height above sea level by measuring atmospheric pressure. Hikers on mountain trips often use altimeters, too.

(10) Before electricity, *metronomes* relied on pendulums that would swing at a fairly constant pace for a while but then slow down. Today, electric metronomes keep a constant tempo.

Scientists continue to invent new measuring devices. Engineers use strain gauges that measure the slightest movements of metals. Some cars use lasers to gauge distances to obstacles or other cars. The future will almost certainly bring more new tools for measuring our world.

barometer

Each sentence below refers to a numbered sentence in the passage. Write the letter of the choice that gives the sentence a meaning that is closest to the original sentence.

_____ **1.** European scientists welcomed the _____ system when it was introduced.
    a. time-measurement   **b.** circle-measurement   **c.** base-10 measurement   **d.** shape-related

_____ **2.** If you want to know the number of meters in _____, just add three zeros.
    a. 1,000 meters   **b.** a mile   **c.** an elevation   **d.** a measurement

_____ **3.** Scientists have expanded the metric system by adding measurements like _____.
    a. grams   **b.** hundredth-meters   **c.** millionth-meters   **d.** feet

_____ **4.** The ancient Greeks developed _____ proofs now taught in schools.
  a. distance-related   **b.** pressurized   **c.** modern   **d.** shape-related

_____ **5.** They figured out the formula for the _____ a circle.
  a. pressure of   **b.** distance around   **c.** distance across   **d.** shape of

_____ **6.** To calculate the perimeter you need only know the _____.
  a. boundary   **b.** distance across   **c.** distance under   **d.** shape

_____ **7.** Vitruvius may have invented the first _____ around 15 BC.
  a. height measurer   **b.** pressure gauge   **c.** timekeeper   **d.** distance measurer

_____ **8.** _____ measure these changes using a column of mercury in a tube.
  a. Pressure measurers   **b.** Rhythm meters   **c.** Kilometers   **d.** Micrometers

_____ **9.** A(n) _____ is a special type of barometer.
  a. time marker   **b.** distance checker   **c.** height measurer   **d.** odor meter

_____ **10.** Before electricity, _____ relied on pendulums.
  a. clockmakers   **b.** musicians   **c.** promise keepers   **d.** rhythm keepers

Indicate whether the statements below are TRUE or FALSE according to the passage.

_____ **1.** In the past, a foot could have been eleven inches long or thirteen inches long.

_____ **2.** The weight of the air pushes on everything it touches.

_____ **3.** *Altimeters* are useful on boats, but not on airplanes.

WRITING EXTENDED RESPONSES

Imagine that you are about to climb a mountain. Describe some
measuring devices that might be useful to you and why. You might use
them before your trip or during your trip. Write at least three paragraphs,
and refer to two or more measuring instruments. Use at least three lesson
words in your response and underline them.

WRITE THE DERIVATIVE

Complete the sentence by writing the correct form of the word shown in
parentheses. You may not need to change the form that is given.

_____ **1.** In the _____ system, 1,000 meters is one kilometer. *(metric)*

_____ **2.** New automobile _____ allow us to measure the distances of two different trips.
  (odometer)

_____ **3.** The quilt was decorated with _____ designs. *(geometry)*

_____ **4.** How many _____ is it from Montreal to Vancouver? *(kilometer)*

_____ **5.** The _____ of a square with an area of one square inch is four inches.
  (perimeter)

_____ 6. Some musicians and dancers seem to have built-in _____. (metronome)

_____ 7. The fall in _____ pressure suggested that bad weather was coming. (barometer)

_____ 8. A _____ can measure the width of a single hair. (micrometer)

_____ 9. The _____ indicated that the plane was falling. (altimeter)

_____ 10. A circle has an infinite number of _____ that are all the same length. (diameter)

FIND THE EXAMPLE

Choose the answer that best describes the action or situation.

_____ 1. An activity that would probably be part of a *geometry* lesson
   a. measuring time **b.** measuring pressure **c.** measuring heat **d.** measuring angles

_____ 2. A distance best expressed in *kilometers*
   a. London to Paris **b.** hand to elbow **c.** kitchen to den **d.** goalpost to goalpost

_____ 3. A measurement that is part of the *metric* system
   a. inches **b.** feet **c.** meters **d.** yards

_____ 4. Something you might measure in *micrometers*
   a. a house **b.** the point of a pin **c.** a highway **d.** your foot

_____ 5. An activity for which a *barometer* would be useful
   a. eating **b.** watching TV **c.** sailing **d.** indoor soccer

_____ 6. A type of business for which *odometers* might be important
   a. taxi company **b.** airline company **c.** shipping company **d.** TV news show

_____ 7. Something used to mark the *perimeter* of a piece of property
   a. a flower **b.** a friendly dog **c.** a foghorn **d.** a fence

_____ 8. Something that has a *diameter*
   a. a box **b.** a shelf **c.** a computer **d.** a ball

_____ 9. A person who would most likely use an *altimeter*
   a. a sea captain **b.** a trucker **c.** a surgeon **d.** a parachutist

_____ 10. A situation in which a *metronome* would be most useful
   a. hiking trip **b.** band practice **c.** rocket launch **d.** geometry class

The Root -mis- or -mit-

WORD LIST

dismiss	emissary	emit	intermittent	missile
mission	missive	omit	submit	transmit

The root *-mis-* or *-mit-* comes from the Latin verb *mittere*, which means "to send." As you can see, the spelling of this root varies in different English words. The words in this lesson all have something to do with sending. The words *dismiss, emit, intermittent,* and *omit* are formed when a prefix is added to the root. Other words, like *mission, missile,* and *missive,* come from the root *-mis-* with a suffix added. This lesson adds useful words to your vocabulary and increases your understanding of how roots, prefixes, and suffixes work together to create meaning.

1. **dismiss** (dĭs-mĭs´) *verb* from Latin *dis-*, "away" or "apart" + *mis*, "send"
   a. To send away or allow to leave
      • The students filled the hall after the teacher **dismissed** the class.
   b. To reject or stop considering
      • With a roll of her eyes, Deborah **dismissed** her mother's suggestion to take an umbrella.

   dismissal *noun* Mr. Jones was relieved at the **dismissal** of the lawsuit.

   dismissive *adjective* The senator's **dismissive** attitude showed that she didn't believe the reports.

2. **emissary** (ĕm´ĭ-sĕr´ē) *noun* from Latin *e-*, "out" + *mis*, "send"
   A person sent to another country or place on official business; representative
   • The doge of Venice sent an **emissary** to set up trade agreements with China.

3. **emit** (ĭ-mĭt´) *verb* from Latin *e-*, "out" + *mit*, "send"
   To send out energy or matter
   • The scientists were concerned that the machine might **emit** harmful radiation.

   emission *noun* The government regulates some tailpipe and power-plant **emissions**.

> Energy *emitted* can include light, heat, other radiation, and sound. Matter can include substances and smells.

emit

4. **intermittent** (ĭn´tər-mĭt´nt) *adjective* from Latin *inter-*, "between" + *mit*, "send"
Stopping and starting; not continuous; periodic
• The forecast was for a cloudy day with **intermittent** showers.

5. **missile** (mĭs´əl) *noun* from *mis*, "send" or "throw"
An object or a weapon sent to a target
• The **missile** was guided by radio waves.

6. **mission** (mĭsh´ən) *noun* from *mis*, "send"
   a. A special duty or assignment given to a person or group
      • His **mission** was to gather information about illegal rhino hunters.
   b. A group of people sent to a foreign country to do diplomatic, educational, or religious work; the building where the group operates
      • California is dotted with Catholic **missions.**

> The word *missionary* usually refers to people who travel abroad to spread their own religion.

7. **missive** (mĭs´ĭv) *noun* from *mis*, "send"
A letter or written communication
• He typed and then e-mailed his **missive** to the editor of the local paper.

8. **omit** (ō-mĭt´) *verb* from Latin *ob-*, "against" or "away" + *mit*, "send"
To leave out; to pass over or not include
• We **omit** periods when we shorten the names of states in mailing addresses.

   omission *noun* The **omission** of one letter from a word can change the meaning of a whole sentence.

9. **submit** (səb-mĭt´) *verb* from Latin *sub-*, "under" + *mit*, "send"
   a. To present a plan or proposal for approval
      • The architect **submitted** plans for a new city hall.
   b. To obey; to allow one's self to be controlled by another person
      • The sailor **submitted** to the captain's orders and cleaned the deck.

   submission *noun* My **submission** to the science fair won Honorable Mention.

> When we *submit* something, we put it "under" someone's consideration. When we *submit* to orders, we are "under" someone's authority.

10. **transmit** (trăns-mĭt´) *verb* from Latin *trans-*, "across" + *mit*, "send"
To send from one person, place, or thing to another
• Insect bites sometimes **transmit** disease.

   transmission *noun* The first **transmission** of a TV commercial took place in 1951.

WORD ENRICHMENT

Omitted words

Our dictionaries are becoming bigger and bigger as more words are added to the English language. But at times, dictionaries also *omit* words that are no longer used. (We say these words have become *obsolete.*) Words *omitted* from English dictionaries include

Shreed — "to clothe or cover," as in "We were *shreed* in battle clothes."
Leuch — "laughed," as in "She smiled and *leuch.*"
Yuly — "beautiful," as in "A woman most *yuly.*"

NAME _____ DATE _____

WRITE THE CORRECT WORD

Write the correct word in the space next to each definition.

_____ 1. not continuous

_____ 2. to send

_____ 3. to reject

_____ 4. a weapon sent to a target

_____ 5. to present for approval

_____ 6. a special assignment

_____ 7. a person sent on an official mission

_____ 8. to give off; to send out

_____ 9. to leave out

_____ 10. a written communication

COMPLETE THE SENTENCE

Write the letter for the word that best completes each sentence.

_____ 1. The diplomat went on a(n) _____ to make peace between the two countries.
   a. missive   b. missile   c. emission   d. mission

_____ 2. The _____ sounds made us think that something was following us.
   a. dismissed   b. submitted   c. intermittent   d. omitted

_____ 3. Does that tower _____ AM or FM radio waves?
   a. transmit   b. omit   c. dismiss   d. submit

_____ 4. When you told me you were locked out, you conveniently _____ the fact that you'd lost the key.
   a. omitted   b. transmitted   c. emitted   d. submitted

_____ 5. "That was quite a(n) _____," said the teacher, while returning the student's letter.
   a. missile   b. missive   c. mission   d. emissary

_____ 6. When fossil fuels such as oil and coal are burned, they _____ gases that trap the sun's heat in the earth's atmosphere.
   a. omit   b. emit   c. submit   d. dismiss

_____ 7. The president often sends the vice president as a(n) _____ to other countries.
   a. dismissal   b. missile   c. omission   d. emissary

_____ 8. "I will penalize papers that are not _____ on time," said the teacher.
   a. emitted   b. submitted   c. dismissed   d. omitted

_____ 9. Don't _____ something just because you have never thought of it before.
   a. submit   b. transmit   c. dismiss   d. emit

_____ 10. In June of 1944, Germany launched the first rocket-powered _____ to be used in a war.
   a. missive   b. emissary   c. submission   d. missile

Challenge: The concerned doctors authored a _____ about the dangers of mercury _____.
_____
   a. missile…transmissions   b. missive…emissions   c. transmission…submissions

An Important Voyage

Our world is barely a tiny dot in an unimaginably huge universe. What would we find if we traveled across our solar system and beyond? **(1)** The twin Voyager 1 and Voyager 2 spacecraft are on a *mission* to answer this complex and fascinating question.

Voyager 1 and Voyager 2 were launched in 1977. They used rocket power to blast off, and they accelerated with the help of gravity from several planets along the way. The Voyagers have now traveled far enough across the solar system to explore its most distant planets. **(2)** Though instrument failures have resulted in the *omission* of certain data that researchers had hoped to get, the mission's overall record of discovery is remarkable.

Both Voyagers have studied Jupiter and Saturn, along with their moons. **(3)** Voyager 2 did the same for Uranus and Neptune, *transmitting* dramatic photographs back to Earth. Voyager 1 even discovered raging volcanoes on Io, a moon of Jupiter. **(4)** *Intermittent* eruptions on Io blast to more than 180 miles above its surface! Of interest to scientists who wonder about the possibility of life beyond the earth, Jupiter's moon Europa was shown to be covered with a layer of ice that might be a thin skin atop a liquid ocean. **(5)** Altogether, the ships *submitted* new evidence of more than twenty moons and other large bodies.

Perhaps most incredibly, both Voyagers are now whizzing through the cold, dark space at the very edge of our solar system. **(6)** There, they meet radiation *emitted* from the sun and from other sources across the galaxy.

(7) Though it's a bit like hoping a message in a tiny bottle is found by a ship sailing a very large ocean, scientists cannot entirely *dismiss* the possibility that one or both of the Voyagers will be found by intelligent life. **(8)** Just in case this happens, the ships were designed to be our first *emissaries* to other worlds. **(9)** They carry *missives* about us and about our planet, written in fifty-five languages. They also have music, including Beethoven compositions and Chuck Berry tunes. **(10)** Scientists think that intelligent beings would be unlikely to mistake a Voyager for some kind of *missile* or other weapon.

A tremendous amount of thought and effort has gone into the journey of the Voyagers. We wish them well as they journey into the uncharted space beyond our solar stem.

Each sentence below refers to a numbered sentence in the passage. Write the letter of the choice that gives the sentence a meaning that is closest to the original sentence.

_____ **1.** The twin Voyager 1 and Voyager 2 spacecraft are on a(n) _____ to answer this question.
     a. target   **b.** transistor   **c.** assignment   **d.** communication

_____ **2.** Instrument failures have resulted in the _____ of certain data.
     a. destruction   **b.** approval   **c.** sending out   **d.** leaving out

_____ **3.** Voyager 2 did the same for Uranus and Neptune, _____ dramatic photographs back to Earth.
     a. expelling   **b.** sending   **c.** leaving out   **d.** rejecting

_____ **4.** _____ eruptions on Io blast to more than 180 miles above its surface!
     a. Dangerous   **b.** Continuous   **c.** Periodic   **d.** Radioactive

_____ **5.** Altogether, the ships _____ evidence of more than twenty moons and other large bodies.
     a. presented   **b.** rejected   **c.** left out   **d.** absorbed

_____ **6.** There, they meet radiation _____ the sun and other sources.
   a. given off by   **b.** rejected by   **c.** ignored by   **d.** taken by

_____ **7.** Scientists cannot entirely _____ the possibility that one or both of the Voyagers will be found by intelligent life.
   a. send by radio   **b.** like or believe   **c.** turn in or give   **d.** reject or ignore

_____ **8.** The ships were designed to be our first _____ to other worlds.
   a. warnings   **b.** representatives   **c.** weapons   **d.** radio signals

_____ **9.** They carry _____ about us and about our planet.
   a. computers   **b.** writings   **c.** weapons   **d.** assignments

_____ **10.** Scientists think that intelligent beings would be unlikely to mistake a Voyager for some kind of _____.
   a. important task   **b.** radio signal   **c.** flying weapon   **d.** written communication

Indicate whether the statements below are TRUE or FALSE according to the passage.

_____ **1.** Only Voyager I made it to Jupiter and Saturn.

_____ **2.** Voyager I discovered volcanoes on one of Jupiter's moons and ice on another.

_____ **3.** The people who planned the Voyager mission thought that music was an important part of what it means to be human.

FINISH THE THOUGHT

Complete each sentence so that it shows the meaning of the italicized word.

1. We *dismissed* his advice because _____

_____

2. The *emissary* _____

_____

WRITE THE DERIVATIVE

Complete the sentence by writing the correct form of the word shown in parentheses. You may not need to change the form that is given.

_____ **1.** The hurricane warnings resulted in early _____ from school. (*dismiss*)

_____ **2.** Interference from the buildings made the _____ weak. (*transmit*)

_____ **3.** Apparently willing to do just about anything to make his point, the columnist was guilty of one key _____ after another. (*omit*)

_____ **4.** Though dangerous secret _____ make for good movies, much of the real work of the CIA is done in offices and libraries. (*mission*)

_____ 5. Simple kinds of _____ have been used in wartime for thousands of years. (*missile*)

_____ 6. "Please limit your _____ to the assigned work," grumbled the teacher as he caught Jesse passing a note to Pat. (*missive*)

_____ 7. Many governments sent _____ to the national celebration. (*emissary*)

_____ 8. The letter said, "We regret to inform you that we cannot accept late _____." (*submit*)

_____ 9. Toxic _____ are now affecting people around the world. (*emit*)

_____ 10. Her good moods were as _____ as starlight in a sky studded with clouds. (*intermittent*)

FIND THE EXAMPLE

Choose the answer that best describes the action or situation.

_____ 1. A type of suggestion most likely to be *dismissed*
     a. helpful   **b.** foolish   **c.** practical   **d.** whispered

_____ 2. Something often *submitted*
     a. a competitor   **b.** a judge   **c.** an entry   **d.** a prize

_____ 3. Something likely to be a charity's *mission*
     a. selling junk food   **b.** causing violence   **c.** eating buffalo   **d.** feeding the hungry

_____ 4. Something *emitted*
     a. diplomats   **b.** apples   **c.** light   **d.** newspapers

_____ 5. Something that is *intermittent*
     a. a foghorn   **b.** time   **c.** an ocean   **d.** Jupiter

_____ 6. One function of *missiles*
     a. to teach   **b.** to destroy   **c.** to feed   **d.** to clean

_____ 7. What an *emissary* might do
     a. swim for a living   **b.** run a country   **c.** make sandwiches   **d.** deliver a message

_____ 8. The best way to make sure you don't *omit* key parts of your speech
     a. whisper   **b.** smile   **c.** rehearse   **d.** scream

_____ 9. An example of a *missive*
     a. a line graph   **b.** a painting   **c.** a letter   **d.** a tape recording

_____ 10. Something *submitted*
     a. a proposal   **b.** a religious center   **c.** a star   **d.** a smell

Prefixes, Roots, and Suffixes

The Prefixes *non-* and *un-*

The prefix *non-* comes from the Latin word *non,* meaning "not." The prefix *un-* comes from Old English. Both of the prefixes *non-* and *un-* mean "not" when they are attached to a word. They usually attach to words that can be used independently in English. You will see these prefixes in hundreds of words.

Prefix-Meaning	Root/Base Word	Word-Meaning
non-, not	fiction	*nonfiction,* not fiction
non-, not	member	*nonmember,* not a member
un-, not	true	*untrue,* not true
un-, not	avoidable	*unavoidable,* not avoidable

Below are some clues to words you can make using *non-* or *un-*. Fill in the blanks with a new word containing one of these prefixes.

1. The prefix *un-* can be added to *believable;* something that is *not believable*

   is _____.

2. The prefix *non-* can be added to *essential;* something that is *not essential*

   is _____.

3. The prefix *un-* can be added to *wanted;* something that is *not wanted*

   is _____.

4. The prefix *non-* can be added to *verbal;* someone who is *not verbal*

   is _____.

5. The prefix *un-* can be added to *comfortable;* someone who is *not comfortable*

   is _____.

Practice

You can combine context clues with your knowledge of these prefixes to make intelligent guesses about the meanings of words. All of the sentences below contain a word formed with *un-* or *non-*. Read the sentences and write down what you think the word in italics means. Then look up the word in the dictionary and write the formal definition.

1. Unfortunately, her suggestions were pure *nonsense,* so we couldn't use them.

   My definition _____

   Dictionary definition _____

2. In the mountains, the winds are often *unpredictable.*

   My definition _____

   Dictionary definition _____

3. The *unmanned* spacecraft was controlled from Earth.

My definition _____

Dictionary definition _____

4. The *nonstandard* replacement part was extremely difficult to find.

My definition _____

Dictionary definition _____

5. Ella, Connor, and I all live here, but Jesse is a *nonresident*.

My definition _____

Dictionary definition _____

6. It was *unfortunate* that she missed the best game of the season.

My definition _____

Dictionary definition _____

At times, *non-* and *un-* are added to roots that do not stand alone as words. (We call these *combining roots*.) The Latin word *calere* used to mean "to be warmed, to be heated up." Today, this word root means "to be concerned." The word *nonchalant* is formed from *non-* + *calere*. It means "*not bothered* by something."

Review of Word Elements

Reviewing word elements helps you remember them and use them when you are reading. Below, write the meaning of the word elements that you have studied. Each one appears italicized in a word.

Word	Word Element	Type of Element	Meaning of Word Element
*non*stop	*non-*	prefix	_____
psych*ology*	*-ology*	suffix	_____
inter*mit*tent	*mit*	root	_____
odo*meter*	*-meter*	suffix	_____
*un*known	*un-*	prefix	_____

The Roots -vid- and -vis-

WORD LIST

improvise	revision	video	viewpoint	visa
visible	visionary	visor	vista	visualize

This lesson presents a word root meaning "see." It comes from the Latin verb *videre*, meaning "to see." In English, this root is usually spelled *-vis-*, *-vid-*, or *-vi-*. Perhaps the most common English words from this root are *view* and *vision*. To get the most out of this lesson, think about how seeing is related to each word. At times, these words deal with things we see using our eyes. At other times, they deal with things we "see" with our minds.

1. **improvise** (ĭm´prə-vīz´) *verb* from Latin *im-*, "not" + *pro-*, "before" + *vis*, "see"
   a. To invent and perform without preparation
   • Many comedians can **improvise** funny lines at a moment's notice.
   b. To make quickly with whatever is available
   • I **improvised** a raincoat by throwing a plastic tablecloth over my head.

   improvisation *noun* The tree house was an **improvisation,** built on the spur of the moment.

> *Improvise* is built from three word elements. It means "not seen before," or "not foreseen."

2. **revision** (rĭ-vĭzh´ən) *noun* from Latin *re-*, "again" + *vis*, "see"
   A corrected or improved version
   • The textbook **revision** included new pictures and a new design.

   revise *verb* Chen **revised** the first draft of his report.

> *Revisions* often refer to written work, such as books, papers, and computer programs.

video camera

3. **video** (vĭd´ē-ō´) from *vid*, "see"
   a. *noun* A videocassette or videotape
   • **Videos** make it possible for people to see movies at home.
   b. *adjective* Referring to electronically produced visual images, such as televised ones
   • Charlie brought a **video** game to play with Ed.

4. **viewpoint** (vyoo´point´) *noun* from *vis*, "see" + English *point*
   A way of looking at or considering something; an opinion
   • From a parent's **viewpoint**, a child's safety is the most important thing.

5. **visa** (vē´zə) *noun* from *vis*, "see"
An official document that allows a foreign person to enter a country
• It took me months to get a **visa** to visit Vietnam.

6. **visible** (vĭz´ə-bəl) *adjective* from *vis*, "see"
Able to be seen
• The planet Venus is **visible** without a telescope.

visibility *noun* **Visibility** was so bad that they could not see the road.

7. **visionary** (vĭzh´ə-nĕr´ē) from *vis*, "see"
   a. *adjective* Able to imagine the future; having foresight
   • The Wright Brothers were **visionary** engineers who developed the airplane.
   b. *noun* Someone who is able to imagine the future
   • Martin Luther King, Jr., was a **visionary** who believed Americans of all backgrounds were entitled to equal opportunities.

8. **visor** (vī´zər) *noun* from *vis*, "see"
A shade or shield on a helmet or cap, to protect the eyes, nose, or forehead
• The baseball cap's **visor** had stars printed on it.

9. **vista** (vĭs´tə) *noun* from *vis*, "see"
A long, far-reaching view
• The west window provided a broad **vista** of ocean and mountains.

10. **visualize** (vĭzh´ōō-ə-līz´) *verb* from *vis*, "see"
To form a mental picture
• Coaches often encourage athletes to **visualize** the plays and moves they will make while competing.

visualization *noun* **Visualization** of a peaceful place can help you relax.

> Cars also have *visors* that can be pulled down to block the sun.

WORD ENRICHMENT

Famous visionaries

Visionaries in many fields have *envisioned*—and helped create—the future.

Albert Einstein, the physicist who developed the theory of relativity, described relationships between time and space, as well as between matter and energy. His vision changed science for all time.

Susan B. Anthony lived in a world where only men could vote. She worked to get suffrage, or voting rights, for women. She and the women who worked with her were even jailed for their beliefs. Finally, in 1920, the United States granted voting rights to women. Susan B. Anthony's vision helped to change the political landscape of the country.

In 1962, at a time when few people thought about the environment, Rachel Carson published the groundbreaking *Silent Spring*, which raised awareness of the destruction of plant and animal life by pollution.

Visionaries who worked from the 1840s to the 1950s to develop the computer included Charles Babbage, George Boole, and Alan Turing.

WRITE THE CORRECT WORD

Write the correct word in the space next to each definition.

_____ 1. referring to an electronic visual image

_____ 2. able to be seen

_____ 3. a corrected version

_____ 4. a document needed to enter a country

_____ 5. a shade on a hat

_____ 6. someone able to imagine the future

_____ 7. a far-reaching view

_____ 8. to picture mentally

_____ 9. to create with little or no preparation

_____ 10. a way of looking at something

COMPLETE THE SENTENCE

Write the letter for the word that best completes each sentence.

_____ 1. The scar from Ben's operation was barely _____.
   a. visible   b. improvised   c. visionary   d. visualized

_____ 2. The knight lowered his _____ and prepared to charge.
   a. visor   b. vista   c. video   d. visa

_____ 3. A(n) _____ leader was needed to help the people imagine a future worth fighting for.
   a. visible   b. revised   c. improvised   d. visionary

_____ 4. The new singer's music _____ was a major success.
   a. visor   b. video   c. visa   d. vista

_____ 5. They stood silent, awed by the _____ of the Grand Canyon.
   a. visionary   b. vista   c. improvisation   d. visa

_____ 6. After checking his history report, Roberto made only one _____.
   a. visualization   b. visor   c. revision   d. video

_____ 7. In one comedy show, the actors have no script and are given situations for which they must _____ their lines.
   a. improvise   b. revise   c. video   d. visualize

_____ 8. The Hungarian official checked my _____ so that I could enter the country.
   a. revision   b. video   c. visa   d. vista

_____ 9. I wrote a letter to the editor to share my _____ on the issue.
   a. visionary   b. viewpoint   c. vista   d. improviser

_____ 10. It was hard to _____ mean old Mr. Martin as a happy, carefree young man.
   a. video   b. revise   c. improvise   d. visualize

Challenge: From the airport employee's _____, the foreigner's _____ was valid.

_____
   a. viewpoint…visa   b. visa…revision   c. revision…vista

The Web: Information for All

Surfing the Net thrills people with its sense of freedom. **(1)** Its seemingly endless sources of information and images become *visible* as we simply sit in front of a computer screen. We can order books and clothes, without going to a store. **(2)** We can get news from Nigeria or Afghanistan, without a passport or *visa* for travel. We can e-mail people who are thousands of miles away. The World Wide Web is a vast, free communication system that everyone can use.

However, the Web could have been something very different. We might have had to pay for an expensive Internet communication system. Or the Internet might have been limited to adults, or even just to professors. **(3)** The wonderful freedom of the World Wide Web is due to a *visionary* scientist named Tim Berners-Lee.

Berners-Lee worked at CERN, an international physics research organization based in Switzerland. **(4)** In a work environment with *vistas* of snowcapped mountains all around him, he cooperated with scientists from across the globe. But these scientists often found it difficult to share information from hundreds of research projects with their colleagues around the world. **(5)** Scientists who wanted to work together on *revisions* to a research procedure first had to get their computers to communicate. **(6)** Sometimes scientists wasted days trying to *improvise* ways for their programs and computers to "talk" to each other. To help fix this situation, Berners-Lee invented a program that he called a "memory substitute."

Later, he began to think that the general public might be able to use similar systems to find information on all sorts of things. He started to develop a new form of translating, sending, and receiving messages.

(7) Berners-Lee *visualized* free and open communication that would be available to everyone. He believed that no person or group should be able to take control of this system. In 1991, he put this system out on the Internet as the World Wide Web.

The Web was immediately viewed as a fast and powerful tool. **(8)** In 1994, the first World Wide Web Consortium advanced Berners-Lee's *viewpoint* that the Web would encourage open and free use of information.

Today, Tim Berners-Lee's invention affects the lives of billions of people. The Web has spread to homes, offices, schools, and stores. **(9)** You can log on for news, information, entertainment, *videos,* and e-mail. **(10)** You can even clip a handheld, Web-capable computer to the *visor* of your cap when you are jogging. Tim Berners-Lee has made it possible for each person who uses the World Wide Web to be in touch with information from around the world.

Each sentence below refers to a numbered sentence in the passage. Write the letter of the choice that gives the sentence a meaning that is closest to the original sentence.

_____ **1.** Its seemingly endless sources of information and images become _____ as we simply sit in front of a computer screen.
    a. imaginative   **b.** corrected   **c.** confusing   **d.** seen

_____ **2.** We can get news from Nigeria or Afghanistan, without a passport or a(n) _____ for travel.
    a. travel agent   **b.** driver's license   **c.** recorded image   **d.** official document

_____ **3.** The wonderful freedom of the World Wide Web is due to a(n) _____ scientist.
    a. computerized   **b.** imaginative   **c.** able to be seen   **d.** opinionated

_____ **4.** In a work environment with _____ of snowcapped mountains all around, he cooperated with scientists from across the globe.
    a. views   **b.** ranges   **c.** borders   **d.** documents

5. Scientists who wanted to work together on _____ to a research procedure first had to get their computers to communicate.
  a. mental pictures   **b.** corrections   **c.** techniques   **d.** opinions

6. Sometimes scientists wasted days trying to _____ ways for their programs and computers to "talk" to each other.
  a. invent   **b.** correct   **c.** research   **d.** study

7. Berners-Lee _____ free and open communication that would be available to everyone.
  a. finally developed   **b.** officially blocked   **c.** mentally pictured   **d.** videotaped

8. In 1994, the first World Wide Web Consortium advanced Berners-Lee's _____ that the Web would encourage open and free use of information.
  a. opinion   **b.** invention   **c.** harsh criticism   **d.** unclear statement

9. You can log on for news, information, entertainment, _____, and e-mail.
  a. official documents   **b.** visual images   **c.** instant messaging   **d.** recipes

10. You can even clip a handheld, Web-capable computer to the _____ of your cap.
  a. corrected version   **b.** mental picture   **c.** top   **d.** shade

Indicate whether the statements below are TRUE or FALSE according to the passage.

1. The World Wide Web is controlled by the government of one country.

2. The Internet uses technology that allows computers to communicate with each other.

3. The World Wide Web was invented in the United States.

WRITING EXTENDED RESPONSES

Imagine you are going on a vacation to a beautiful or exotic place. It could be a majestic mountain range, an active volcano, an underwater coral reef with colorful fish, or any other place. In a descriptive letter, write home to your family or friends about what you see. Try to describe the sights so that others can imagine them. Your letter should be at least three paragraphs long. Remember to use proper letter form. Use at least three lesson words in your letter and underline them.

WRITE THE DERIVATIVE

Complete the sentence by writing the correct form of the word shown in parentheses. You may not need to change the form that is given.

1. The heavy fog made _____ very bad. (*visible*)

2. Children often enjoy _____ themselves as superheroes or princesses. (*visualize*)

_____ **3.** One of the features of jazz music is _____. *(improvise)*

_____ **4.** Wearing a hat with a _____ helps protect your eyes from harmful UV rays. *(visor)*

_____ **5.** The official made sure Juanita had a _____ to enter Norway. *(visa)*

_____ **6.** Every room in the hotel featured a breathtaking _____. *(vista)*

_____ **7.** Mohammed put the _____ into the machine and turned on the television. *(video)*

_____ **8.** _____ an essay is always a good idea. *(revision)*

_____ **9.** The president's _____ on raising taxes was controversial. *(viewpoint)*

_____ **10.** The inventor of the automobile assembly line was a _____ named Henry Ford. *(visionary)*

FIND THE EXAMPLE

Choose the answer that best describes the action or situation.

_____ **1.** A place you might need a *visa* to visit
  a. another state **b.** a new school **c.** another country **d.** a campground

_____ **2.** Something that is made *visible* by a microscope
  a. a tiny insect **b.** a nearby star **c.** a distant planet **d.** a household pet

_____ **3.** Something that most likely needs *revision*
  a. a published book **b.** a photo album **c.** a framed painting **d.** a first draft of a report

_____ **4.** Something that someone stranded on an island might have to *improvise*
  a. sand **b.** shelter **c.** poison **d.** peace and quiet

_____ **5.** Something that is a *viewpoint*
  a. Bowling is fun. **b.** Ice is cold. **c.** Fire is hot. **d.** Plants create oxygen.

_____ **6.** A *vista* you might see in the Arctic
  a. sunny coastline **b.** field of flowers **c.** skyscrapers **d.** snow-covered land

_____ **7.** What a sports coach might ask her team to *visualize*
  a. falling **b.** catching a cold **c.** napping **d.** winning a trophy

_____ **8.** The time of day when a *visor* would be most needed
  a. evening **b.** noon **c.** dusk **d.** midnight

_____ **9.** A group of *visionary* people
  a. burglars **b.** couch potatoes **c.** the 1912 Red Sox **d.** the Founding Fathers

_____ **10.** Something that might be influenced by events caught on *video*
  a. fancy pens **b.** exhaust pipes **c.** novels **d.** court cases

The Roots -man- and -ped-

WORD LIST

emancipate	impede	manacle	maneuver	manipulate
manual	manuscript	pedestal	pedestrian	pedigree

The root *-man-* refers to "hand"; *-ped-* refers to "foot." They come from the Latin words *manus,* meaning "hand," and *ped,* meaning "foot." These roots are used in common English words. For example, we use our feet to press on *pedals,* a word that contains the root *-ped-*. Words using these roots often give us glimpses into history. The word *manufactured* once meant "made by hand." Today, of course, most *manufactured* goods are made by machine. As you study each word, think of how it relates to the meaning of "hand" or "foot."

1. **emancipate** (ĭ-mǎn´sə-pāt´) *verb* from Latin *ex-,* "out" + *mancipare,* "to take in hand" or "buy"
   To set free; liberate
   • In 1833, England **emancipated** the slaves in its colonies.

   emancipation *noun* Mahatma Gandhi worked for the **emancipation** of India from English rule.

   emancipator *noun* President Lincoln is sometimes called The Great **Emancipator.**

> Many words that end in *-or* and *-er*, like *emancipator,* refer to a person who does a certain action.

2. **impede** (ĭm-pēd´) *verb* from Latin *in-,* "not" + *ped,* "foot"
   To slow down or block the progress of
   • Just one stalled car can **impede** the flow of rush-hour traffic.

   impediment *noun* Not having a high-school diploma is an **impediment** to getting a good job.

> The combination of *im-* ("not") and *ped* ("foot") probably came from an earlier word meaning "not able to move by foot."

3. **manacle** (mǎn´ə-kəl) from *man,* "hand"
   a. *noun* Handcuffs; anything that prevents hands from being moved
      • A guard removed the **manacle** so that the prisoner could sign his name.
   b. *verb* To put hands in something that prevents movement
      • The police officer **manacled** the suspect.

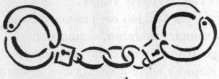

manacle

4. **maneuver** (mə-nōō´vər) from *man,* "hand"
   a. *noun* A skillful action, move, or plan
      • The dancer tried a new **maneuver** using a cane and top hat.
   b. *verb* To make a skillful move
      • The racecar driver **maneuvered** around the stalled car just in time to avoid hitting it.

   maneuverable *adjective* The heavy door was not easily **maneuverable.**

5. **manipulate** (mə-nĭp´yə-lāt´) *verb* from *man*, "hand"
   a. To arrange or operate skillfully, usually by hand
      • It takes training to **manipulate** a large video camera.
   b. To influence or manage cleverly, often by secret means
      • Promising to mow the lawn in the morning, Ray tried to **manipulate** his dad into letting him stay out late.

6. **manual** (măn´yoo-əl) from *man*, "hand"
   a. *adjective* Done by hand or with physical labor
      • Because George's job involved **manual** labor, he was usually exhausted by the end of the day.
   b. *noun* A guidebook on how to do or use something
      • A car's **manual** gives instructions for maintaining the car.

7. **manuscript** (măn´yə-skrĭpt´) *noun* from *man*, "hand"+ Latin *scribere*, "to write"
   A handwritten document; an original text before being set in print
      • The **manuscript** of a speech by Thomas Jefferson is on display at the library.

8. **pedestal** (pĕd´ĭ-stəl) *noun* from *ped*, "foot"
   A support or base for a column or statue
      • The Statue of Liberty stands on a large, strong **pedestal.**

9. **pedestrian** (pə-dĕs´trē-ən) from *ped*, "foot"
   a. *noun* A person traveling on foot
      • **Pedestrians** in high-traffic areas need to walk very carefully.
   b. *adjective* Ordinary; not distinguished
      • Mary was surprised by the famous singer's **pedestrian** performance.

10. **pedigree** (pĕd´ĭ-grē´) *noun* from *ped*, "foot" + Latin *grue*, "crane"
    A record of ancestors or a family tree for persons, dogs, horses, or other animals
       • A member of the nobility has an impressive **pedigree.**

> *Maneuver* and *manipulate* come from the act of moving things by hand. Over time, both words have come to mean "to move or control" mentally, as well as by hand.

> To put someone *on a pedestal* means "to idealize or idolize someone."

> People thought that *pedigree* charts looked like the foot of a bird called a crane.

WORD ENRICHMENT

The lowly foot

The foot has been associated with humble words. *Pedestrian*, for example, can mean "ordinary." In the Middle Ages (about 500–1500), gentlemen went to war using horses. The word *cavalier*, taken from the word for horse, actually came to mean "gentleman." In contrast, poor men battled on foot, and *pedon* meant "foot soldier." From this root comes the word *pawn*, somebody under the control of others (or the lowest figure on a chess board). *Peon*, a lowly worker, and *pioneer*, originally a soldier who built forts, also descend from *pedon*. All these words refer to people who are poor or occupy lowly positions.

WRITE THE CORRECT WORD

Write the correct word in the space next to each definition.

_____ 1. to slow progress

_____ 2. done by hand

_____ 3. a person who is walking

_____ 4. a skillful move

_____ 5. to influence or control someone

_____ 6. a hand-created document

_____ 7. a statue base

_____ 8. to set free

_____ 9. record of ancestors

_____ 10. handcuffs

COMPLETE THE SENTENCE

Write the letter for the word that best completes each sentence.

_____ 1. The promising racehorse had a _____ that included several former champions.
   a. manacle   **b.** pedestal   **c.** pedigree   **d.** impediment

_____ 2. The bicycle rider stopped suddenly to avoid the _____ crossing the street.
   a. pedestrian   **b.** manuscript   **c.** manual   **d.** pedestal

_____ 3. The construction worker had to _____ the crane into place.
   a. manacle   **b.** maneuver   **c.** impede   **d.** emancipate

_____ 4. Using persuasive arguments, Sue tried to _____ her brother into taking her side.
   a. maneuver   **b.** manipulate   **c.** impede   **d.** emancipate

_____ 5. The guard removed the _____ from the woman's wrists.
   a. impediment   **b.** pedigree   **c.** pedestrian   **d.** manacle

_____ 6. The artist put her sculpture on a tall _____.
   a. pedestrian   **b.** manacle   **c.** pedigree   **d.** pedestal

_____ 7. The novelist worked on her _____ for three years.
   a. manuscript   **b.** maneuver   **c.** pedestal   **d.** pedigree

_____ 8. Most large companies have a _____ that explains the rules of the workplace.
   a. manipulation   **b.** maneuver   **c.** manual   **d.** manacle

_____ 9. The revolution _____ the country from the dictator's harsh rule.
   a. manacled   **b.** impeded   **c.** manipulated   **d.** emancipated

_____ 10. The bus driver tried not to _____ the flow of traffic when he stopped.
   a. manacle   **b.** impede   **c.** maneuver   **d.** manipulate

Challenge: The ancient _____ was mounted on a(n) _____ for all to see.

_____   **a.** pedestal…impediment   **b.** pedigree…manacle   **c.** manuscript…pedestal

Australia: Prison to Paradise

(1) The year 1776 marked the beginning of our nation's *emancipation* from Britain. In that same year, British people were being loaded onto ships bound for another distant land. **(2)** They were not going of their own free will, but as prisoners in *manacles* and leg chains.

The hardships of poverty had led to high crime rates in Britain. **(3)** *Pedestrians* coped daily with pickpockets. Serious crime was also increasing. Pressure built for police and judges to do something.

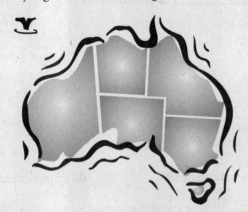

(4) For many years, British prisoners had been shipped to America to serve sentences as *manual* laborers. But with the establishment of the United States as an independent country, this practice stopped. As a result, British jails were soon overflowing with prisoners. It did not help that the punishments even for small crimes were often very harsh. **(5)** As described in an eighteenth-century *manuscript,* the penalties for crimes such as stealing vegetables or a loaf of bread could be prison or death. The justice system of the time also had other problems. **(6)** Corrupt judges could be *manipulated* by bribes to pass judgment without evidence.

Under these conditions, it made sense to ship prisoners to foreign places. The prisoners who were loaded on the ships in 1776, however, did not set sail for months. They were kept at anchor, aboard the crowded ships, because Britain suddenly had nowhere to send them.

Finally, a man named Joseph Banks made a suggestion. **(7)** He had been to Australia and thought it would be a good *maneuver* to send prisoners there. Britain had already declared Australia to be its colony and needed settlers to protect its claim.

In 1787, the first British prisoners arrived in Australia. They were followed by roughly 150,000 more who came in shipments lasting until the mid-1800s. These convicts were added to the 300,000 Australian natives, known as Aborigines, already living there.

(8) Although they were *impeded* by harsh living conditions and a difficult climate, the prisoners were able to build settlements and cities in Australia. They constructed many towns on the shore.

In contrast, the Aborigines (native Australians) tended to live in the interior and did not have much contact with the British. Because of this, the Aborigines were able to keep their culture intact. Aboriginal culture is recognized today as the oldest surviving one in the world; it dates back at least 50,000 years.

Eventually, prisoners who served out their terms were freed, and they established successful lives in Australia. Today, Australia is a relatively rich country with a very low crime rate. **(9)** On a sturdy *pedestal* at the site of an early settlement, tourists can see a monument that tells of the work the prisoners did. **(10)** Many Australians claim British ancestry, and some can trace their *pedigrees* all the way back to convicts.

Each sentence below refers to a numbered sentence in the passage. Write the letter of the choice that gives the sentence a meaning that is closest to the original sentence.

_____ **1.** The year 1776 marked the beginning of our nation's _____ from Britain.
 a. lineage **b.** origin **c.** freedom **d.** war

_____ **2.** They were going as prisoners in _____ and leg chains.
 a. slavery **b.** handcuffs **c.** steamboats **d.** old clothes

_____ **3.** _____ coped daily with pickpockets.
 a. The police **b.** English prisoners **c.** Australian people **d.** Walkers

_____ **4.** Prisoners had been shipped to America to serve sentences as _____ laborers.
 a. artistic **b.** criminal **c.** physical **d.** liberated

_____ **5.** As described in an eighteenth-century _____, the penalties for crimes such as stealing vegetables or a loaf of bread could be prison or death.
    a. document   **b.** law   **c.** judge   **d.** crime

_____ **6.** Corrupt judges could be _____ by bribes to pass judgment without evidence.
    a. tolerated   **b.** handcuffed   **c.** influenced   **d.** arrested

_____ **7.** He had been to Australia and thought it would be a good _____ to send prisoners there.
    a. plan   **b.** benefit   **c.** construction   **d.** settlement

_____ **8.** Although they were _____ by harsh living conditions and a difficult climate, the prisoners were able to build settlement and cities in Australia.
    a. impressed   **b.** unable to walk   **c.** slowed   **d.** imprisoned

_____ **9.** On a sturdy _____ at the site of an early settlement, tourists can see a monument that tells of the work the prisoners did.
    a. base   **b.** sculpture   **c.** book   **d.** artwork

_____ **10.** Some Australians can trace their _____ all the way back to convicts.
    a. traditions   **b.** wealth   **c.** crimes   **d.** ancestry

Indicate whether the statements below are TRUE or FALSE according to the passage.

_____ **1.** The Aborigines and the British convicts worked together to build Australia's cities.

_____ **2.** In the 1700s, British convicts were sent to do hard labor in far-off places.

_____ **3.** The convicts who were sent to Australia helped England settle a new colony.

FINISH THE THOUGHT

Complete each sentence so that it shows the meaning of the italicized word.

1. The *pedestrian* was surprised when _____

_____

2. Our progress on the trip was *impeded* when _____

_____

WRITE THE DERIVATIVE

Complete the sentence by writing the correct form of the word shown in parentheses. You may not need to change the form that is given.

_____ **1.** It is not possible to roll down this car's windows _____. *(manual)*

_____ **2.** The fallen tree was an _____ to drivers. *(impede)*

_____ 3. Children often try to _____ their parents. (*manipulate*)

_____ 4. One result of the Civil War was the _____ of slaves. (*emancipate*)

_____ 5. The iron block was not _____; no one could move it. (*maneuver*)

_____ 6. Hilda wanted a puppy with a very fine _____. (*pedigree*)

_____ 7. Jorge's soccer trophy had an engraved _____. (*pedestal*)

_____ 8. The prisoners were _____, one to the other. (*manacle*)

_____ 9. Fans were expecting great things from the baseball slugger, but on the day of the playoff game, his hitting was just _____. (*pedestrian*)

_____ 10. Yossi submitted his _____ to the publisher last Friday. (*manuscript*)

FIND THE EXAMPLE

Choose the answer that best describes the action or situation.

_____ 1. Someone most likely to wear *manacles*
   a. a teacher   **b.** a firefighter   **c.** a crime suspect   **d.** a defense lawyer

_____ 2. Something that would appear in a *manual* for a new television
   a. how to return it   **b.** a TV schedule   **c.** the price   **d.** how to set it up

_____ 3. Someone who would normally want to be *emancipated*
   a. a police officer   **b.** a prisoner   **c.** an actor   **d.** a politician

_____ 4. This would be useful to a *pedestrian*
   a. a highway   **b.** a sidewalk   **c.** a bike trail   **d.** a railroad track

_____ 5. Something that would *impede* a teacher during his class
   a. a free period   **b.** a teacher's aide   **c.** a quiet student   **d.** a headache

_____ 6. The one most likely to have a *pedigree*
   a. purebred horse   **b.** lost bird   **c.** stray cat   **d.** large roach

_____ 7. The most likely object to be displayed on a *pedestal*
   a. bike lock   **b.** science notebook   **c.** sculpture   **d.** fashion model

_____ 8. A place where it would be difficult to *maneuver* a bicycle
   a. a bike path   **b.** a muddy road   **c.** an indoor gym   **d.** a paved sidewalk

_____ 9. The format of a *manuscript* from the eighteenth century
   a. stone tablet   **b.** e-mail   **c.** typed   **d.** handwritten

_____ 10. Writing that aims to *manipulate* its readers into buying something
   a. a short story   **b.** a business letter   **c.** an advertisement   **d.** a children's book

The Root -sta-

WORD LIST

circumstance	constitution	destitute	institution	obstacle
obstinate	stately	stationary	stature	status

The word root *-sta-* means "standing" or "placed." It is found in Greek, Latin, and Old English. This word root, which can be spelled *-sta-*, *-stat-*, or *-stit-*, relates to words in different ways. *Stationary* simply means "standing still," or "not moving." Sometimes, however, it takes a little imagination to understand how the root *-sta-* relates to words. *Circumstance,* which is formed from *circum,* meaning "around," and *-stat-,* meaning "standing," refers to the things that are *standing around* a main event and influencing it. As you study the vocabulary words, look for their connections with the meanings of *-sta-*.

1. **circumstance** (sûr′kəm-stăns′) *noun* from *circum-,* "around" + *sta,* "stand"
   A condition affecting someone or something
   • Considering the difficult **circumstances** she has had to work under, she has done a remarkable job.

   > *Circumstantial* evidence means that the evidence is not direct, but is part of the *circumstances* around the crime.

2. **constitution** (kŏn′stĭ-tōō′shən) *noun* from *con-,* "together" + *sta,* "placed"
   a. Basic principles, usually written down, of a nation or an organization
      • After the country gained its independence, it needed a **constitution.**
   b. One's general physical makeup or health
      • He had such a delicate **constitution** that he was not strong enough to make the journey.

   constitutional *adjective* **Constitutional** amendments modify the original document.

3. **destitute** (dĕs′tĭ-tōōt′) *adjective* from *de-,* "remove from" + *sta,* "place"
   Very poor; without anything
   • The Great Depression of the 1930s left many people **destitute.**

   > When people's "standing" or "place" is removed, they are left *destitute.*

4. **institution** (ĭn′stĭ-tōō′shən) *noun* from *in-,* "in" + *stat,* "placed"
   An established organization or custom
   • A university is an **institution** of higher learning.

5. **obstacle** (ŏb′stə-kəl) *noun* from *ob-* "against" + *sta,* "stand"
   Something that stands in the way
   • The mountain bikers had to weave around rocks, branches, and other **obstacles** in the path.

obstacle

6. **obstinate** (ŏb´stə-nĭt) *adjective* from *ob-*, "against" + *sta*, "stand"
   Stubborn
   • Despite his mother's best efforts to persuade him, the **obstinate** child refused to eat any vegetables.

   obstinacy *noun* Sheer **obstinacy** prevented the lost man from asking for help.

7. **stately** (stāt´lē) *adjective* from *sta*, "stand"
   Dignified; impressive; majestic
   • The long gown made Maggie look **stately** and elegant.

8. **stationary** (stā´shə-nĕr´ē) *adjective* from *sta*, "stand"
   Not moving; standing still
   • The squirrel remained completely **stationary**, as it watched us with fearful curiosity.

   > Don't confuse *stationary* with *stationery*. *Stationery* is paper used for writing letters.

9. **stature** (stăch´ər) *noun* from *sta*, "stand"
   a. The natural height of a person or an animal
      • The **stature** of basketball players is generally above average.
   b. A high level of achievement
      • Her old classmates were impressed by her **stature** in the field of journalism.

10. **status** (stăt´əs) *noun* from *stat*, "place"
    Prestige, honor, and social position
    • People listened to her opinion because she had **status** in the community.

WORD ENRICHMENT

Sta and the Indo-European language family

Words with the root *sta* are found in ancient Greek, Latin, and Old English. Where, then, did this root originate? All these languages belong to the Indo-European language family, thought to have come from the area around present-day Turkey more than 6,000 years ago. English, German, Spanish, Greek, Swedish, Farsi (a language of Iran), and Hindi (a language of India), as well as many other languages, are in this family. However, other languages, like Hebrew, Arabic, Mandarin, and Finnish are not.

Because *sta* has been used for so long, it has acquired many spellings and senses. The word *stature* has two meanings. In one, *sta* means "physical height," or "how tall a person stands." *Stature* can also be "social height" or "social standing."

In another meaning for *sta*, *institutions* and *constitutions* "stay around" for a long time. *Stay, stage, statue,* and *static* also come from this root. These words, as well as hundreds of others from *sta*, are part of the Indo-European family of languages.

WRITE THE CORRECT WORD

Write the correct word in the space next to each definition.

_____ 1. basic written principles of an organization

_____ 2. height

_____ 3. something in the way

_____ 4. social position

_____ 5. very poor

_____ 6. a condition affecting something

_____ 7. dignified; impressive

_____ 8. an established organization

_____ 9. stubborn

_____ 10. not moving

COMPLETE THE SENTENCE

Write the letter for the word that best completes each sentence.

_____ 1. The _____ student refused to follow directions.
a. stately   b. destitute   c. obstinate   d. circumstantial

_____ 2. His small _____ enabled him to fit in the magician's box.
a. obstacle   b. stature   c. constitution   d. status

_____ 3. The writers of the _____ agreed to include a clause ensuring equal rights for all.
a. institution   b. stationary   c. circumstance   d. constitution

_____ 4. When the weather was bad, the cyclist trained inside on a(n) _____ bike.
a. stationary   b. destitute   c. stately   d. obstinate

_____ 5. According to most religions, it is one's duty to help those who are _____.
a. constitutional   b. circumstantial   c. stately   d. obstinate

_____ 6. Even during a crisis, she somehow managed to appear calm and _____.
a. obstinate   b. stately   c. destitute   d. stationary

_____ 7. "We must continue to uphold the high standards that have earned this _____ its excellent reputation," the chairmen told his employees.
a. obstacle   b. circumstance   c. institution   d. status

_____ 8. His position as a judge gave him great _____ in his community.
a. status   b. institutions   c. constitutions   d. obstinacy

_____ 9. He has so many _____ to overcome that it seems impossible for him to succeed.
a. obstacles   b. institutions   c. constitutions   d. statures

_____ 10. The judge asked the suspect to describe the _____ that led to the crime.
a. obstinacy   b. circumstances   c. status   d. stature

Challenge: The _____ called for the creation of a(n) _____ to oversee public health.
_____   a. status…obstacle   b. circumstance…stature   c. constitution…institution

"Aloha-oe": The Voice of a Queen

(1) Hawaii's last queen was a strong and *stately* woman who loved her country and her people. Her name was Liliuokalani. **(2)** A musician of some *stature*, Liliuokalani composed many songs, including "Aloha-Oe." This popular Hawaiian song is now known all over the world. But Liliuokalani should be remembered for much more than her songs.

She was born in 1838 and became queen when her brother, King Kalakaua, died in 1891. Liliuokalani ruled until 1893. In this era, Hawaii was changing rapidly.

During the 1800s, faster transportation, such as clipper ships and steamboats, made it easier for immigrants to come to the islands. Hawaii became the destination for many wealthy Americans. They knew they could make a lot of money operating sugar plantations and selling the product to the United States. These people gained a great deal of power. **(3)** Some felt that Hawaiian society was *stationary,* and they wanted to change traditional life.

As the sugar industry thrived, a special trade agreement between the United States and Hawaii increased American influence. **(4)** Many *institutions* in Hawaii began to change. Schools run by Americans paved the way for English to become the main language, largely replacing Hawaii's native

languages. **(5)** In 1887, the king of Hawaii was forced to sign a *constitution* that weakened his power.

(6) When Liliuokalani became queen, she wanted to restore the former *status* of the monarchy. **(7)** With the power of the crown restored, she hoped to help many *destitute* native Hawaiians. The queen's goal was to bring her people into the world economy and improve living conditions on the islands. **(8)** The main *obstacle* was the resistance of American businessmen, who wanted to control the profitable fruit and sugar crops of Hawaii. **(9)** They opposed the queen's goals and fought *obstinately* against her. Liliuokalani tried to get the American government to listen to her. She even wrote a book about what was happening to Hawaii, but it was no use.

The situation grew worse when a new U.S. law made it more expensive to export Hawaiian sugar to the United States. American businessmen in Hawaii felt that the only solution was to make Hawaii part of the United States. In 1893, Liliuokalani was overthrown, and Hawaii became a territory of the United States. (Later, in 1959, it became the fiftieth state.)

The brave queen Liliuokalani was arrested during the overthrow. When she was released, her power and title were gone. Although she was no longer a queen, she was still respected by her people. She spent the rest of her life working for charities. **(10)** When she died in 1917, she was living in comfortable *circumstances* in a beautiful home in Honolulu. She died a well-loved figure and a symbol of Hawaiian resistance. Her voice is still heard in "Aloha-Oe," and in the Hawaiian people's fierce pride in their past.

Each sentence below refers to a numbered sentence in the passage. Write the letter of the choice that gives the sentence a meaning that is closest to the original sentence.

_____ **1.** Hawaii's last queen was a strong and _____ woman who loved her country.
    a. poor   **b.** dignified   **c.** tall   **d.** still

_____ **2.** A musician of some _____, Liliuokalani composed many songs.
    a. achievement   **b.** height   **c.** organization   **d.** country

_____ **3.** Some felt that Hawaiian society was _____.
    a. quite friendly   **b.** very poor   **c.** standing still   **d.** very impressive

_____ **4.** Many _____ in Hawaii began to change.
    a. basic principles   **b.** living conditions   **c.** poor people   **d.** established customs

_____ **5.** The king of Hawaii was forced to sign a(n) _____ that weakened his power.
     a. official letter   **b.** marble statue   **c.** document of principles   **d.** medical form

_____ **6.** Liliuokalani wanted to restore the former _____ of the monarchy.
     a. height   **b.** prestige   **c.** principles   **d.** stubbornness

_____ **7.** The queen hoped to help many _____ native Hawaiians.
     a. very tall   **b.** very hopeful   **c.** very poor   **d.** very angry

_____ **8.** The main _____ was the resistance of American businessmen.
     a. thing in the way   **b.** source of hope   **c.** established custom   **d.** social position

_____ **9.** They opposed the queen's goals and fought _____ against her.
     a. honorably   **b.** poorly   **c.** impressively   **d.** stubbornly

_____ **10.** When she died in 1917, she was living in comfortable _____.
     a. principles   **b.** palaces   **c.** conditions   **d.** customs

Indicate whether the statements below are TRUE or FALSE according to the passage.

_____ **1.** Queen Liliuokalani tried to improve the lives of her people.

_____ **2.** American businessmen who went to Hawaii to make money in the sugar industry wanted Hawaii to be part of the United States.

_____ **3.** American businessmen in Hawaii tried to help the queen regain her power.

WRITING EXTENDED RESPONSES

The same word often brings different ideas or images to mind for different people. Choose three words from this list. Then, prepare a piece of paper with three columns. In the first column, list the word. In the second column, write down what comes to your mind when you think of each word. For instance, what do you think of when you hear the word *obstinate?* Then, interview an adult about each word. What images, ideas, or behavior does the adult associate with each word? Write the adult's association in the third column. Your paper should contain these headings: Word, My Examples, Adult's Examples.

WRITE THE DERIVATIVE

Complete the sentence by writing the correct form of the word shown in parentheses. You may not need to change the form that is given.

_____ **1.** A U.S. _____ amendment must be approved by two-thirds of Congress. *(constitution)*

_____ **2.** The students were sent to the principal's office to explain the _____ that led to their fight. *(circumstance)*

_____ **3.** Throughout her imprisonment, the queen maintained a _____ air. *(stately)*

_____ **4.** The boy's _____ infuriated his mother. *(obstinate)*

_____ 5. She has made it past all the _____ on the course and has now almost completed the race. (obstacle)

_____ 6. His greatest fear was losing his social _____. (status)

_____ 7. The karate students were told to remain _____ for five minutes. (stationary)

_____ 8. The educational _____ in our country are among the best in the world. (institution)

_____ 9. In some countries, the majority of the population is _____. (destitute)

_____ 10. Although the wrestler is short in _____, he is powerful. (stature)

FIND THE EXAMPLE

Choose the answer that best describes the action or situation.

_____ 1. Something that a person of great *stature* would most likely be
a. famous   b. poor   c. stubborn   d. still

_____ 2. Something that a *destitute* person might have
a. large yacht   b. nice car   c. ragged clothing   d. plenty to eat

_____ 3. A *circumstance* that might cause someone to miss work
a. good weather   b. reliable transportation   c. positive attitude   d. serious illness

_____ 4. An *obstacle* to getting a part in the school play
a. singing well   b. missing tryouts   c. acting well   d. working hard

_____ 5. Something that might need a *constitution*
a. sick person   b. established company   c. historic museum   d. new country

_____ 6. A person who is most likely to be *stately*
a. princess   b. football player   c. rock star   d. plumber

_____ 7. Another way to describe an *obstinate* person
a. easygoing   b. mildly friendly   c. strong-willed   d. cruel

_____ 8. Something that is always *stationary*
a. car   b. statue   c. kite   d. lawn mower

_____ 9. A person who is likely to have *status* in his or her community
a. a child   b. a clerk   c. a mayor   d. a clown

_____ 10. Something that is an *institution*
a. a county hospital   b. a backyard   c. a statue   d. a pen pal

Prefixes, Roots, and Suffixes

The Prefixes *pre-* and *post-*

The prefixes *pre-* and *post-* have opposite meanings. *Pre-* means "before" or "in front." *Post-* means "after" or "behind." These two prefixes can be attached to many words to form new words.

Prefix-Meaning	Root/Base Word	Word-Meaning
pre-, before	game	*pregame*, before the game
post-, after	game	*postgame*, after the game

People often watch broadcasts before a game. These are called *pregame* shows. Programs after the game are called *postgame* shows. *Pregame* shows often consist of predictions about how the game will go. *Postgame* shows generally analyze what happened.

Below are some clues to words you can make using *pre-* or *post-*. Fill in the blanks with a new word containing one of these prefixes.

1. A test taken *before* we receive instruction is called a _____.

2. A test taken *after* we receive instruction is called a _____.

3. *Before* we take a *flight*, an attendant makes _____ announcements.

4. *After* we *graduate* from college, we can take _____ courses.

At other times, *pre-* and *post-* may be added to a root that cannot stand alone. For example, to *prepare* means to arrange things ahead of time. It is made of *pre-* + *parare*, a Latin word meaning "to equip." In English, *pare* (or *parare*) cannot stand alone as a word.

Practice

You can combine context clues with your knowledge of these prefixes to make intelligent guesses about the meanings of words containing *pre-* and *post-*. All of the sentences below contain words formed with these prefixes. Read the sentences and write down what you think the word in italics means. Then look up the word in the dictionary and write the formal definition.

1. A *postscript* added to the letter said, "Hope to see you soon."

My definition _____

Dictionary definition _____

2. The patient had to carefully follow the *postoperative* instructions.

My definition _____

Dictionary definition _____

3. We got special invitations for a *preview* of the theater production.

My definition _____

Dictionary definition _____

4. The cloudy skies gave us a *premonition* of rain.

My definition _____

Dictionary definition _____

5. In the days after her birth, the baby had excellent *postnatal* care.

My definition _____

Dictionary definition _____

6. *Postnasal* drip often annoys people who suffer from colds or allergies.

My definition _____

Dictionary definition _____

7. Because of rain, the game was *postponed* for a week.

Your definition _____

Dictionary definition _____

8. I *predict* the weather will change.

My definition _____

Dictionary definition _____

Review of Word Elements

Reviewing word elements helps you remember them and use them when you are
reading. Below, write the meaning of each word element that you have studied. Each
one appears italicized in a word.

Word	Word Element	Type of Element	Meaning of Word Element
*stat*ionary	*stat*	root	_____
*ped*estrian	*ped*	root	_____
*man*ual	*man*	root	_____
*vis*ionary	*vis*	root	_____
*un*limited	*un-*	prefix	_____
*non*stop	*non-*	prefix	_____
archae*ology*	*-logy*	suffix	_____
*pre*school	*pre-*	prefix	_____
*post*meridian	*post-*	prefix	_____

Health and Illness

WORD LIST

alleviate	contagious	donor	endurance	fracture
nutrient	paralysis	revitalize	soothe	thrive

The words in this lesson relate to health and illness. However, many of the words can also be used in other contexts. As you study this vocabulary, look for both medical and general ways to use it.

1. **alleviate** (ə-lē´vē-āt´) *verb*
To relieve, lessen, or make more bearable
• Nurses gave the patient medication after surgery to **alleviate** her pain.

   alleviation *noun* The **alleviation** of poverty was the president's highest priority.

2. **contagious** (kən-tā´jəs) *adjective*
Able to spread from person to person
• I stayed home from school until my flu was no longer **contagious.**

   contagion *noun* The medical staff used masks and rubber gloves to avoid **contagion.**

3. **donor** (dō´nər) *noun*
   a. A person who contributes money to a cause
      • The school depends on **donors** to fund band uniforms.
   b. A person who contributes blood, tissue, or an organ to another
      • The doctor finally found a **donor** for the boy who needed a kidney transplant.

   donation *noun* I made a **donation** to the shelter for homeless veterans.

   donate *verb* I **donated** some books to the school library.

endurance

4. **endurance** (ĕn-door´əns) *noun*
Strength to withstand or continue under stress or strain
• The long race required great **endurance.**

   endure *verb* I'm not sure how long I can **endure** this loud music.

5. **fracture** (frăk´chər)
   a. *noun* A break or crack
      • The fall caused a **fracture** to the bone in his arm.
   b. *verb* To break or crack
      • The sharp hammer blow **fractured** the stone.

> *Endurance* is one of many nouns that can also be used as an adjective. We can say, "A marathon is an *endurance* test."

6. **nutrient** (noo´trē-ənt) *noun*
   A component of food that is needed for health
   • The cereal's **nutrients** were listed on the label.

   nutritious *adjective* Experts say it's important to eat a **nutritious** breakfast.

7. **paralysis** (pə-răl´ĭ-sĭs) *noun*
   Loss of ability to move the body or certain parts of the body
   • Polio often causes **paralysis** of the legs.

   paralyze *verb* Some spiders attack insects by **paralyzing** them.

8. **revitalize** (rē-vīt´l-īz´) *verb*
   To give new life or vigor
   • A good watering **revitalized** the plants in the yard.

   revitalization *noun* The neighborhood's **revitalization** turned it into a fashionable place to live.

9. **soothe** (sooth) *verb*
   To calm or comfort; to relieve pain
   • She sang a lullaby to **soothe** the baby.

   soothing *adjective* The sound of rain was so **soothing** that he fell asleep.

10. **thrive** (thrīv) *verb*
    To grow well; to do well
    • Plants need water and light to **thrive**.

> The plural of *paralysis* is *paralyses* (pronounced pə-răl´ĭ-sēz´).

WORD ENRICHMENT

Avoiding contagion

It was only in the 1800s that people began to develop an understanding of what caused disease. Before cures were developed, it was essential to avoid *contagion* in order to stay healthy.

Malaria got its name because people thought that breathing in bad (*mal*) air got them sick. As a result, people tried to stay away from smelly swamps. Today, we know that mosquitoes, not the swamps they are found in, spread malaria.

People knew that diseases like smallpox, bubonic plague, whooping cough, and typhus were *contagious*. To prevent their spread, sick sailors or those coming in from infected ports often had to stay on their ships, away from anyone on shore, for forty days. The word *quarantine* comes from *quaranta*, the Italian word for "forty." We still *quarantine* animals, plants, and sometimes people to prevent the spread of diseases.

WRITE THE CORRECT WORD

Write the correct word in the space next to each definition.

_____ **1.** to break   _____ **6.** to grow well

_____ **2.** to calm   _____ **7.** able to spread

_____ **3.** to relieve   _____ **8.** a person who gives money

_____ **4.** strength under stress   _____ **9.** a healthy part of food

_____ **5.** to give new life   _____ **10.** inability to move

COMPLETE THE SENTENCE

Write the letter for the word that best completes each sentence.

_____ **1.** Unless they are held and fed, babies will fail to _____ .
  a. revitalize   **b.** soothe   **c.** alleviate   **d.** thrive

_____ **2.** Vitamin A is an important _____ that can be found in carrots, sweet potatoes, and red peppers.
  a. donor   **b.** nutrient   **c.** endurance   **d.** fracture

_____ **3.** The blood _____ felt dizzy after her blood was drawn.
  a. contagion   **b.** fracture   **c.** donor   **d.** nutrient

_____ **4.** This shampoo promises to _____ dull, unhealthy hair.
  a. thrive   **b.** paralyze   **c.** revitalize   **d.** endure

_____ **5.** I wore a bandage so that the _____ in my little toe would heal.
  a. nutrient   **b.** fracture   **c.** donor   **d.** alleviation

_____ **6.** The lotion really works to _____ painful sunburns.
  a. soothe   **b.** revitalize   **c.** donate   **d.** thrive

_____ **7.** Weightlifters need good training, will, and _____ .
  a. alleviation   **b.** revitalization   **c.** paralysis   **d.** endurance

_____ **8.** Thanks to new technology, people who suffer from _____ have many ways to get around.
  a. endurance   **b.** nutrition   **c.** paralysis   **d.** revitalization

_____ **9.** If you have a _____ illness, avoid contact with other people.
  a. nutritious   **b.** contagious   **c.** soothing   **d.** fractured

_____ **10.** He hired an assistant to _____ the burden of his workload.
  a. alleviate   **b.** soothe   **c.** fracture   **d.** paralyze

Challenge: We need _____ to help _____ our school building.

_____   **a.** endurance...soothe   **b.** nutrients...thrive   **c.** donors...revitalize

Test-Tube Skin

Each year, more than two million Americans suffer burn injuries. In most cases, the burns are minor. Such injuries can be treated at home by holding the burned skin under cold, running water for about fifteen minutes. **(1)** Then, if the burned area is not charred or blistering, a variety of ointments can be used to *soothe* the pain.

If the burn injury is serious, however, immediate medical care is required, and the process of recovery may be a long one. Second- and third-degree burns (the most severe) may require one or more surgeries. **(2)** Victims often *endure* extreme pain. **(3)** Burn pain is far more intense than that caused by a *fracture* to an arm or a leg. **(4)** A body weakened by burns can easily become infected with *contagious* diseases. **(5)** Although burns don't usually result in *paralysis*, burn victims may have difficulty moving because of skin and muscle damage.

(6) Because burned skin cannot always be *revitalized*, it must often be replaced with new skin. But where does this skin come from? **(7)** People can actually *donate* skin to themselves. Skin can be taken from a donor site, a healthy area of the burn victim's body. It is then put on the damaged site in a process called "skin grafting." However, if burns cover more than 90 percent of the body surface, it is hard to find enough healthy skin to graft. **(8)** Fortunately, a technique has been developed to help *alleviate* this problem.

Using a special procedure, skin can actually be grown in laboratory test tubes. First, cells are taken from a tiny area of healthy skin on the burn victim's body.

(9) These are then placed in a test tube containing special *nutrients* that stimulate rapid growth. **(10)** The new population of cells can *thrive* for up to a year if stored in a very cold freezer. When the patient is ready for surgery, a natural protein called collagen is applied to the affected area. The area is then covered with a protective coating, either a manmade material or skin from another donor. The collagen is left in place for about two weeks—enough time for blood vessels to grow into the collagen. Finally, physicians can graft the new skin from the test tube onto the patient's body.

The use of "test-tube skin," in combination with proper care by an experienced hospital team, can lead to speedier recoveries for badly burned patients. This is good news for burn victims and their families.

Each sentence below refers to a numbered sentence in the passage. Write the letter of the choice that gives the sentence a meaning that is closest to the original sentence.

_____ **1.** A variety of ointments can be used to _____ the pain.
    a. break   **b.** strengthen   **c.** grow   **d.** relieve

_____ **2.** Victims often _____ extreme discomfort.
    a. strengthen   **b.** avoid   **c.** bear   **d.** relieve

_____ **3.** Burn pain is far more intense than pain caused by a _____ to an arm or a leg.
    a. burn   **b.** break   **c.** cramp   **d.** fall

_____ **4.** A body weakened by burns can easily become infected with _____ diseases.
    a. treatable   **b.** fool-related   **c.** burn-related   **d.** catching

_____ **5.** Although burns don't usually result in _____, burn victims may have difficulty moving because of skin and muscle damage.
    a. loss of vision   **b.** loss of movement   **c.** loss of growth   **d.** loss of pain

_____ 6. Since burned skin cannot always be _____, it must often be replaced with
             new skin.
             a. healthy   **b.** restored   **c.** taken   **d.** spread

_____ 7. People can actually _____ skin to themselves.
             a. give   **b.** send   **c.** spread   **d.** lose

_____ 8. Fortunately, a technique has been developed to help _____ the problem.
             a. medicate   **b.** complicate   **c.** relieve   **d.** calm

_____ 9. These are then placed in a test tube containing special _____ that stimulate
             rapid growth.
             a. fresh vegetables **b.** thin glasses   **c.** burn compounds **d.** food components

_____ 10. The new population of cells can _____ for up to a year if stored in a very
             cold freezer.
             a. bear   **b.** live   **c.** contribute   **d.** crack

Indicate whether the statements below are TRUE or FALSE according to the passage.

_____ 1. Test-tube skin is produced from the skin cells of one person, and then donated
             to another.

_____ 2. Second- and third-degree burns may require medical treatment.

_____ 3. For severe burns, letting burned skin grow back naturally is more effective than
             grafting new skin onto the burn site.

FINISH THE THOUGHT

Complete each sentence so that it shows the meaning of the italicized word.

1. You can *alleviate* a headache by _____

_____

2. Because her illness was *contagious* _____

_____

WRITE THE DERIVATIVE

**Complete the sentence by writing the correct form of the word shown in
parentheses. You may not need to change the form that is given.**

_____ **1.** Slow and quiet music often is _____ to people. *(soothe)*

_____ **2.** The new medication contributed to the _____ of the pain. *(alleviate)*

_____ **3.** An ad campaign helped to _____ the nearly bankrupt company. *(revitalize)*

_____ **4.** It is particularly important for children to eat _____ foods at every meal. (*nutrient*)

_____ **5.** She was _____ by fear, unable to take even one step. (*paralysis*)

_____ **6.** The Salvation Army accepts _____ of used clothing, furniture, and appliances. (*donor*)

_____ **7.** Do you think you can _____ one more set of push-ups? (*endurance*)

_____ **8.** Because of the increase in sales during the holiday season, the toy store is now _____. (*thrive*)

_____ **9.** The surgeon reset the boy's _____ leg. (*fracture*)

_____ **10.** Vaccines are vital to the prevention and elimination of _____ diseases. (*contagious*)

FIND THE EXAMPLE

Choose the answer that best describes the action or situation.

_____ **1.** An activity that tests *endurance*
   a. ten-mile walk　　**b.** half-mile walk　　**c.** sleeping　　**d.** watching TV

_____ **2.** Something that might *alleviate* heavy rush-hour traffic
   a. fewer road lanes　　**b.** bigger cars　　**c.** accidents　　**d.** public transportation

_____ **3.** The most likely *donor* to a new art exhibit at a museum
   a. wheat farmer　　**b.** music student　　**c.** hockey player　　**d.** sculpture collector

_____ **4.** Most likely to cause *paralysis*
   a. mild headache　　**b.** stuffy nose　　**c.** spinal injury　　**d.** burn injury

_____ **5.** A *soothing* sound
   a. loud music　　**b.** the ocean　　**c.** a jack hammer　　**d.** a police siren

_____ **6.** The most *nutritious* food
   a. buttered popcorn　　**b.** birthday cake　　**c.** vegetable soup　　**d.** lollipops

_____ **7.** Something that is NOT required for children to *thrive*
   a. television　　**b.** nutritious food　　**c.** love　　**d.** sleep

_____ **8.** A condition that is *contagious*
   a. broken leg　　**b.** common cold　　**c.** a toothache　　**d.** high blood pressure

_____ **9.** Something that one who *fractures* her ankle might say
   a. "I'm hungry."　　**b.** "I'm in a rush."　　**c.** "That's better."　　**d.** "It hurts!"

_____ **10.** Something that might *revitalize* a city park
   a. making it safer　　**b.** making it dirty　　**c.** tearing it down　　**d.** discouraging picnics

Government

WORD LIST

congress	democratic	dictator	endorse	forum
judicial	legislation	monarchy	municipality	veto

Any group of people, from a tiny tribe to a nation of millions, needs rules or restraints in order to survive and function. In modern times, governments play a role in creating and enforcing rules. The many forms of government include *monarchies* ruled by kings and *democracies* governed by the people. Some countries, including Great Britain, are both a *monarchy* and a *democracy*. In this lesson, you will learn words that describe how nations govern themselves.

Congress meets in the Capitol.

1. **congress** (kŏng´grĭs) *noun*
   a. A large meeting to discuss issues
      • An international **congress** of educators met in Sweden last summer.
   b. The lawmaking body of the United States
      • Members of **Congress** are elected by citizens from their state or district.

   Congressional *adjective* A **Congressional** aide did research for the Senator.

2. **democratic** (dĕm´ə-krăt´ĭk) *adjective*
   Governed by the people, directly or through elected representatives
   • A **democratic** government must answer to its citizens.

   democracy *noun* The United States is a **democracy.**

   Democrat *noun* A member of the U.S. Democratic Party
   • Both **Democrats** and Republicans supported increased money for education.

3. **dictator** (dĭk´tā´tər) *noun*
   A ruler with complete power
   • In a country ruled by a **dictator,** the people have no political power.

   dictate *verb* The king **dictated** an increase in taxes.

   dictatorship *noun* A country ruled by a dictator
   • People in **dictatorships** often have no freedom of speech or press.

> The U.S. Congress has two parts, the Senate and the House of Representatives.

> In ancient Greek, *demos* means "people" and *kratos* means "rule." *Democracy* is the "rule of the people."

4. endorse (ĕn-dôrs´) *verb*
To give support or approval
• Fifty physicians **endorsed** the lotion for use in preventing infection.

endorsement *noun* The principal's **endorsement** of the new school
policy encouraged the teachers to support it as well.

5. forum (fôr´əm) *noun*
A gathering (or a gathering place) for public discussion
• The United States Congress is a national **forum.**

6. judicial (jōō-dĭsh´əl) *adjective*
Related to courts, judges, and trials
• The highest court in the U.S. **judicial** system is the Supreme Court.

7. legislation (lĕj´ĭ-slā´shən) *noun*
A law or a group of laws
• The new **legislation** provides funds for building highways.

legislate *verb* The Congress may **legislate** new tax laws this year.

legislative *adjective* Parliament is the chief **legislative** body of
Great Britain.

legislator *noun* The **legislator** voted for the law to regulate pollution.

legislature *noun* The **legislature** considered several bills during
this session.

8. monarchy (mŏn´ər-kē) *noun*
A country or government headed by a king or queen
• The country of Thailand is a **monarchy.**

monarch *noun* One of Great Britain's most popular **monarchs** was
Queen Elizabeth I.

9. municipality (myōō-nĭs´ə-păl´ĭ-tē) *noun*
A town or city that has local powers of government
• The 1951 plumbing code of Evanston, Illinois, became a model for
  other **municipalities.**

municipal *adjective* Police officers are **municipal** employees.

10. veto (vē´tō)
  a. *verb* To reject or forbid something
    • Dad **vetoed** our plan to go camping.
  b. *noun* A vote that rejects or forbids a decision
    • Everyone was surprised by the **veto.**

> The U.S. government has three
> branches. The *legislative*, or
> *Congress*, makes laws. The
> *executive*, the president, sees
> that the laws are carried out,
> or "executed." The *judicial*, or
> court system, judges whether
> laws have been broken.

> The U.S. president may *veto*
> a bill passed by a majority
> in *Congress*. *Congress* can
> then override the *veto* if
> the bill is passed again by
> a two-thirds vote.

WORD ENRICHMENT

One ruler

Monarchy, the word for a government ruled by a king or queen,
comes from the word elements *mono-* (one) and *-arch* (rule). More than
110 words in the American Heritage Dictionary begin with the prefix *mono-.*
A *monogram* is an initial, or one letter. A *monologue* is a performance given
by one actor or speaker. A *monosyllabic* word has one syllable. A *monopoly* is
control by one person or group. Of course, number-related prefixes are not
limited to *mono-:* A *bicycle* has two wheels and a *tricycle* has three.

WRITE THE CORRECT WORD

Write the correct word in the space next to each definition.

_____ **1.** to refuse or reject

_____ **2.** laws

_____ **3.** government run by a king or queen

_____ **4.** a gathering for discussion

_____ **5.** relating to courts

_____ **6.** to give support

_____ **7.** a self-governing city

_____ **8.** governed by the people

_____ **9.** U.S. lawmaking organization

_____ **10.** ruler with complete power

COMPLETE THE SENTENCE

Write the letter for the word that best completes each sentence.

_____ **1.** The mayor called for a _____ to discuss the new library.
  a. forum   **b.** dictator   **c.** legislation   **d.** veto

_____ **2.** Our _____ system has many kinds of courts.
  a. judicial   **b.** veto   **c.** monarchy   **d.** dictator

_____ **3.** New _____ was needed to regulate the use of scooters on sidewalks.
  a. forum   **b.** legislation   **c.** endorsement   **d.** veto

_____ **4.** The senator asked for the governor's _____ of her plan to reduce air pollution.
  a. monarchy   **b.** dictatorship   **c.** democracy   **d.** endorsement

_____ **5.** In a _____, people give their allegiance to the king or queen.
  a. democracy   **b.** monarchy   **c.** legislation   **d.** congress

_____ **6.** The _____ ruled the land cruelly.
  a. dictator   **b.** veto   **c.** judiciary   **d.** democracy

_____ **7.** The town hall is often in the downtown section of a _____.
  a. judiciary   **b.** dictatorship   **c.** municipality   **d.** congress

_____ **8.** If the president does not _____ it, the bill will become law.
  a. veto   **b.** legislate   **c.** endorse   **d.** dictate

_____ **9.** The citizens of the small country fought to establish a(n) _____ government.
  a. congressional   **b.** democratic   **c.** endorsement   **d.** judicial

_____ **10.** The U.S. _____ consists of the Senate and the House of Representatives.
  a. legislation   **b.** municipality   **c.** monarchy   **d.** Congress

Challenge: In the American Revolution, colonists fought against rule by the British _____, and when they gained independence, they set up a _____.
_____   **a.** dictatorship…monarchy   **b.** monarchy…democracy   **c.** monarchy…veto

The Child Queen

In 1890, on a gray and wintry day in Holland, a small blond girl sat quietly beside her mother in a black carriage. They headed a long procession, with men in top hats and women in black veils. **(1)** The girl's name was Wilhelmina, and the funeral procession was for her father, the *monarch* of the Netherlands.

When her father passed away, ten-year-old Wilhelmina inherited the throne. However, her mother actually reigned until Wilhelmina turned eighteen. To prepare for her rule, the child studied government, economics, and history.

At eighteen, Wilhelmina was crowned Queen of the Netherlands. **(2)** Although the country was a constitutional monarchy, the queen had absolute power to *veto* the acts of government. **(3)** She could approve or deny any new *legislation*. **(4)** She had the power to make *judicial* appointments. **(5)** She could also name *municipal* officials.

(6) Wilhelmina's ministers did not always *endorse* what she did. When she was only twenty, British warships were threatening the president of the Transvaal in Africa. The young queen's advisors did not want her to interfere.

Against their wishes, however, she sent a Dutch warship to rescue the president. Her people came to respect her for this and other brave moves.

As queen, Wilhelmina instituted reforms to benefit people in factory and manual labor jobs. Under her leadership, her country grew wealthier. She also strengthened the Netherlands's educational system.

(7) In 1940, the Nazi *dictator* Adolph Hitler invaded the Netherlands. In response, Wilhelmina moved the Dutch government to England. From London, she led the Dutch resistance to the Nazi invasion. Throughout World War II, she radioed messages to her people on a Dutch station called Radio Orange. She encouraged them to remain strong in the face of violence and starvation. To honor her, they planted orange flowers in their gardens.

(8) In 1942, Wilhelmina crossed the Atlantic to address the U.S. *Congress*. She made a famous speech urging people to continue the fight to save democracy. She said:

"Those of us who have the . . . privilege of being free feel that it is our holy duty . . . to do whatever we can to hasten victory. **(9)** *Democracy* is our most precious heritage. We cannot breathe in the sullen atmosphere of [the dictator's] rule."

When the war was over, Wilhelmina returned to Holland and went to work helping her people rebuild their country. **(10)** She offered her castle in The Hague as a *forum* for world peace. Since World War II, The Hague has served as a place where nations can work out their differences through discussion instead of war. Queen Wilhelmina's ideas became the foundation for the International Court of The Hague.

She was queen for fifty years and left a lasting legacy to her country and the world. Today, her granddaughter, Beatrix, is the monarch of the Netherlands.

Each sentence below refers to a numbered sentence in the passage. Write the letter of the choice that gives the sentence a meaning that is closest to the original sentence.

_____ **1.** The funeral procession was for her father, the _____ of the Netherlands.
    a. congress   **b.** judge   **c.** dictator   **d.** king

_____ **2.** The queen had absolute power to _____ the acts of government.
    a. reject   **b.** compromise   **c.** support   **d.** discuss

_____ **3.** She could approve or deny any new _____.
    a. war   **b.** law   **c.** officer   **d.** town

_____ **4.** She had the power to make _____ appointments.
   a. government   **b.** meeting   **c.** court   **d.** city

_____ **5.** She could also name _____ officials.
   a. important   **b.** court   **c.** city   **d.** school

_____ **6.** Wilhelmina's ministers did not always _____ what she did.
   a. support   **b.** fight against   **c.** meet about   **d.** discuss

_____ **7.** In 1940, the Nazi _____ Adolph Hitler invaded the Netherlands.
   a. supporter   **b.** king   **c.** absolute leader   **d.** president

_____ **8.** In 1942, Wilhelmina crossed the Atlantic to address the U.S. _____.
   a. absolute ruler   **b.** education system   **c.** court system   **d.** lawmaking body

_____ **9.** _____ is our most precious heritage.
   a. The Netherlands   **b.** The court system   **c.** Rule by a queen   **d.** Rule by the people

_____ **10.** She offered her castle in The Hague as a(n) _____ for world peace.
   a. city   **b.** school   **c.** absolute ruler   **d.** gathering place

Indicate whether the statements below are TRUE or FALSE according to the passage.

_____ **1.** Queen Wilhelmina was crowned at the age of eighteen.

_____ **2.** Queen Wilhelmina went to Africa to rescue the president.

_____ **3.** The Hague is a place where nations can come together to discuss ways to create peace.

WRITING EXTENDED RESPONSES

People from other countries have often lived under different forms of government. Interview one person who immigrated to your country. (If you cannot find such a person, read about an immigrant's experience or ask someone who knows an immigrant.) Ask this person (or read about) how our governmental system is the same as and different from the one he or she lived under before. Use a recorder or take notes. Finally, write an essay that compares and contrasts the two forms of government. Your essay should be at least three paragraphs. Use at least three lesson words in your piece and underline them.

WRITE THE DERIVATIVE

Complete the sentence by writing the correct form of the word shown in parentheses. You may not need to change the form that is given.

_____ **1.** The candidate received an important _____ from her senator. *(endorse)*

_____ **2.** Each state has the power to create its own _____. *(legislation)*

_____ **3.** In a _____, most citizens have the right to vote. *(democratic)*

_____ **4.** A _____ session was in progress. *(congress)*

_____ **5.** The _____ system includes judges and courts. *(judicial)*

_____ **6.** The _____ swimming pool is open to all town residents. *(municipality)*

_____ **7.** William the Conqueror was one of England's _____ . *(monarchy)*

_____ **8.** Without a congress or parliament, a ruler can often _____ freely. *(dictator)*

_____ **9.** The president _____ the tax plan. *(veto)*

_____ **10.** The conference was a _____ for transportation issues. *(forum)*

FIND THE EXAMPLE

Choose the answer that best describes the action or situation.

_____ **1.** A nursery rhyme that mentions a *monarch*
   a. Little Miss Muffet   **b.** The Queen of Hearts   **c.** Jack and Jill   **d.** Little Jack Horner

_____ **2.** The best person to *endorse* a new restaurant
   a. a food reviewer   **b.** the owner   **c.** a librarian   **d.** a teenager

_____ **3.** How people who live under a *dictator* might feel
   a. free to vote   **b.** very powerful   **c.** powerless   **d.** in charge

_____ **4.** A right and privilege in a *democracy*
   a. owning land   **b.** voting   **c.** recycling   **d.** working

_____ **5.** A *municipal* employee
   a. a king or queen   **b.** a business owner   **c.** a private tutor   **d.** a police officer

_____ **6.** Something many parents might *veto*
   a. doing homework   **b.** dyeing your hair   **c.** washing dishes   **d.** taking a bath

_____ **7.** Something most likely to be addressed in a state *forum*
   a. music awards   **b.** movie reviews   **c.** national forests   **d.** educational standards

_____ **8.** Something that is NOT part of the *judicial* system
   a. the Senate   **b.** state courts   **c.** judges   **d.** the Supreme Court

_____ **9.** Something a member of *Congress* does
   a. makes laws   **b.** vetoes laws   **c.** enforces laws   **d.** teaches about laws

_____ **10.** An issue about which a town council would be most likely to pass *legislation*
   a. eating vegetables   **b.** watching TV   **c.** street parking   **d.** hair length

Law and Order

WORD LIST

| bankrupt | defendant | evident | fugitive | just |
| larceny | lenient | testimony | verdict | witness |

A law is a rule for behavior. At times, people are accused of committing crimes, or breaking laws. In our legal system, every person charged with a crime is entitled to a trial. Prosecutors present the case against the accused person, and defense lawyers defend him or her. A jury, a panel made up of regular citizens, hears many cases and determines whether the person is guilty. The words in this lesson are often used in courtrooms. Learning them will help you understand books, movies, television programs, and discussions about law and order.

1. bankrupt (băngk´rŭpt´) *adjective*
Unable to pay debts; financially ruined
• The court declared the company to be **bankrupt.**

bankruptcy *noun* "This foolish spending will put us in **bankruptcy!**" yelled the company treasurer.

2. defendant (dĭ-fĕn´dənt) *noun*
A person being accused in a court of law
• The lawyer told the **defendant** to state where he was on the day of the robbery.

defend *verb* The lawyer will **defend** the accused man.

defense *noun* The lawyer's **defense** was convincing.

3. evident (ĕv´ĭ-dənt) *adjective*
Easily seen or understood; obvious
• After five innings, it was **evident** that our team was going to win the game.

evidence *noun* The chocolate on the boy's face was **evidence** that he had gotten into the cookie jar.

> *Evident* contains the word root *vid*, meaning "see." Something that can be easily seen is *evident*.

4. fugitive (fyoo´jĭ-tĭv)
a. *noun* A person who runs from the law
• The citizens of the town volunteered to help the sheriff find the **fugitive.**
b. *adjective* Running away or fleeing from the law
• The **fugitive** thief fled to South America.

fugitive

5. just (jŭst) *adjective*
Fair or morally right; honorable
• The judge was greatly respected for his **just** opinions.

justice *noun* The goal of our court system is to ensure **justice.**

6. larceny (lär´sə-nē) *noun*
The crime of stealing
• Shoplifting is a common form of **larceny.**

7. lenient (lē´nē-ənt) *adjective*
Not strict or demanding; forgiving; generous
• The **lenient** baby sitter let Joshua stay up past his bedtime.

leniency *noun* Due to the judge's **leniency,** the prisoner's sentence was reduced.

8. testimony (tĕs´tə-mō´nē) *noun*
A statement given as evidence in a trial
• The gardener's **testimony** established that the suspect was in the house at the time of the robbery.

testify *verb* Morgan **testified** that she saw the defendant enter the store at noon on Friday.

9. verdict (vûr´dĭkt) *noun*
a. The decision reached by a jury
• The jury carefully reviewed the case before announcing its **verdict.**
b. A conclusion or judgment
• Historians have reached the **verdict** that Franklin Delano Roosevelt was an important president.

10. witness (wĭt´nĭs)
a. *noun* Someone who has heard or seen something
• The statements of the **witnesses** helped to make a case for the defendant's innocence.
b. *verb* To see something
• The woman **witnessed** the boy stealing some of her apples.

WORD ENRICHMENT

Speaking the truth

The word *verdict* is made up of two word elements. The root *ver* (from Latin *verus*) means "truth." The root *dict* (from Latin *dicere*) means "say." When a jury or judge reaches a *verdict,* they "speak the truth" based on what they have determined. These two word elements are found in many other English words.

Ver is used in words like *veracity* (truth) and *verify* (to determine the truth of something). The common word *very* is related to this root; it can mean "truly" or "really."

Words with *dict* are also common in English. A teacher might *dictate* or "say aloud" the words on a spelling test. What a *dictator* says must be done by the people. When we speak, we try to use good *diction* so people will understand exactly what we are saying.

WRITE THE CORRECT WORD

Write the correct word in the space next to each definition.

_____ 1. financially ruined

_____ 2. person on trial

_____ 3. easily understood

_____ 4. fair

_____ 5. statement given as evidence

_____ 6. not strict

_____ 7. stealing

_____ 8. a person running from the law

_____ 9. to see something

_____ 10. a jury's decision

COMPLETE THE SENTENCE

Write the letter for the word that best completes each sentence.

_____ 1. Everyone admired the king for being powerful and _____.
    a. evident   **b.** just   **c.** bankrupt   **d.** fugitive

_____ 2. It is _____ from your report card that you worked very hard this year.
    a. bankrupt   **b.** just   **c.** evident   **d.** lenient

_____ 3. The _____ was shackled when he was brought into the courtroom.
    a. testimony   **b.** defendant   **c.** witness   **d.** verdict

_____ 4. The store clerk was convicted of _____.
    a. testimony   **b.** evidence   **c.** leniency   **d.** larceny

_____ 5. The defendant had been a _____ before she was caught and brought to trial.
    a. fugitive   **b.** testimony   **c.** verdict   **d.** justice

_____ 6. The "Out of Business" sign was a clue that the store owner had gone _____.
    a. bankrupt   **b.** witness   **c.** evident   **d.** lenient

_____ 7. After seeing the car accident, Mario was called to be a(n) _____.
    a. evidence   **b.** fugitive   **c.** witness   **d.** justice

_____ 8. The jury spent a week in discussion, but they couldn't come up with a _____.
    a. testimony   **b.** witness   **c.** justice   **d.** verdict

_____ 9. Because this was the defendant's first crime, the judge was _____.
    a. lenient   **b.** evident   **c.** bankrupt   **d.** fugitive

_____ 10. The _____ of the expert witness convinced everyone that the defendant was guilty.
    a. leniency   **b.** bankruptcy   **c.** testimony   **d.** fugitive

Challenge: It was only _____ that the pickpocket was punished for _____.

_____   **a.** evident…leniency   **b.** just…larceny   **c.** lenient…bankruptcy

O. Henry: Master Short-Story Writer

In 1897, prison doors slammed shut on William Sydney Porter. In 1901, they opened, and Porter walked out with a new name and a second chance. **(1)** The one-time *fugitive* turned that new chance into lasting fame.

Porter (1862–1910) was born in North Carolina. When he was three, his mother died. Porter and the rest of his family went to live with his grandmother and his aunt, who educated him and encouraged him to read.

In 1892, because of poor health, Porter went to a Texas ranch to rest. For two years, he listened to the tales of cowhands, drifters, and outlaws.

In 1894, Porter moved to Austin, Texas, where he met his wife. There, he was struck by a series of misfortunes. His wife became ill, and their baby died. His humor magazine, called *The Rolling Stone,* was not successful.

Porter worked as a bank teller and then quit to go to work for a newspaper. After he left the bank, Porter was accused of stealing money. **(2)** He was forced to stand trial for embezzlement, a form of *larceny.*

(3) Convinced that he would not be treated in a *just* manner, Porter fled to Central America. However, he returned to visit his dying wife and was arrested.

(4) From the beginning, it was *evident* that the case against Porter was not very strong. Bad bookkeeping may have been more to blame than criminal behavior. **(5)** The bank officials' *testimony* was not very convincing. **(6)** Still, there were few *witnesses* to speak in Porter's defense. **(7)** The jury returned a *verdict* of guilty. **(8)** The *defendant,* William Sydney Porter, had lost.

Once in jail, Porter became a model prisoner. **(9)** A *lenient* judge reduced Porter's five-year sentence

to three. While in prison, Porter began to write stories. He also took the pen name O. Henry, which some said he adopted from a kindly prison guard.

National magazines began to buy his work. In 1904, a book of O. Henry's short stories was published, and more collections quickly followed. One tale, "The Gift of the Magi," is famous for its moving portrayal of poor people making sacrifices for love. O. Henry had a gift for narrative, with characters whose words and actions bring them to life on the page.

In 1907, the O. Henry Memorial Award was established. It is given each year to an outstanding short-story writer.

Like his stories, O. Henry's life was brief, adventurous, and marked by sudden twists of fate. **(10)** In 1910, O. Henry died nearly *bankrupt,* but he left the world a treasure in his hundreds of stories.

Each sentence below refers to a numbered sentence in the passage. Write the letter of the choice that gives the sentence a meaning that is closest to the original sentence.

_____ **1.** The one-time _____ turned that new chance into lasting fame.
    a. judge   **b.** runaway   **c.** writer   **d.** lawyer

_____ **2.** He was forced to stand trial for embezzlement, a form of _____.
    a. stealing   **b.** murder   **c.** debts   **d.** bookkeeping

_____ **3.** Convinced that he would not be treated in a(n) _____ manner, Porter fled to Central America.
    a. strict   **b.** fair   **c.** obvious   **d.** gracious

_____ **4.** From the beginning, it was _____ that the case against Porter was not very strong.
    a. judged   **b.** fair   **c.** obvious   **d.** unknown

5. The bank officials' _____ was not very convincing.
a. defense of Porter   b. bad bookkeeping   c. strange decision   d. statement of evidence

6. Still, there were few _____ to speak in Porter's defense.
a. bank tellers   b. judges and juries   c. runaways   d. people who saw

7. The jury returned a(n) _____ of guilty.
a. judgment   b. discussion   c. crime   d. evidence

8. The _____, William Sydney Porter, had lost.
a. terrible crime   b. jury panel   c. unfair judge   d. person being charged

9. A _____ judge reduced the five-year sentence to three.
a. fair   b. crazy   c. forgiving   d. strict

10. O. Henry died almost _____, but he left a treasure of more than six hundred stories.
a. financially ruined   b. famous   c. easily understood   d. in jail

Indicate whether the statements below are TRUE or FALSE according to the passage.

_____ **1.** Porter was convicted despite the fact that the case against him was weak.

_____ **2.** Porter learned how to read and write while in prison.

_____ **3.** O. Henry's stories are known for their sudden twists.

FINISH THE THOUGHT

Complete each sentence so that it shows the meaning of the italicized word.

1. I hoped my teacher would be *lenient* after _____

_____

2. When the company went *bankrupt,* _____

_____

WRITE THE DERIVATIVE

Complete the sentence by writing the correct form of the word shown in parentheses. You may not need to change the form that is given.

_____ **1.** The woman did not want to _____ against her neighbor. *(testimony)*

_____ **2.** Two of America's main values are freedom and _____ for all. *(just)*

_____ **3.** Some feel that _____ should be applied when the criminal is very young. *(lenient)*

_____ **4.** Because he couldn't pay his debts, Mr. Wilson had to declare _____. *(bankrupt)*

_____ **5.** The lawyer presented a good _____ of her client. *(defendant)*

_____ **6.** The robber was a _____ for a few months before he returned to stand trial. (*fugitive*)

_____ **7.** Without any solid _____ against him, the defendant will go free. (*evident*)

_____ **8.** The jury reached a _____ of "not guilty." (*verdict*)

_____ **9.** While looking out her window, Sally _____ a crime on the street below. (*witness*)

_____ **10.** John received ten years in prison for grand _____ . (*larceny*)

FIND THE EXAMPLE

Choose the answer that best describes the action or situation.

_____ **1.** Someone who commits *larceny*
   a. a murderer   **b.** a judge   **c.** a thief   **d.** a juror

_____ **2.** Something a *fugitive* would most likely do
   a. go into hiding **b.** go back to school **c.** become a judge   **d.** run for president

_____ **3.** A *just* punishment for NOT doing your homework
   a. ten years in prison **b.** a large fine **c.** getting sent home **d.** zero on the paper

_____ **4.** Something a *lenient* teacher might do
   a. give many tests **b.** require silence **c.** give pop quizzes **d.** give little homework

_____ **5.** Megan took Jesse's pen. Harry saw the event and told Karen. Who is the *witness*?
   a. Megan   **b.** Karen   **c.** Harry   **d.** Jesse

_____ **6.** *Evidence* of lack of sleep
   a. high energy   **b.** good appetite   **c.** glowing skin   **d.** bags under eyes

_____ **7.** Something a store that went *bankrupt* would do
   a. expand the store **b.** open another store **c.** close the store **d.** hire new workers

_____ **8.** The person with the most reliable *testimony* in a murder trial
   a. an eyewitness **b.** the defendant   **c.** the lawyer   **d.** the judge

_____ **9.** Something *defendants* often do in court
   a. juggle   **b.** testify   **c.** steal   **d.** cook

_____ **10.** A *verdict* that would make the defendant happy
   a. not guilty   **b.** guilty   **c.** ten years   **d.** a big fine

Prefixes, Roots, and Suffixes

The Prefixes *sub-* and *super-*

The prefixes *sub-* and *super-* mean "below" and "above." Either may be added to the root word *script*, which means "writing." In chemistry, a *subscript* is written in small letters below a symbol. The "$_2$" in the symbol H_2O is a subscript. A *superscript* is written above another symbol. For example, in x^2, the "^{2}" is a superscript.

Look at the italicized word in this sentence: Do the stars of some of your favorite movies have *superhuman* powers? Here the word, *super-* means "beyond." One of the first *superhuman* heroes was a comic book figure, later made into a TV show and a movie. His name is *Superman*. On the other hand, some fictional monsters seem to have intelligence that is "under," or less than, that of human beings. We might call this *subhuman* intelligence. *Sub-* can also mean "part of," as in the word *subdivision*.

Prefix-Meaning	Root/Base Word	Word-Meaning
sub-, under	script	*subscript*, letters under text
sub-, part of	committee	*subcommittee*, part of a committee
super-, over	script	*superscript*, letters above text
super-, beyond, extremely	human	*superhuman*, having powers that are beyond human

Below are some clues to help you make words using *sub-* or *super-*. Fill in the blanks with a new word containing one of these prefixes.

1. *Part* of a *total* may be called a _____ .

2. When something is *very abundant* it can be called _____ .

3. Something *under* the *soil* is _____ .

4. A country that is *very powerful* is called a _____ .

At times, the prefixes *sub-* and *super-* simply attach to English words that may stand alone. The words *subsoil* and *superpower* are examples of this. At other times, *sub-* and *super-* may be added to roots that cannot stand alone. You studied some words in this book that use the prefixes *super-* and *sub-* with this type of root.

superlative is made from *super-* + *lat*, past tense of "to carry" in Latin
   A *superlative* carries a *very* positive meaning.

supervise is made from *super-* + *vis*, to "see"
   When we *supervise* someone, we *oversee* them.

submit is made from *sub-* + *mit*, a root meaning "send"
   When we *submit* something, we *send* it in so that it may be *under* consideration by others. We might *submit* a science project for a prize.

Practice

You can combine context clues with your knowledge of these prefixes to make intelligent guesses about the meanings of words containing *sub-* and *super-*. All of the sentences below contain words formed with these prefixes. Read the sentences and write down what you think the word in italics means. Then look up the word in the dictionary and write the formal definition.

1. Using reactors, scientists searched for unbelievably small *subatomic* particles.

   My definition _____

   Dictionary definition _____

2. My skin is *supersensitive* to sunlight, so I burn after only a few minutes exposure to it.

   My definition _____

   Dictionary definition _____

3. Our car is a *subcompact*.

   My definition _____

   Dictionary definition _____

4. The powerful system was run by a *supercomputer*.

   My definition _____

   Dictionary definition _____

5. The *submarine* had over a hundred sailors in its crew.

   My definition _____

   Dictionary definition _____

6. We only needed three batteries; the other two were *superfluous*.

   My definition _____

   Dictionary definition _____

Review of Word Elements

Reviewing word elements helps you remember them and use them when you are reading. Below, write the meaning of each word element that you have studied. Each one appears italicized in a word.

Word	Word Element	Type of Element	Meaning of Word Element
*sub*standard	*sub-*	prefix	_____
*vis*ible	*vis*	root	_____
*e*mit	*mis, mit*	root	_____
kilo*meter*	*-meter*	suffix	_____
*super*sonic	*super-*	prefix	_____

LESSON 1 antonym	LESSON 1 glossary	LESSON 2 beastly	LESSON 2 mammoth	LESSON 3 affable	LESSON 3 enchanting
LESSON 1 concept	LESSON 1 retain	LESSON 2 hog	LESSON 2 parrot	LESSON 3 awe	LESSON 3 fascinate
LESSON 1 context	LESSON 1 specialized	LESSON 2 horseplay	LESSON 2 pigheaded	LESSON 3 contempt	LESSON 3 loathe
LESSON 1 derivative	LESSON 1 synonym	LESSON 2 hound	LESSON 2 scapegoat	LESSON 3 crave	LESSON 3 rave
LESSON 1 effective	LESSON 1 terminology	LESSON 2 lionize	LESSON 2 sheepish	LESSON 3 detestable	LESSON 3 recoil

antonym
(ăn´tə-nĭm´) n.
A word with an opposite meaning of another word

© Great Source

concept
(kŏn´sĕpt´) n.
A thought or an idea

© Great Source

context
(kŏn´tĕkst´) n.
Writing or speech surrounding a word

© Great Source

derivative
(dĭ-rĭv´ə-tĭv) n.
A word formed from another word

© Great Source

effective
(ĭ-fĕk´tĭv) adj.
Successful in bringing results

© Great Source

glossary
(glô´sə-rē) n.
A list of terms used in a text

© Great Source

retain
(rĭ-tān´) v.
To hold or keep

© Great Source

specialized
(spĕsh´ə-līzd) adj.
Having one particular use

© Great Source

synonym
(sĭn´ə-nĭm´) n.
A word with a similar meaning

© Great Source

terminology
(tûr´mə-nŏl´ə-jē) n.
Special vocabulary of a subject

© Great Source

beastly
(bēst´lē) adj.
Awful; unpleasant

© Great Source

hog
(hŏg) v.
To be greedy

© Great Source

horseplay
(hôrs´plā´) n.
Rough play

© Great Source

hound
(hound) v.
To pursue without stopping

© Great Source

lionize
(lī´ə-nīz´) v.
To greatly admire

© Great Source

mammoth
(măm´əth) adj.
Enormous

© Great Source

parrot
(păr´ət) v.
To repeat without understanding

© Great Source

pigheaded
(pĭg´hĕd´ĭd) adj.
Stupidly stubborn

© Great Source

scapegoat
(skāp´gōt´) n.
Someone unfairly blamed

© Great Source

sheepish
(shē´pĭsh) adj.
Embarrassed

© Great Source

affable
(ăf´ə-bəl) adj.
Friendly

© Great Source

awe
(ô) n.
Wonder

© Great Source

contempt
(kən-tĕmpt´) n.
Hateful scorn

© Great Source

crave
(krāv) v.
To need or desire

© Great Source

detestable
(dĭ-tĕs´tə-bəl) adj.
Deserving hatred

© Great Source

enchanting
(ĕn-chăn´tĭng) adj.
Charming

© Great Source

fascinate
(făs´ə-nāt´) v.
To capture interest

© Great Source

loathe
(lōth) v.
To hate intensely

© Great Source

rave
(rāv) v.
To praise with much enthusiasm

© Great Source

recoil
(rĭ-koil´) v.
To shrink back in disgust

© Great Source

LESSON 4 bluff	LESSON 4 fabricate	LESSON 4 frank	LESSON 4 genuine	LESSON 4 impartial
LESSON 4 integrity	LESSON 4 obvious	LESSON 4 plagiarize	LESSON 4 reliable	LESSON 4 suppress
LESSON 5 accumulate	LESSON 5 ample	LESSON 5 barren	LESSON 5 comprehensive	LESSON 5 extensive
LESSON 5 meager	LESSON 5 pervasive	LESSON 5 sparse	LESSON 5 surpass	LESSON 5 trifle
LESSON 6 accord	LESSON 6 consent	LESSON 6 contrary	LESSON 6 corroborate	LESSON 6 friction
LESSON 6 insolent	LESSON 6 negotiate	LESSON 6 pact	LESSON 6 rapport	LESSON 6 rift

bluff
(blŭf) *v.*
To try to frighten
with false threats

© Great Source

fabricate
(făb´rĭ-kāt´) *v.*
To invent in order
to deceive

© Great Source

frank
(frăngk) *adj.*
Completely honest

© Great Source

genuine
(jĕn´yoo-ĭn) *adj.*
Real

© Great Source

impartial
(ĭm-pär´shəl) *adj.*
Fair

© Great Source

integrity
(ĭn-tĕg´rĭ-tē) *n.*
Strong moral
character

© Great Source

obvious
(ŏb´vē-əs) *adj.*
Easy to see

© Great Source

plagiarize
(plā´jə-rīz´) *v.*
To copy the
work of another

© Great Source

reliable
(rĭ-lī´ə-bəl) *adj.*
Dependable

© Great Source

suppress
(sə-prĕs´) *v.*
To prevent something
from being known

© Great Source

accumulate
(ə-kyoom´yə-lāt´) *v.*
To collect

© Great Source

ample
(ăm´pəl) *adj.*
More than enough

© Great Source

barren
(băr´ən) *adj.*
Unable to grow crops

© Great Source

comprehensive
(kŏm´prĭ-hĕn´sĭv) *adj.*
Including everything

© Great Source

extensive
(ĭk-stĕn´sĭv) *adj.*
Far-reaching

© Great Source

meager
(mē´gər) *adj.*
Less than enough

© Great Source

pervasive
(pər-vā´sĭv) *adj.*
Found throughout

© Great Source

sparse
(spärs) *adj.*
Not thick or
dense; scattered

© Great Source

surpass
(sər-păs´) *v.*
To be better
than expected

© Great Source

trifle
(trī´fəl) *n.*
Something not
important

© Great Source

accord
(ə-kôrd´) *v.*
To give or grant

© Great Source

consent
(kən-sĕnt´) *n.*
Permission or
acceptance

© Great Source

contrary
(kŏn´trĕr´ē) *adj.*
Opposite or opposed to;
completely different

© Great Source

corroborate
(kə-rŏb´ə-rāt´) *v.*
To support with new
facts or evidence

© Great Source

friction
(frĭk´shən) *n.*
Conflict or clash

© Great Source

insolent
(ĭn´sə-lənt) *adj.*
Rude; disrespectfully
bold; insulting

© Great Source

negotiate
(nĭ-gō´shē-āt´) *v.*
To discuss in order to
reach agreement

© Great Source

pact
(păkt) *n.*
A formal agreement

© Great Source

rapport
(ră-pôr´) *n.*
A relationship of shared
trust and understanding

© Great Source

rift
(rĭft) *n.*
A disagreement or
break in relations

© Great Source

LESSON 7	LESSON 7	LESSON 8	LESSON 8	LESSON 9	LESSON 9
brisk	saunter	appease	penitent	barrio	mesa
linger	scurry	condone	reconcile	escapade	mustang
mingle	sedentary	indignant	resent	fiesta	poncho
nimble	stride	infuriate	retaliate	guerrilla	siesta
perpetual	totter	malicious	wrath	lariat	stampede

brisk (brĭsk) *adj.*
Moving quickly, as in walking

© Great Source

linger (lĭng´gər) *v.*
To stay for a while before leaving

© Great Source

mingle (mĭng´gəl) *v.*
To mix or join with others

© Great Source

nimble (nĭm´bəl) *adj.*
Having quick and skillful movements

© Great Source

perpetual (pər-pĕch´ oo -əl) *adj.*
Lasting forever for a very long time

© Great Source

---

saunter (sôn´tər) *v.*
To walk in a slow, relaxed manner

© Great Source

scurry (skûr´ē) *v.*
To run hurriedly with quick, short steps

© Great Source

sedentary (sĕd´n-tĕr´ē) *adj.*
Staying in one place

© Great Source

stride (strīd) *v.*
To walk with long steps

© Great Source

totter (tŏt´ər) *v.*
To move unsteadily

---

appease (ə-pēz´) *v.*
To calm by giving in

© Great Source

condone (kən-dōn´) *v.*
To allow a wrong

© Great Source

indignant (ĭn-dĭg´nənt) *adj.*
Angry about something unfair

© Great Source

infuriate (ĭn-fyŏor´ē-āt´) *v.*
To enrage

© Great Source

malicious (mə-lĭsh´əs) *adj.*
With intent to harm

© Great Source

---

penitent (pĕn´ĭ-tənt) *adj.*
Regretful

© Great Source

reconcile (rĕk´ən-sīl´) *v.*
To settle differences

© Great Source

resent (rĭ-zĕnt´) *v.*
To feel bitter about something

© Great Source

retaliate (rĭ-tăl´ē-āt´) *v.*
To fight back

© Great Source

wrath (răth) *n.*
Rage

© Great Source

---

barrio (bä´rē-ō´) *n.*
A Spanish-speaking neighborhood

© Great Source

escapade (ĕs´kə-pād´) *n.*
An adventure filled with mischief and danger.

© Great Source

fiesta (fē-ĕs´tə) *n.*
A celebration

© Great Source

guerrilla (gə-rĭl´ə) *n.*
A soldier in an unofficial army

© Great Source

lariat (lăr´ē-ət) *n.*
A lasso

© Great Source

---

mesa (mā´sə) *n.*
A high, flat-topped hill

© Great Source

mustang (mŭs´tăng´) *n.*
A wild horse

© Great Source

poncho (pŏn´chō) *n.*
A sleeveless, blanket-like cloak

© Great Source

siesta (sē-ĕs´tə) *n.*
An afternoon nap

© Great Source

stampede (stăm-pēd´) *n.*
The sudden rush of a herd of animals

© Great Source

LESSON 10 **acquaint**	LESSON 10 **aloof**	LESSON 10 **amiable**	LESSON 10 **betray**	LESSON 10 **enmity**	
LESSON 10 **idealize**	LESSON 10 **protégé**	LESSON 10 **recluse**	LESSON 10 **solitary**	LESSON 10 **treacherous**	
LESSON 11 **accessory**	LESSON 11 **auxiliary**	LESSON 11 **entail**	LESSON 11 **essence**	LESSON 11 **excess**	
LESSON 11 **frivolous**	LESSON 11 **imperative**	LESSON 11 **notable**	LESSON 11 **pertinent**	LESSON 11 **significant**	
LESSON 12 **dormant**	LESSON 12 **frenetic**	LESSON 12 **industrious**	LESSON 12 **loiter**	LESSON 12 **lull**	
LESSON 12 **restless**	LESSON 12 **sluggish**	LESSON 12 **spry**	LESSON 12 **strenuous**	LESSON 12 **vigor**	

acquaint (ə-kwānt´) *v.* To make familiar with	**idealize** (ī-dē´ə-līz´) *v.* To think of as perfect	**accessory** (ăk-sĕs´ə-rē) *n.* Something that adds attractiveness	**frivolous** (frĭv´ə-ləs) *adj.* Silly; trivial	**dormant** (dôr´mənt) *adj.* Temporarily inactive
© Great Source	© Great Source	© Great Source	© Great Source	© Great Source
aloof (ə-lōōf´) *adj.* Unfriendly; distant	**protégé** (prō´tə-zhā´) *n.* A student of a more experienced person	**auxiliary** (ôg-zĭl´yə-rē) *adj.* Providing extra help or support	**imperative** (ĭm-pĕr´ə-tĭv) *adj.* Necessary	**frenetic** (frə-nĕt´ĭk) *adj.* Wildly active
© Great Source	© Great Source	© Great Source	© Great Source	© Great Source
amiable (ā´mē-ə-bəl) *adj.* Friendly	**recluse** (rĕk´lōōs´) *n.* A hermit	**entail** (ĕn-tāl´) *v.* To require or involve	**notable** (nō´tə-bəl) *adj.* Worth attention or notice	**industrious** (ĭn-dŭs´trē-əs) *adj.* Hardworking
© Great Source	© Great Source	© Great Source	© Great Source	© Great Source
betray (bĭ-trā´) *v.* To be disloyal or unfaithful	**solitary** (sŏl´ĭ-tĕr´ē) *adj.* Living or being alone	**essence** (ĕs´əns) *n.* The most basic part	**pertinent** (pûr´tn-ənt) *adj.* Relevant	**loiter** (loi´tər) *v.* To stand around doing nothing
© Great Source	© Great Source	© Great Source	© Great Source	© Great Source
enmity (ĕn´mĭ-tē) *n.* Deep hatred	**treacherous** (trĕch´ər-əs) *adj.* Dangerous	**excess** (ĕk´sĕs´) *n.* An extra amount	**significant** (sĭg-nĭf´ĭ-kənt) *adj.* Important; meaningful	**lull** (lŭl) *n.* A slowing down or stopping of activity
© Great Source	© Great Source	© Great Source	© Great Source	© Great Source
				restless (rĕst´lĭs) *adj.* Not able to relax or rest
				© Great Source
				sluggish (slŭg´ĭsh) *adj.* Slow; lacking energy
				© Great Source
				spry (sprī) *adj.* Active; energetic; lively
				© Great Source
				strenuous (strĕn´yōō-əs) *adj.* Requiring great effort
				© Great Source
				vigor (vĭg´ər) *n.* Strength or physical energy
				© Great Source

LESSON 13	LESSON 13	LESSON 14	LESSON 14	LESSON 15
blunt	opaque	adjourn	absurd	exotic
LESSON 13	LESSON 13	LESSON 14	LESSON 14	LESSON 15
coarse	radiant	cease	prolong	habitual
LESSON 13	LESSON 13	LESSON 14	LESSON 14	LESSON 15
dense	sheen	decisive	repel	authentic
LESSON 13	LESSON 13	LESSON 14	LESSON 14	LESSON 15	LESSON 15
dingy	tinge	detain	shackle	bizarre	norm
LESSON 13	LESSON 13	LESSON 14	LESSON 14	LESSON 15	LESSON 15
iridescent	transparent	hinder	undermine	conventional	novel
			LESSON 15	LESSON 15	
			exception	superlative	

blunt (blŭnt) *adj.*	Not sharp or pointed
coarse (kôrs) *adj.*	Rough in texture
dense (děns) *adj.*	Tightly crowded together
dingy (dĭn´jē) *adj.*	Dirty and discolored
iridescent (ĭr´ĭ-děs´ənt) *adj.*	Having shiny, rainbow-like colors
opaque (ō-pāk´) *adj.*	Not letting light through
radiant (rā´dē-ənt) *adj.*	Giving out light or heat
sheen (shēn) *n.*	Shine; brightness
tinge (tĭnj) *n.*	A hint or small amount of color
transparent (trăns-pâr´ənt) *adj.*	Letting light through
adjourn (ə-jûrn´) *v.*	To stop or end a meeting
cease (sēs) *v.*	To end; to stop
decisive (dĭ-sī´sĭv) *adj.*	Settled in a final way
detain (dĭ-tān´) *v.*	To delay
hinder (hĭn´dər) *v.*	To interfere with
prolong (prə-lông´) *v.*	To lengthen in time
repel (rĭ-pĕl´) *v.*	To drive away
shackle (shăk´əl) *n.*	Something that limits
tarry (tăr´ē) *v.*	To stay for a while
undermine (ŭn´dər-mīn´) *v.*	To weaken or affect negatively
absurd (əb-sûrd´) *adj.*	Ridiculous
authentic (ô-thěn´tĭk) *adj.*	Not fake or copied; real
bizarre (bĭ-zär´) *adj.*	Extremely strange or odd
conventional (kən-věn´shə-nəl) *adj.*	Generally accepted
exception (ĭk-sĕp´shən) *n.*	Something outside a rule or convention
exotic (ĭg-zŏt´ĭk) *adj.*	Foreign; unusual
habitual (hə-bĭch´ōō-əl) *adj.*	Done regularly
norm (nôrm) *n.*	The usual standard
novel (nŏv´əl) *adj.*	New
superlative (sōō-pûr´lə-tĭv) *adj.*	The best

LESSON 16	LESSON 16	LESSON 17	LESSON 17	LESSON 18	LESSON 18
ancestor	hereditary	ballad	rhythmically	autobiography	metaphor
clan	kin	choral	serenade	biography	onomatopoeia
compatible	lineage	lyrics	shrill	flashback	prose
domestic	matrimony	opera	symphony	folklore	proverb
filial	spouse	resonant	vocal	genre	simile

ancestor
(ăn´sĕs´tər) n.
A person from whom one is descended

clan
(klăn) n.
A group that shares a common background

compatible
(kəm-păt´ə-bəl) adj.
Working well together

domestic
(də-mĕs´tĭk) adj.
Not wild; tame

filial
(fĭl´ē-əl) adj.
Relating to a son or a daughter

hereditary
(hə-rĕd´ĭ-tĕr´ē) adj.
Passed down through genes

kin
(kĭn) n.
A person's relatives

lineage
(lĭn´ē-ĭj) n.
Direct descent from a particular ancestor

matrimony
(măt´rə-mō´nē) n.
Marriage

spouse
(spous) n.
A wife or husband

ballad
(băl´əd) n.
A song that tells a story

choral
(kôr´əl) adj.
Relating to music sung by a choir

lyrics
(lĭr´ĭks) n.
The words to a song

opera
(ŏp´ər-ə) n.
A type of musical theater

resonant
(rĕz´ə-nənt) adj.
Having a strong, deep sound

rhythmically
(rĭth´mĭ-kə-lē) adv.
With a regular beat

serenade
(sĕr´ə-nād´) n.
A love song

shrill
(shrĭl) adj.
High-pitched and piercing

symphony
(sĭm´fə-nē) n.
A long piece of music written for an orchestra

vocal
(vō´kəl) adj.
Relating to the voice

autobiography
(ô´tō-bī-ŏg´rə-fē) n.
A story of one's life, written by that person

biography
(bī-ŏg´rə-fē) n.
A story of someone's life, written by another

flashback
(flăsh´băk´) n.
A scene set at an earlier time

folklore
(fōk´lôr´) n.
Traditional stories

genre
(zhän´rə) n.
Type of literature or art

metaphor
(mĕt´ə-fôr´) n.
Description of something as if it were another thing

onomatopoeia
(ŏn´ə-măt´ə-pē´ə) n.
The use of words that imitate sounds

prose
(prōz) n.
Ordinary writing without a regular rhythm

proverb
(prŏv´ûrb´) n.
A short saying

simile
(sĭm´ə-lē) n.
A comparison using the words like or as

LESSON 19	LESSON 19	LESSON 19	LESSON 19	LESSON 19
approximate	assumption	certify	contend	hypothesis

LESSON 19	LESSON 19	LESSON 19	LESSON 19	LESSON 19
illusion	inevitable	inquire	presume	vague

LESSON 20	LESSON 20	LESSON 20	LESSON 20	LESSON 20
compress	concise	eject	exclusion	expulsion

LESSON 20	LESSON 20	LESSON 20	LESSON 20	LESSON 20
liberate	propel	regulate	restrain	restriction

LESSON 21	LESSON 21	LESSON 21	LESSON 21	LESSON 21
battalion	casualty	corps	encampment	formidable

LESSON 21	LESSON 21	LESSON 21	LESSON 21	LESSON 21
garrison	infiltrate	provoke	sentry	siege

approximate (ə-prŏk´sə-mĭt) *adj.* Almost exact or correct

© Great Source

assumption (ə-sŭmp´shən) *n.* Something accepted as true

© Great Source

certify (sûr´tə-fī´) *v.* To guarantee

© Great Source

contend (kən-tĕnd´) *v.* To struggle against difficulties

© Great Source

hypothesis (hī-pŏth´ĭ-sĭs) *n.* A theory

© Great Source

illusion (ĭ-lōō´zhən) *n.* A mistaken idea or belief

© Great Source

inevitable (ĭn-ĕv´ĭ-tə-bəl) *adj.* Impossible to prevent

© Great Source

inquire (ĭn-kwīr´) *v.* To ask for information

© Great Source

presume (prĭ-zōōm´) *v.* To believe without proof

© Great Source

vague (vāg) *adj.* Unclear

© Great Source

compress (kəm-prĕs´) *v.* To press together

© Great Source

concise (kən-sīs´) *adj.* Using few words; short and clear

© Great Source

eject (ĭ-jĕkt´) *v.* To push out by force

© Great Source

exclusion (ĭk-sklōō´zhən) *n.* The act of keeping out

© Great Source

expulsion (ĭk-spŭl´shən) *n.* Forcing or driving out

© Great Source

liberate (lĭb´ə-rāt´) *v.* To release or set free

© Great Source

propel (prə-pĕl´) *v.* To cause to move forward

© Great Source

regulate (rĕg´yə-lāt´) *v.* To control with rules

© Great Source

restrain (rĭ-strān´) *v.* To hold back

© Great Source

restriction (rĭ-strĭk´shən) *n.* A limit or limitation

© Great Source

battalion (bə-tăl´yən) *n.* A large unit of soldiers

© Great Source

casualty (kăzh´ōō-əl-tē) *n.* A soldier who is injured or killed

© Great Source

corps (kôr) *n.* A group with a specialized function

© Great Source

encampment (ĕn-kămp´mənt) *n.* A campsite

© Great Source

formidable (fôr´mĭ-də-bəl) *adj.* Inspiring fear

© Great Source

garrison (găr´ĭ-sən) *n.* A place where soldiers are stationed

© Great Source

infiltrate (ĭn-fĭl´trāt´) *v.* To enter secretly

© Great Source

provoke (prə-vōk´) *v.* To cause to act

© Great Source

sentry (sĕn´trē) *n.* A guard

© Great Source

siege (sēj) *n.* The act of surrounding a place

© Great Source

LESSON 22	LESSON 22	LESSON 22	LESSON 22	LESSON 22
anthropology	archaeology	biology	criminology	geology
LESSON 22	LESSON 22	LESSON 22	LESSON 22	LESSON 22
paleontology	physiology	sociology	technology	theology
LESSON 23	LESSON 23	LESSON 23	LESSON 23	LESSON 23
altimeter	barometer	diameter	geometry	kilometer
LESSON 23	LESSON 23	LESSON 23	LESSON 23	LESSON 23
metric	metronome	micrometer	odometer	perimeter
LESSON 24	LESSON 24	LESSON 24	LESSON 24	LESSON 24
dismiss	emissary	emit	intermittent	missile
LESSON 24	LESSON 24	LESSON 24	LESSON 24	LESSON 24
mission	missive	omit	submit	transmit

anthropology
(ăn´thrə-pŏl´ə-jē) n.
The study of humans

© Great Source

archaeology
(är´kē-ŏl´ə-jē) n.
The study of past human life

© Great Source

biology
(bī-ŏl´ə-jē) n.
The study of living things

© Great Source

criminology
(krĭm´ə-nŏl´ə-jē) n.
The study of crime and criminals

© Great Source

geology
(jē-ŏl´ə-jē) n.
The study of Earth's structure

© Great Source

paleontology
(pā´lē-ŏn-tŏl´ə-jē) n.
The study of fossils

© Great Source

physiology
(fĭz´ē-ŏl´ə-jē) n.
The study of the organs and parts of living things

© Great Source

sociology
(sō´sē-ŏl´ə-jē) n.
The study of human social behavior

© Great Source

technology
(tĕk-nŏl´ə-jē) n.
The application of science to practical uses

© Great Source

theology
(thē-ŏl´ə-jē) n.
The study of religious questions

© Great Source

altimeter
(ăl-tĭm´ĭ-tər) n.
An instrument that measures altitude

© Great Source

barometer
(bə-rŏm´ĭ-tər) n.
An instrument that measures atmospheric pressure

© Great Source

diameter
(dī-ăm´ĭ-tər) n.
A line through the exact center of a figure

© Great Source

geometry
(jē-ŏm´ĭ-trē) n.
The study of points, lines, angles, and shapes

© Great Source

kilometer
(kĭ-lŏm´ĭ-tər) n.
One thousand meters

© Great Source

metric
(mĕt´rĭk) adj.
Referring to a measurement system

© Great Source

metronome
(mĕt´rə-nōm´) n.
An instrument that marks time with regular beats

© Great Source

micrometer
(mī-krŏm´ĭ-tər) n.
An instrument that measures very small things

© Great Source

odometer
(ō-dŏm´ĭ-tər) n.
An instrument that measures distance traveled

© Great Source

perimeter
(pə-rĭm´ĭ-tər) n.
An outer boundary

© Great Source

dismiss
(dĭs-mĭs´) v.
To reject

© Great Source

emissary
(ĕm´ĭ-sĕr´ē) n.
A person sent on an official mission

© Great Source

emit
(ĭ-mĭt´) v.
To send out energy

© Great Source

intermittent
(ĭn´tər-mĭt´nt) adj.
Not continuous

© Great Source

missile
(mĭs´əl) n.
A weapon sent to a target

© Great Source

mission
(mĭsh´ən) n.
A special duty or assignment

© Great Source

missive
(mĭs´ĭv) n.
Written communication

© Great Source

omit
(ō-mĭt´) v.
To leave out

© Great Source

submit
(səb-mĭt´) v.
To present for approval

© Great Source

transmit
(trăns-mĭt´) v.
To send

© Great Source

LESSON 25 improvise

LESSON 25 visible

LESSON 25 revision

LESSON 25 visionary

LESSON 25 video

LESSON 25 visor

LESSON 25 viewpoint

LESSON 25 vista

LESSON 25 visa

LESSON 25 visualize

LESSON 26 emancipate

LESSON 26 impede

LESSON 26 manacle

LESSON 26 maneuver

LESSON 26 manipulate

LESSON 26 manual

LESSON 26 manuscript

LESSON 26 pedestal

LESSON 26 pedestrian

LESSON 26 pedigree

LESSON 27 circumstance

LESSON 27 constitution

LESSON 27 destitute

LESSON 27 institution

LESSON 27 obstacle

LESSON 27 obstinate

LESSON 27 stately

LESSON 27 stationary

LESSON 27 stature

LESSON 27 status

improvise (ĭm´prə-vīz´) v. To invent and perform without preparation
© Great Source

revision (rĭ-vĭzh´ən) n. A corrected version
© Great Source

video (vĭd´ē-ō´) adj. Referring to an electronic visual image
© Great Source

viewpoint (vyōō´point´) n. A way of looking at something
© Great Source

visa (vē´zə) n. A document needed to enter a country
© Great Source

visible (vĭz´ə-bəl) adj. Able to be seen
© Great Source

visionary (vĭzh´ə-něr´ē) n. Someone able to imagine the future
© Great Source

visor (vī´zər) n. A shade on a hat
© Great Source

vista (vĭs´tə) n. A far-reaching view
© Great Source

visualize (vĭzh´ōō-ə-līz´) v. To picture mentally
© Great Source

emancipate (ĭ-măn´sə-pāt´) v. To set free
© Great Source

impede (ĭm-pēd´) v. To slow progress
© Great Source

manacle (măn´ə-kəl) n. Handcuffs
© Great Source

maneuver (mə-nōō´vər) n. A skillful move
© Great Source

manipulate (mə-nĭp´yə-lāt´) v. To influence or manage cleverly
© Great Source

manual (măn´yōō-əl) adj. Done by hand
© Great Source

manuscript (măn´yə-skrĭpt´) n. A handwritten document
© Great Source

pedestal (pĕd´ĭ-stəl) n. A statue base
© Great Source

pedestrian (pə-dĕs´trē-ən) n. A person who walks
© Great Source

pedigree (pĕd´ĭ-grē´) n. Record of ancestors
© Great Source

circumstance (sûr´kəm-stăns´) n. A condition affecting something
© Great Source

constitution (kŏn´stĭ-tōō´shən) n. Basic written principles of an organization
© Great Source

destitute (dĕs´tĭ-tōōt´) adj. Very poor
© Great Source

institution (ĭn´stĭ-tōō´shən) n. An established organization
© Great Source

obstacle (ŏb´stə-kəl) n. Something in the way
© Great Source

obstinate (ŏb´stə-nĭt) adj. Stubborn
© Great Source

stately (stāt´lē) adj. Dignified; impressive
© Great Source

stationary (stā´shə-něr´ē) adj. Not moving
© Great Source

stature (stăch´ər) n. Height
© Great Source

status (stāt´əs) n. Social position
© Great Source

LESSON 28 fracture	**LESSON 28** endurance	**LESSON 28** donor	**LESSON 28** contagious	**LESSON 28** alleviate	**LESSON 28**
LESSON 28 thrive	**LESSON 28** soothe	**LESSON 28** revitalize	**LESSON 28** paralysis	**LESSON 28** nutrient	**LESSON 29**
LESSON 28 forum	**LESSON 29** endorse	**LESSON 29** dictator	**LESSON 29** democratic	**LESSON 29** congress	**LESSON 29**
LESSON 29 veto	**LESSON 29** municipality	**LESSON 29** monarchy	**LESSON 29** legislation	**LESSON 29** judicial	**LESSON 30**
LESSON 30 just	**LESSON 30** fugitive	**LESSON 30** evident	**LESSON 30** defendant	**LESSON 30** bankrupt	**LESSON 30**
LESSON 30 witness	**LESSON 30** verdict	**LESSON 30** testimony	**LESSON 30** lenient	**LESSON 30** larceny	

alleviate	(ə-lē´ vē-āt´)	v.	To relieve
contagious	(kən-tā´ jəs)	adj.	Able to spread
donor	(dō´ nər)	n.	A person who gives money to a cause
endurance	(ĕn-door´əns)	n.	Strength under difficult conditions
fracture	(frăk´ chər)	v.	To break
nutrient	(noo´ trē-ənt)	n.	A healthy part of food
paralysis	(pə-răl´ĭ-sĭs)	n.	Inability to move
revitalize	(rē-vīt´l-īz´)	v.	To give new life
soothe	(sooth)	v.	To calm
thrive	(thrīv)	v.	To grow well
congress	(kŏng´ grĭs)	n.	A large meeting to discuss issues
democratic	(dĕm´ə-krăt´ĭk)	adj.	Governed by the people
dictator	(dĭk´ tā´ tər)	n.	A ruler with complete power
endorse	(ĕn-dôrs´)	v.	To give support
forum	(fôr´əm)	n.	A gathering for public discussions
judicial	(joo-dĭsh´əl)	adj.	Relating to courts
legislation	(lĕj´ĭ-slā´ shən)	n.	Laws
monarchy	(mŏn´ ər-kē)	n.	A government run by a king or queen
municipality	(myoo-nĭs´ə-păl´ĭ-tē)	n.	A self-governing city
veto	(vē´ tō)	v.	To forbid or reject
bankrupt	(băngk´ rŭpt´)	adj.	Financially ruined
defendant	(dĭ-fĕn´ dənt)	n.	Person on trial
evident	(ĕv´ĭ-dənt)	adj.	Easily seen or understood
fugitive	(fyoo´ jĭ-tĭv)	n.	A person running from the law
just	(jŭst)	adj.	Fair
larceny	(lär´ sə-nē)	n.	The crime of stealing
lenient	(lē´ nē-ənt)	adj.	Not strict
testimony	(tĕs´ tə-mō´ nē)	n.	A statement given as evidence
verdict	(vûr´ dĭkt)	n.	A jury's decision
witness	(wĭt´ nĭs)	v.	To see something